WHAT EVE

FUTURE

MISSIONARY

& THEIR PARENTS

NEED TO KNOW

ED J. PINEGAR

WHAT EVERY
FUTURE
MISSIONARY

& THEIR PARENTS
NEED TO KNOW

ED J. PINEGAR

CFI

AN IMPRINT OF CEDAR FORT, INC.
SPRINGVILLE, UTAH

© 2016 Ed J. Pinegar

ISBN 13: 978-1-4621-1776-5

Published by CFI, an imprint of Cedar Fort, Inc.
2373 W. 700 S., Springville, UT 84663
Distributed by Cedar Fort, Inc., www.cedarfort.com

LIBRARY OF CONGRESS CATALOGING-IN-PUBLICATION DATA

Names: Pinegar, Ed J., author.
Title: What every future missionary and their parents need to know / Ed J.
 Pinegar.
Description: Springville, Utah : CFI, an imprint of Cedar Fort, Inc., [2016]
 | "2016 | Includes bibliographical references.
Identifiers: LCCN 2015038457 | ISBN 9781462117765 (perfect bound : alk. paper)
Subjects: LCSH: Church of Jesus Christ of Latter-day Saints--Missions. |
 Mormon missionaries. | Missionaries--Training of.
Classification: LCC BX8661 .P574 2016 | DDC 266/.9332--dc23
LC record available at http://lccn.loc.gov/2015038457

Cover design by Shawnda T. Craig
Cover design © 2016 by Cedar Fort, Inc.
Edited and typeset by Deborah Spencer

Printed in the United States of America

10 9 8 7 6 5 4 3 2 1

Printed on acid-free paper

To all the faithful missionaries of the past and to the future.

Also by Ed Pinegar

Gethsemane, Golgotha and the Garden Tomb

*The Temple: Gaining Knowledge
and Power in the House of the Lord*

A Mighty Change

*Preparing for the Melchizedek
Priesthood and My Mission*

The Christmas Code

Leadership for Saints

Series of latter-day teachings and commentaries, unlocking,
and who's who—Old Testament, New Testament, Book of
Mormon, and Doctrine and Covenants

Soon to be released:

The Little Book of Gratitude for Latter-Day Saints

The Christmas List

CONTENTS

ACKNOWLEDGMENTS

It is with gratitude I express my appreciation for the thousands of missionaries I have had the honor and privilege of serving with. Thanks to Eschler Editing for their help in the beginning stages. Special thanks to Ryan Weller and Ann Jamison, who made suggestions that have made the book better, and to Garfield Cook, who reviewed the manuscript as well.

I am grateful to my dear friend Dave Wirthlin, who read the manuscript and provided a generous endorsement. To my Cedar Fort friends, McKell Parsons, Emily Chambers, Deborah Spencer, and the staff there, I express my gratitude.

And to my sweetheart, Pat, who is always so supportive of my time spent hunched over the computer, typing with three fingers, I am forever grateful. All of these wonderful people made this book possible.

INTRODUCTION

In my years of serving in the Lord's kingdom here upon the earth, I have had many opportunities and blessings of serving in the missionary effort. I have served on many Church committees, taught at the Missionary Training Center (MTC), served as a mission president in England, and as the president of the Provo MTC. I have taught mission preparation courses at BYU and the Orem Institute. I have interviewed thousands of missionaries. In these experiences I have learned much from the Lord's missionaries. I have observed the importance of their preparation as well as the results of a lack thereof. I know they want to do well but often haven't had enough instruction or paid the price of preparation.

The best missionary preparation occurs as parents and missionaries work together in that great process. The process of becoming a missionary for the Lord is not easy. It takes work. It takes dedication. It takes sacrifice. You have to learn by your own experience to do hard things. Some missionaries struggle to the point of anxiety and frustration. Some young men and women are not fully prepared even though the desire is there.

To aid this process, this book is designed to let you and your parents know what is expected of you and when. It will take you through every major event within your mission. It is designed to help you make the change from everyday life to the life of a missionary. It will help prepare you for each special event of your missionary life. It will help you face difficult moments in your mission.

Unrealized expectations often bring negative responses, and to be forewarned is to be forearmed. This will help in your preparation because you will know of the things you need to do in order to be better prepared. This book is the journey of a full-time missionary from beginning to serve to returning with honor. It is taken from real-life experiences that will inspire and teach you things you need to know to serve as a disciple of the Lord Jesus Christ. You have to learn by your own experience!

You, the promised generation, have been called to hasten the Lord's work (see D&C 88:73). Never has there been a time like this. Much is expected of you because you are the ones to hasten the work of the Lord. The prophet has provided an earlier departure date on this grand and glorious opportunity to serve the Lord and your fellowman. New inventions and tools have been provided for you in this great work. You have often heard that your mission becomes a defining moment in your life. As I speak with some of the missionaries I have had the privilege of serving with, their words are something like this, "President, it seems like that every time something comes up at work or in the family I reflect back to things that I learned on my mission that can help me." This missionary's eyes were glistening and I could see gratitude in his heart and soul. Yes, a mission can be this moment in life when great growth and understanding begin.

This great opportunity depends upon how you embrace it—is your desire to learn and be strong in the strength of the Lord? Have you received your patriarchal blessing? Are you living worthy to receive your promised temple blessings? Is your diligence and work ethic full of enthusiasm? Is your love for your fellowman observable and expressed in your actions? Is obedience your quest and pleasing God your pursuit? Has faith become your power to the point that doubt and fear have flown away? Have you prepared well to receive your own endowments so that you can go forward being endowed with power from on high? Do you live worthy of the Holy Spirit's direction? Do you recognize that the missionary name tag indicates the wearer to be a minister of the Lord Jesus Christ? Do you realize that the Holy Ghost can be your constant companion? All these questions will help you to prepare well, serve with honor, and return with no regrets.

Preparing for your mission and receiving your own endowment requires great effort, but the pay is indescribably delicious. The Lord's disciples who have been to the holy temple receive blessings that will protect them through their faithful obedience and empower them from on high. These blessings will allow God to be with them as He was with the Savior *"who went about doing good*, and healing all that were oppressed of the devil; *for God was with him"* (Acts 10:38; emphasis added). You indeed will go about doing good, preaching the gospel and inviting people to come unto Christ—for the Holy Ghost can always be with you (see D&C 20:77). And being an instrument in the hands of God will become your joy and glory (see Alma 29:9–10).

You are prayed for daily by your family and loved ones and by patrons in the temples of our God that you will be protected and led to those seeking to know the truth. You will be the instrument through whom many lives will be saved and great joy shall be shared.

Plead and pray for the Holy Ghost to become your constant companion and for a portion of the Spirit to be upon those that you teach. Pray that they may hear the word of God, come to the knowledge of the truth through your preaching, and be converted unto the Lord—never to fall away (see Alma 23:6).

Now is the time to prepare. Prepare well and reap the blessings of finding joy in the service of the Lord.

CHAPTER 1

Ready to Serve

Taught to Serve: Your Early Years

Many of you, when you received a name and blessing at birth, were blessed with a desire to serve the Lord as a full-time missionary. You have heard the stories of missionaries who have served the Lord, and of the joy they felt in helping others come unto Christ. You can remember your primary teacher, with her sweet smile, the tender way she would teach you the gospel, and the way her eyes twinkled as you sang, "I hope they call me on a mission!"[1]

Those words can still echo in your mind and heart as you serve in the Aaronic Priesthood and in the Young Women organization. Your lessons in Sunday School, Young Women, and Priesthood contain some of the material you will teach in the mission field. You practice teaching them every Sunday. Your confidence of becoming a missionary is getting stronger every day. You know you can do it, and when you sing "Called to Serve," you are really fired up.

In April 1985, my wife and I were in the Assembly Hall with all the mission presidents, their wives, and the General Authorities of the Church, receiving the new discussions for missionaries. The stirring hymn "Called to Serve" was introduced as our missionary anthem. Elder Packer had invited missionaries to come from the MTC, and they entered every door singing this hymn with the organ at triple fortissimo. There was not a dry eye as we all stood

1

with gratitude and amazement. While serving at the Provo MTC, we sang this hymn with every departing missionary. The words and music are awe-inspiring. Each time it is sung with great gusto, I feel goose bumps.

Let the words of this glorious hymn remind you that you can serve your Heavenly King and teach His glorious plan of redemption and His love to the people you meet. You will have the strength of the Lord to do all things and to bring His children to the knowledge of the truth and the Lord (see Alma 23:5–6).

It seems there is a song or hymn in every aspect of being taught the importance of serving a mission. We sing the thrilling song by Janice Kapp Perry, "We'll Bring the World His Truth." Oh, how I love Sister Kapp's beautiful music. This song echoes in my heart as my children sang it at the funeral of their brother, Cory, to wish him well when he was called to serve in the spirit world in 1986.

All of the missionary songs inspire and teach eternal truths and the importance of sharing the gospel with our fellowman. From your time in Primary, Sunday School, and the Young Men and Young Women organizations, you have been continually inspired with the desire to serve. Some of your friends have struggled in these early years of their lives and have often wandered off the path, having a difficult time deciding whether or not they would serve. Love them and help them keep this commitment.

Deciding to Serve

Some of you have had a "mighty change" occur within your soul that inspired you to want to serve. Many of you have decided, even before you were baptized, that you would be a missionary. And as time went on, your commitment to be a missionary grew deep within your soul. It is simply what you had been taught and what you wanted to do. You felt that it was the least you could do for your Savior, who has done everything for you. You and I are indebted forever to our Savior for everything, especially for His suffering and His sacrifice in Gethsemane and on Golgotha's hill to fulfill His infinite Atonement.

This motive to serve was rooted in your love for your Heavenly Father and your Savior, which kindled your love for your fellowmen. "Now they were desirous that salvation should be declared to every creature, *for they could not bear that any human soul should perish; yea, even the very thoughts that any soul should endure endless torment did cause them to quake and tremble*" (Mosiah 28:3; emphasis added). The sons of Mosiah served their missions because they cared about other people. They were no longer thinking of themselves and all the fun they wanted to have. They cared, and because of them and the sweet whisperings of the Holy Spirit, you started to care about others too!

One day, in my mission preparation class, a student expressed his doubts concerning his abilities and his testimony of the gospel. I realized that his conversion was not deep enough to make the commitment, so I bore my testimony to him. We talked about the gospel when we were together, and slowly but surely, his spirit felt the Holy Ghost witness to him the truthfulness of the gospel, and his desire became stronger each week. It was miraculous.

Sometimes my students simply knew it was the right thing to do. Even though they were not strong in the gospel, they were willing to try and, years later, would bear witness as they became deeply converted and committed in the MTC. As they served the Lord, they knew of the truthfulness of His gospel (see John 7:17).

Some go on missions because all of their friends are going, and gradually through the influence of the Holy Spirit they "put [their] trust in that Spirit which leadeth to do good—yea, to do justly, to walk humbly, to judge righteously; and this is my Spirit. Verily, verily, I say unto you, I will impart unto you of my Spirit, which shall enlighten your mind, which shall fill your soul with joy" (D&C 11:12–13). When that happens for any missionary, it is not only a miracle, but also a manifestation to all of us that the Lord will always be there for us; that He will always provide a way for us to accomplish His work, if we but try (see 1 Nephi 3:7).

For example, one missionary told me of some difficult times he experienced during his mission: "There was a moment where I was kind of struggling. It was a really long day and I was exhausted. Feeling a little down and anxious, I said a quick prayer in my heart for comfort. Then, I was looking down at my name tag, looking at my name, and below it was the name of my Savior Jesus Christ. I immediately just felt uplifted and confident, knowing that I could take on whatever came at me next. I knew that our Savior Jesus Christ is with us at all times and in all places (see D&C 84:88). I felt the confirmation that I am working shoulder to shoulder with my brother and Savior in our Father in Heaven's holy work. Most importantly, you don't need to be a missionary to know that He is there for you, and that He knows what you are going through more than anybody else. He is there for you. Fighting side by side with you through every trial that you face. He loves you, as does our Father in Heaven." This missionary's experience is an example of pure revelation to one of the Lord's chosen disciples.

Perhaps one of your friends has to delay his mission call because he is not fully prepared. Maybe all you can do to help is to pray for him. It may not be long before he will be prepared and will become a magnificent missionary. You must never judge and never find fault. You simply encourage and express your love. It is each individual's right to make his own choices.

I heard a young man say, "I am so glad that we get to go out on a mission earlier, so there is not a break from high school. There is no time to be distracted. It seems so inspired to me that the Lord trusts us with His holy work at a younger age. And what is exciting to see is that more of our priests are deciding to go immediately following high school." Amazing! The Lord is hastening His work (see D&C 88:73), and you are the ones to do the work. What an honor and privilege. Deciding to go on a mission is a life-changing decision. It will affect your life forever, as it does all missionaries. If you turn your life over to the Lord, you will be changed.

President Ezra Taft Benson taught us this transcending truth: "Men and women who turn their lives over to God will discover that He can make a lot more out of their lives than they can. He will deepen their joys, expand their vision, quicken their minds, strengthen their muscles, lift their spirits, multiply their blessings, increase their opportunities, comfort their souls, raise up friends, and pour out peace. Whoever will lose his life in the service of God will find eternal life."[2]

You must also remember that the Lord has said, "Behold, I stand at the door, and knock: if any man hear my voice, and open the door, I will come in to him, and will sup with him, and he with me. To him that overcometh will I grant to sit with me in my throne, even as I also overcame, and am set down with my Father in his throne" (Revelation 3:20–21). The Lord will always be there for us.

One of my friends told me that all of the young men in his ward's priests quorum wanted to serve a mission, so they promised each other that they would all go and help each other if one began to struggle with his commitment to serve. They all decided to go, and they all served honorable missions.

Remember there are promised blessings for serving an honorable mission:

- Your sins will be forgiven (see D&C 31:5; 58:42–43; 88:85)
- You will have glory and joy as you bring souls to Christ (see Alma 29: 9–10; D&C 15:6)
- You will bring joy to the Lord and share the joy with your converts (see D&C 18:10–16)
- You—and the souls you bring unto Christ—will be perfected in Him (see Moroni 10:32–33)
- You will be strengthened and watched over. The Lord said to the early missionaries of this dispensation, "Any man [or woman] that shall go and preach this gospel of the kingdom, and fail not to continue faithful in all things, shall not be weary in mind, neither darkened, neither in body, limb, nor joint; and a hair of his head shall not fall to the ground unnoticed. And they shall not go hungry, neither athirst" (D&C 84:80).
- You will find success and happiness as you bring souls unto Christ, as did Ammon:

My brothers and my brethren, behold I say unto you, how great reason have we to rejoice; for could we have supposed when we started from the land of Zarahemla that God would have granted unto us such great blessings?

And now, I ask, what great blessings has he bestowed upon us? Can ye tell?

Behold, I answer for you; for our brethren, the Lamanites, were in darkness, yea, even in the darkest abyss, but behold, how many of them are brought to behold the marvelous light of God! And this is the blessing which hath been bestowed upon us, that we have been made instruments in the hands of God to bring about this great work.

Behold, thousands of them do rejoice, and have been brought into the fold of God. (Alma 26:1–4)

- Your losses will be compensated for. The Lord taught, "Every one that hath forsaken houses, or brethren, or sisters, or father, or mother, or wife, or children, or lands, for my name's sake, shall receive an hundredfold, and shall inherit everlasting life" (Matthew 19:29).

- You will reap eternal rewards. The Savior reminds us, "Say not ye, There are yet four months, and then cometh harvest? behold, I say unto you, Lift up your eyes, and look on the fields; for they are white already to harvest. And he that reapeth receiveth wages, and gathereth fruit unto life eternal: that both he that soweth and he that reapeth may rejoice together" (John 4:35–36).

- You will find a multitude of blessings for serving the Lord, for He will train you to be a leader. You will gain friendships for a lifetime. You will learn how to get along with others. You will learn how to love and to serve. You will assimilate the divine nature of Christ. You will increase in your faith and the virtues of holiness. Your testimony will grow. You will learn how to recognize the Holy Spirit. You will wax strong in the knowledge of the truth. You will feel close to your Heavenly Father, and your gratitude for your Savior will increase a hundredfold.

As I think of the promised blessings that Heavenly Father provides for us, I am astonished at the complete and perfect love that Heavenly Father and our Savior have for us. All that They do is motivated by Their love for us (see John 3:16; 2 Nephi 26:24). Missionary work is the lifeblood of the kingdom of God. Remember that deciding to go is wonderful, but you must be worthy as well. And the better prepared you are, the better you can serve the Lord.

Ready to Serve

As you begin to prepare for the magnificent journey of serving the Lord, I write to you after the manner of Mormon, the great prophet of the Book of Mormon and the abridger of this sublime record. Mormon came to the attention of a record keeper named Ammaron, who said of him, "I perceive that thou art a sober child, and art quick to observe" (Mormon 1:2).

Similarly, Alma counseled his sons before they left on their missions to be sober-minded as they declared the word of God (see Alma 37:47; 38:15; 42:31). To be sober-minded means to be serious about matters of importance and to keep your heart and mind focused on such matters.

Like Mormon and the sons of Alma, you too will need to be sober-minded and quick to observe. This work of saving souls and bringing them to Christ is sacred and vitally important. And, like Alma's sons, you will *declare* the word of God. The word *declare* connotes that we will make God's word known clearly, proclaim it with authority, and affirm its truthfulness. Along these lines the Prophet Joseph declared, "After all that has been said, the greatest and most important duty is to preach the Gospel."[3]

It will be necessary for you to study and prepare, just as you would study and prepare for a major test in school. Becoming a true disciple of Christ takes a great deal of effort. You will grow spiritually as you prepare to receive your own endowments in the temple, and as you study the words of the prophets. As you prepare to serve, read *For The Strength of Youth—Fulfilling Our Duty to God,* which was written specifically for the young women and young men. Take special note of the message from the First Presidency, which describes you as beloved, young people in whom they have great confidence, as choice spirits with great responsibilities and opportunities. That's you. You have been called and especially chosen to help the Lord hasten His work.

As you prepare, it is also important for you to remember that you have agency—moral agency. This means that you choose whether you will act or be acted upon. It also means that you are accountable for these actions and that each one of your actions will have consequences. As President Monson would remind us, "Your decisions will determine your destiny." You will do well to remember this great truth throughout your life. Agency and accountability fulfill the law of the harvest. You will reap what you sow—no more and no less. In other words, the seeds of preparation you sow now will yield a bountiful harvest of blessings, for both yourself and others.

Understanding the Pattern of Spiritual Growth

Spiritual growth most often develops in the following pattern: As we humble ourselves, we can then be taught and brought to the knowledge of the truth. We are then able to understand and appreciate the word of God with all its doctrines, principles, commandments, covenants, and ordinances. We are then filled with gratitude and are able to receive the love of God into our hearts. As our love of God increases, we will begin to feel an overwhelming desire to do good and to love our fellowmen. This is what disciples of the Lord do. "A new commandment I give unto you, That ye love one another; as I have loved you, that ye also love one another. By this shall all men know that ye are my disciples, if ye have love one to another" (John 13:34–35).

We will carefully review this pattern:

Humility is necessarily the starting point for all spiritual growth. We develop humility when we acknowledge and understand our relationship to and our dependence on God. In this state of humility, we become submissive, easily entreated, and teachable. We are able to receive inspiration and revelation. We allow ourselves to be nurtured by the good word of God. Humility allows us to relate to God in gratitude and love. We worship Him in humility through prayer, as well as through our worship in His holy house—and in all things.

Knowledge is the next marker in the pattern of spiritual growth. Knowledge always precedes understanding, and for this reason it is critical to seek the knowledge of truth, as contained in the word of God. This knowledge will lead to your conversion to the Lord (see Alma 23:6). We must seek knowledge in the word of God to understand any doctrine or principle. We can feast upon the scriptures, the words of living prophets, and words spoken by the power of the Holy Ghost (see D&C 68:3–7). As we read in Proverbs, "A man of understanding hath wisdom" (10:23).

Understanding comes as we couple effort and desire with faith, diligence, and patience. Turning knowledge into understanding is not a passive exercise, however. We must be prepared to exert effort, whether in our studies or our relationships. Understanding gospel truths is a critical step in the process of change. As we humble ourselves and seek for knowledge, the Holy Spirit will help us understand and bear witness of the truth. It is worth noting that we will often need to adjust our perspectives to fully understand a principle of the gospel and that we must exercise empathy as we attempt to understand another person's behavior.

Appreciation comes as we gain greater understanding. With that understanding, we will develop an appreciation for the blessings and knowledge that we have obtained. Where there is no understanding, there can be no appreciation. Alternatively, where we have gained understanding, we will feel a natural feeling of appreciation for the principles of the gospel and the blessings we have been given by a loving Heavenly Father.

Appreciation for someone or something happens when our hearts are softened and when we have come to understand and delight in that which is good. For example, we come to appreciate the power of the word of God as we reach an understanding of God's infinite goodness, grace, and mercy.

The transition from understanding to appreciation is a process of discovery—one that requires mighty prayer and pondering on the mercies of God (see Moroni 10:3). This enlightening process often feels like a series of "ah-ha" moments as understanding unfolds into appreciation. It is possible to become so obsessed with the acquisition of knowledge that one never comes to see, understand, or fully appreciate—to only know *about* something rather than to really *know* it. Knowledge in and of itself is not enough. Satan, the father of all lies, knows that Jesus is the Christ, but he does not acknowledge or appreciate the blessings that are available to mankind because of the Savior's Atonement. Knowledge must be applied in order for it to be effective in our lives. This application of knowledge to understanding and appreciation comes through the power of the Holy Ghost. Without the Spirit, we cannot righteously act upon or appreciate gospel truths. For example, it was only after Peter was endowed and received the Holy Ghost in its fulness that he could reach his full potential as the mighty chief Apostle (see Luke 24:49; Acts 2,3, 5:15). We become enlightened by the power of the Holy Ghost: "Verily, verily, I say unto you, I will impart unto you of my Spirit, which shall enlighten your mind" (D&C 11:13).

Gratitude comes after appreciation. Only after we gain a sense of appreciation can we feel gratitude—a force so powerful that it moves us to action. Appreciation is the beginning of gratitude in that we start to see the worth of something or someone. Gratitude often brings with it a sense of indebtedness as we recognize sacrifices that have been made in our behalf, love that has been shown to us, or blessings that have been bestowed on us.

For example, as you come to understand and appreciate the goodness and mercy of God, your heart will be filled with gratitude for the love of God. This gratitude will develop into a desire to do good (or in other words, to share and exemplify the love of God that we have come to understand and appreciate), and thus gratitude becomes the catalyst for change—and in fact creates the desire to change! Pure motivation is always centered in gratitude, which is so closely tied to love. The importance of gratitude—the motivating virtue in the pattern of spiritual growth—must be ingrained in our very souls, for it will determine our power to change, to repent, and to be converted to Christ the Lord and receive the mighty change in our hearts. Alma spoke with such tenderness and emotion when he said, "And now behold, I ask of you, my brethren of the church, have ye spiritually been born of God? Have ye received his image in your countenances? Have ye experienced this mighty change in your hearts?" (Alma 5:14). He wanted us to know, understand, and appreciate this transcending step in our lives as we become converted to Christ.

Gratitude—The Catalyst of Change

All steps within the spiritual growth process build from interaction with one another synergistically. *This pattern of spiritual growth, culminating in gratitude, is a catalyst of change.* It is critical to understand that we literally preach and teach what we *are*. If we have experienced growth and change, we can better help others change. If we have exercised faith unto repentance, we can better help others exercise faith unto repentance. As we prepare to serve, we should be prepared to change.

We must continue to learn and grow in order to develop a deeper capacity for gratitude, the cardinal virtue. We must then express this gratitude as often as possible to bring joy to the souls of the giver and the receiver. The *True to the Faith* pamphlet offers wonderful counsel in regard to gratitude and thanksgiving:

> The Lord has promised, "He who receiveth all things with thankfulness shall be made glorious" (D&C 78:19). Gratitude is an uplifting, exalting attitude. You can probably say from experience that you are happier when you have gratitude in your heart. You cannot be bitter, resentful, or mean-spirited when you are grateful.
>
> Be thankful for the wonderful blessings that are yours. Be grateful for the tremendous opportunities you have. Be thankful to your parents. Let them know of your gratitude. Thank your friends and your teachers. Express appreciation to everyone who does you a favor or assists you in any way.

Thank your Heavenly Father for His goodness to you. You can express your gratitude to God by acknowledging His hand in all things, thanking Him for all that He gives you, keeping His commandments, and serving others. Thank Him for His Beloved Son, Jesus Christ. Express thanks for the Savior's great example, for His teachings, for His outreaching hand to lift and help, for His infinite Atonement.

Thank the Lord for His restored Church. Thank Him for all that it offers you. Thank Him for friends and family. Let a spirit of thanksgiving guide and bless your days and nights. Work at being grateful. You will find that it yields wonderful results.[4]

Likewise, we learn from *For the Strength of Youth*,

The Lord wants you to have a spirit of gratitude in all you do and say. Live with a spirit of thanksgiving and you will have greater happiness and satisfaction in life. Gratitude will turn your heart to the Lord and help you recognize His influence and blessings in your life. Even in your most difficult times, you can find much to be grateful for. Doing so will strengthen and bless you.

In your prayers, pour out your heart to your Father in Heaven in thanks for the blessings you have already received. Be specific in thanking Him for His goodness, for your family, for friends, for leaders and teachers, for the gospel, and for His Son, Jesus Christ.

You can also express gratitude to the Lord by the way you live. When you keep His commandments and serve others, you show that you love Him and are grateful to Him. Express your gratitude to others for the many ways they bless your life.[5]

Indeed, as Amulek admonishes, we are to "live in thanksgiving daily, for the many mercies and blessings which [God] doth bestow upon you" (Alma 34:38). We should likewise, "thank the Lord thy God in all things" (D&C 59:7) and remember that "in nothing doth man offend God, or against none is his wrath kindled, save those who confess not his hand in all things, and obey not his commandments" (D&C 59:21).

Gratitude, the great governing principle of change, is intrinsically connected with every aspect of life.

When our goal is spiritual growth and change, we must internalize this the governing principle of gratitude in all aspects of our being. We must have grateful eyes. We must have grateful ears, hands, hearts, and mouths. All our senses must become attuned with gratitude. As we develop gratitude, our souls will be transformed to look for and express gratitude for *all* things.

The love of God is the ultimate fruit of gratitude. This catalyst empowers us and gives us incentive to change, filling our hearts with the love of our heavenly parents. An attitude of gratitude becomes firmly rooted in us as we continue to come to a greater understanding and appreciation of the knowledge and blessings of God in our lives.

As we speak of the necessity of gratitude, it would be wise to remember a caution given about the sin of ingratitude. President Ezra Taft Benson reminds us,

> The Prophet Joseph is reported to have said at one time that one of the greatest sins for which the Latter-day Saints would be guilty would be the sin of ingratitude. I presume most of us have not thought of that as a serious sin. There is a great tendency for us in our prayers—in our pleadings with the Lord—to ask for additional blessings. Sometimes I feel we need to devote more of our prayers to expressions of gratitude and thanksgiving for blessings already received. Of course we need the daily blessings of the Lord. But if we sin in the matter of prayer, I think it is in our lack of the expressions of thanksgiving for daily blessings.[6]

Receiving and Recognizing the Love of God

The ove of God fills our heart and soul when our hearts are filled with gratitude. And as we receive the love of God we receive the gift of His Beloved Son. The love of God is expressed in all things and especially through the infinite Atonement of our Savior. This Atonement is the enabling power of all spiritual growth and change. A wonderful example is seen in the ancient Nephite nation.

> And it came to pass that there was no contention in the land, because of the love of God which did dwell in the hearts of the people.
>
> And there were no envyings, nor strifes, nor tumults, nor whoredoms, nor lyings, nor murders, nor any manner of lasciviousness; and surely there could not be a happier people among all the people who had been created by the hand of God. (4 Nephi 1:15–16)

The Nephite people changed! They received the love of God into their hearts. They received the Atonement of our Savior Jesus Christ into their very souls. This is the end goal of the gospel of Jesus Christ. When we understand and appreciate, then we can feel gratitude for the love of God, as expressed through our Savior's infinite Atonement and all the tender mercies of the Lord, we can receive this love into our hearts and souls. We will then be inspired and motivated to love God more and more deeply. We will love others more. We will live according to a higher law.

This great truth was demonstrated in a tender moment while I was presiding at the Provo MTC. A young missionary was struggling in every way possible. He was frustrated, overwhelmed, and anxious to go home. It was evident that he was not ready or prepared to serve as a missionary. The branch president explained that the young man was upset at everybody, his companion was distraught, and the district was upset. Everyone was troubled by the young missionary and his behavior. I invited the young missionary in. He expressed distaste for the mission and the Missionary Training Center and explained why he really didn't want to come on a mission in the first place. We visited at length, and I hoped I could assess his needs and his real concerns. He continually expressed his desire to go home and get out of this trying and troubling situation. Since we had several hours before he would be able to leave, simply because of packing and transportation concerns, I suggested that we visit. I asked him questions like, "How do you feel about your Heavenly Father?" Indeed, he loved His Heavenly Father. "How do you feel about life?" Then he mentioned that he was so distraught and discouraged and overwhelmed. He didn't like life. He didn't understand life. He was beside himself.

Then the Spirit taught me what to teach: teach of Christ, preach of Christ—all things of Christ. Teach of the magnificent and eternal atoning sacrifice and how it can heal us through its enabling power. For it is through Christ that we are nurtured and blessed. And so for forty minutes we talked of the Lord Jesus Christ and His atoning sacrifice. Then the missionary's heart softened, and his eyes brightened. His countenance changed.

After this lovely visit, I again asked the question, "How do you feel?" With tears streaming down his face, he said, "Oh, President Pinegar, I want to serve a mission. I love my Heavenly Father and my Savior. I need help. I understand better the goodness and mercy of my Heavenly Father and my Savior in my life. I am just so mixed up; I wanted to get out of here, but not anymore. I want to do it. I want to be a missionary."

A blessing was given. His heart was further softened and reassured at the same time. He understood. He stayed and served his mission. He understood and appreciated the Atonement and its power to heal. He had a mighty change in just an hour, as empowered by the Atonement and the power of the Holy Ghost.

The story doesn't end. I saw him in the temple twenty-four years later, and he reminded me of this life-changing moment. He is a mighty man of God. He radiates the love of God. He has the image of Christ in his countenance. With his beautiful wife beside him, he told me how he has been a seminary teacher for many years, and he loves it. We embraced. Gratitude for the goodness of God filled our souls as we departed. My heart swelled with eternal joy for the tender mercies of God our Father and our Beloved Savior Jesus Christ. And life was good, because this young missionary felt the love of God as he came to understand and appreciate the infinite and eternal Atonement of our Savior Jesus Christ.

The sermon given by the Savior on the mount and then at the temple in the land of Bountiful are indeed the celestial law and the law of the gospel that we should receive into our hearts. The result of a community living these laws creates a society in which there is no envy! No greed! No contention! As we live a celestial law, we live after the manner of happiness. We seek and find the glory of God: "And if your eye be single to my glory, your whole bodies shall be filled with light, and there shall be no darkness in you; and that body which is filled with light comprehendeth all things" (D&C 88:67). As we learn and comprehend all good things, we truly will understand and appreciate all things and be filled with gratitude and the love of God—which will give us a desire to go about doing good.

It is significant to note that love is the great motivating force in all that our Father and Savior do. So it should be with us (see John 3:16; 2 Nephi 26:24; Matthew 22:36–40; John 13:34–35; John 21:15–17). Love should be the motive of every righteous act and deed.

Love—or charity, as Mormon describes it—is the pure love of Christ (see Moroni 7:47). True charity will never fail or fall (see Moroni 7:46). Charity permeates every doctrine, principle, and righteous act that is acceptable before God and is integrally connected to every aspect of the gospel plan. This is why the love of God and our fellowmen fulfills "all the law and the prophets" and is known as "the great commandment" (see Matthew 22:36–40).

While I was serving as president of the England London South Mission (1985–88), we had the privilege of having Elder Russell M. Nelson of the Quorum of the Twelve Apostles come and give a fireside. We were to pick up Elder Nelson at the Heathrow airport in London. We arrived early and were excited and anxious to have him come and be with us and teach the saints in England. As it came time for his plane to land, an announcement came over the loud speakers, "Flight [such and such] has been diverted to an airport north of London due to fuel issues." I quickly went to the desk and asked, "Where is this airport?" I was told the mileage. It was totally out of range to pick him up and make it to the fireside. I was sick. Over two thousand Saints would be at the Crawley Stake Centre for the fireside. I prayed.

I went and pleaded with the clerk at the desk. He smiled and said he was sorry. I said, "There is an Apostle of the Lord on that plane and he needs to be in Crawley to speak." "Again, I am sorry" was his only response. I pleaded with the Lord to intervene somehow. It was now just one hour before the fireside was scheduled to begin. I went to the clerk and asked, "Why don't they land at Gatwick?" Gatwick was only a few minutes from the Crawley Stake Centre. He reminded me that he was merely relaying the message from the air controller to the people at Heathrow. Within a minute or so, an announcement of Elder Nelson's flight was changed and the plane had again been diverted, this time to the Gatwick airport. I couldn't believe it. What a miracle. I called the stake center and told them to send a car to Gatwick to pick up Elder Nelson ASAP. Meanwhile, I drove on the edge of the M-25 from Heathrow to the Crawley exit. I hurried to the stake center and pulled in the little driveway, and a car with Elder Nelson pulled in behind us. My sweetheart and I jumped out, and I opened his door. He smiled and asked, "Have you waited long?" I smiled, and said everything was fine. The fireside started a few minutes late, but we were all relieved and thankful for his save arrival, and we were spiritually uplifted, enlightened, and felt a great desire to go about doing good (see D&C 11:12–13).

On the drive home after the fireside, I related the story to Elder Nelson. He had been calm and full of faith, merely asking the Lord to get him down so he could deliver the message the Lord wanted us to hear. Then he said, "When we touched down at Gatwick for fuel, I went to the flight attendant and mentioned that I had to deplane here. They said I couldn't." He said, "You don't understand, I have to get off here." They then checked with the captain and he said, "We cannot open the baggage area to get your bags. You have to stay on the plane." Elder Nelson said, "I have no bags, simply my carry-on." The pilot shrugged and told the crew to let him off. He walked in to the terminal and the car was waiting. There were miracles at every turn so that the Lord's servant could bless our lives.

When we got home, Elder Nelson was invigorated. Due to the time change, he was not tired at all, so he suggested we have scripture time. We sat around the table with finger food and treats and searched the scriptures for a couple of hours. The following story is one of the things he taught us that night.

Elder Nelson said, "Peter was asked if he loved the Lord. The conversation between the Savior and Peter is recorded in John 21:15–17: 'So when they had dined, Jesus saith to Simon Peter, Simon, son of Jonas, lovest thou me more than these? He saith unto him, Yea, Lord; thou knowest that I love thee. He saith unto him, Feed my lambs.

He saith to him again the second time, Simon, son of Jonas, lovest thou me? He saith unto him, Yea, Lord; thou knowest that I love thee. He saith unto him, Feed my sheep.

He saith unto him the third time, Simon, son of Jonas, lovest thou me? Peter was grieved because he said unto him the third time, Lovest thou me? And he said unto him, Lord, thou knowest all things; thou knowest that I love thee. Jesus saith unto him, Feed my sheep.'"

Going on, Elder Nelson said, "Why would the Lord ask Peter three times? In the Greek translation, the word *love* as a verb has three forms: *agapao*, the perfect love of God; *phileo*, brotherly or reciprocating love; and *erao*, physical love. When the Lord would express love in the form of *agapao*, Peter would answer with *phileo*, which is not enough love to truly feed the Lord's sheep. So, the Lord asked again, and finally, the third time the Lord uses the *phileo*, and Peter was grieved because of being asked three times. This teaches us a great principle about loving. Our love must be complete, perfect, and constant for all mankind, for that is the way the Lord's disciples are known (see John 13:34–35). Indeed, we must have charity—the pure love of Christ, which never fails. We show our love to the Lord by loving and serving everyone (see Matthew 25:40). We show our love by keeping the commandments (see John 14:15)."

Elder Nelson taught clearly that the love necessary to feed the Lord's sheep is a Godlike love, else it will not be strong enough or give us enough of a motive to care for our fellowmen. Needless to say, we taught this to our wonderful missionaries as a prophet of God had taught us.

Listen to the words of the Lord as he has counseled us concerning our qualifications to serve:

"And faith, hope, charity and love, with an eye single to the glory of God, qualify him for the work." (D&C 4:5) "And see that ye have faith, hope, and charity, and then ye will always abound in good works" (Alma 7:24). "A new commandment I give unto you, that ye love one another; as I have loved you, that ye also love one another.

By this shall all men know that ye are my disciples, if ye have love one to another" (John 13:34–35).

The goodness and love of God is ever present if we but seek to see His wondrous hand in all things. Moroni exhorted us to ponder on the mercy the Lord has shown us since the beginning of time (see Moroni 10:3). When we ponder and pray, we will see more clearly the love of God evidenced in every aspect of our lives through His grace, goodness, and mercy. We will have an overwhelming desire to change. We will become more like our Savior, Jesus Christ, and thus go about doing good.

Desire to Do Good

The desire to do good, like need, is often referred to as "the mother of change." Real desire is not a wish or a whim. It is a passion and yearning for something of real import. With this definition, we can better understand the feelings of the sons of Mosiah as they prepared to embark on their missions: "Now they were *desirous* that salvation should be declared to every creature, for they could not bear that any human soul should perish; yea, even the very thoughts that any soul should endure endless torment did cause them to quake and tremble" (Mosiah 28:3; emphasis added). Their hearts were pure, their desires were righteous, and they exemplified true love for their fellowmen.

Those things that we seek after often express the desire of our hearts. We are counseled, "Wherefore, seek not the things of this world but seek ye first to build up the kingdom of God, and to establish his righteousness; and all these things shall be added unto you" (Joseph Smith Translation, Matthew 6:38 [see Matthew 6:33, footnote a]). This desire to bring about righteousness, and to save souls, is a reflection of a converted soul (see Luke 22:32; Colossians 1:9; 2 Nephi 1:16; Jacob 2:3; Enos 1:9, 11, 13; Mosiah 18:11; Alma 32:27; D&C 63:57; 137:9).

We see the importance of desire in the fact that we will be judged according to the desires of our hearts (see D&C 137:9). These desires come from the wellspring of life, even the depths of our hearts, when we possess the love of God. We must then act upon these desires and seek to bless others.

What does it take to have righteous desires constantly within our heart and soul, so that what we do is a natural expression of who we are and what we feel? We see an example in many of the early brethren, who had great desires to know the will of God for them and would come to the Prophet Joseph seeking a revelation. The Whitmer brothers both received identical revelations (sections 15 and 16).

> For many times you have *desired* of me to know that which would be of the most worth unto you.
>
> Behold, blessed are you for this thing, and for speaking my words, which I have given you according to my commandments.
>
> And now, behold, I say unto you, that *the thing which will be of the most worth unto you will be to declare repentance unto this people, that you may bring souls unto me, that you may rest with them in the kingdom of my Father.* (D&C 15:4–6; emphasis added).

Those who are truly converted will have a desire to care for their fellowmen; thus we see that the revelation given to the Whitmer brothers instructed them to seek to bring souls unto Christ. Do the words asking them to invite all to come unto Christ seem familiar to you? They should—for this is the purpose of every missionary! The goal of all missionaries is to build up the kingdom of God and further the purpose of God our Father and our Savior Jesus Christ, which is to bring about our immortality and eternal life. When our desires are to please our Heavenly Father, we all are part of that great work.

Our supreme example is, as always, the Savior. Pleasing God the Father was our Savior's constant goal: "And he that sent me is with me: the Father hath not left me alone; for I do always those things that please him" (John 8:29).

This desire to do good is also expressed consistently throughout the Book of Mormon. We read, "And they all cried with one voice, saying: Yea, we believe all the words which thou hast spoken unto us; and also, we know of their surety and truth, because of the Spirit of the Lord Omnipotent, which has wrought a mighty change in us, or in our hearts, that we have no more disposition to do evil, but to do good continually" (Mosiah 5:2).

This desire to do good is both the result of the enabling power of the Atonement and of being truly converted to Christ. When the love of God fills our hearts, we are empowered to do good by following the example of our Savior.

What does it mean to do good? We "are willing to bear one another's burdens, that they may be light; Yea, and are willing to mourn with those that mourn; yea, and comfort those that stand in need of comfort, and to stand as witnesses of God at all times and in all things, and in all places that ye may be in" (Mosiah 18:8–9). As James tells us, "Pure religion and undefiled before God and the Father is this, To visit the fatherless and widows in their affliction, and to keep himself unspotted from the world" (James 1:27). "Wherefore, be faithful; stand in the office which I have appointed unto you; succor the weak, lift up the hands which hang down, and strengthen the feeble knees" (D&C 81:5). And "strengthen your brethren in all your conversation, in all your prayers, in all your exhortations, and in all your doings" (D&C 108:7). Doing good is all about serving and blessing others. It is about being kind and generous. It is being nonjudgmental and forgiving. It is doing as Jesus would do.

Remember

The Lord trusts you. He is counting on you to hasten His work in these latter days. Why would He allow teenagers to be His missionaries and disciples, to spread his gospel to every nation, kindred, tongue, and people, if He did not? Joseph, the boy prophet, was fourteen and a half years old when he received the first vision. He was seventeen when the angel Moroni appeared to him and taught him concerning Elijah and the coming forth of the Book of Mormon.

Do not live below your privilege. Heavenly Father and our Savior Jesus Christ love and trust you. They will make you equal to your task. So let us do our part in preparing for that task. You will be a magnificent missionary, as disciples of Christ endowed with power from on high, a saver of souls as you assist in this great and glorious work. You are the best the Lord has!

CHAPTER 2

Your Mission Call

Preparing Your Mission Papers

You can submit your missionary papers 120 days prior to your availability date. By filling out your missionary recommendation forms, you are declaring your desire to be called as a full-time missionary for the Lord. "Therefore, if ye have desires to serve God ye are called to the work" (D&C 4:3). The bishop will help you prepare your mission recommendation form online and explain all that you need to do in order to receive your call. You maybe surprised at all the things you need to do just to submit the form. You will need the following information:

Identification information—driver's license or passport
Family information and contact information, including where they served as missionaries
Personal health history
Physician's evaluation of your personal health and well-being
Dental evaluation
Educational experience, Seminary and Institute experience, language skills, your desire to learn a language and your confidence in learning a language, work experience including special skills, extracurricular activities, military experience, and how your mission will be funded
Any special circumstance that could affect your mission call

Information about the sponsoring unit (your ward), provided by the bishop

Medical and dental forms. There is a page (Instructions for the Missionary Candidate) that directs you through preparing the missionary forms and the particular things you need to do. This can take some time if you require medical and dental treatment

Medical and dental records, financial forms, and proof of medical insurance should be completed by parents and missionaries and additional personal information is provided.

Personal insurance information

Privacy agreements needed to process your missionary recommendation form

Bishop or branch president recommendations and suggestions. A special page concerning your worthiness and willingness to serve, as well as confidential information. The bishop or branch president verifies that everything is correct and you are capable to serve a mission in every way, and the page is forwarded on to the stake president

You can tell the prophets really care about you as a missionary after preparing your recommendation forms. Every detail is considered for you to be prepared and healthy in order to serve and have a successful mission.

The stake president recommends you to the First Presidency as willing and worthy to serve. After your recommendation is sent in to the Missionary Department, you will usually have your call within two to three weeks.

Calls Are Inspired

In describing the assigning process, Elder M. Russell Ballard said,

A member of the Quorum of the Twelve assigns every missionary to his or her mission. Although this is done without a traditional face-to-face interview, technology and revelation combine to provide an experience that is remarkably intimate and personal. Let me tell you how this happens.

Your photograph comes up on a computer screen, together with key information provided by your bishop and stake president. When your picture appears, we look into your eyes and review your answers to the missionary recommendation questions. For that brief moment, it seems as if you are present and responding to us directly.

As we look at your photograph, we trust that you have cleared in every way the "raised bar" required today to be a faithful, successful missionary. Then, by the power of the Spirit of the Lord and under the direction of President Thomas S. Monson, we assign you to one of the Church's 406 worldwide missions.[1]

Remember that you are assigned by a prophet, and called by the prophet, to serve under the inspiration of the All Mighty God by the power of the Holy Ghost. A story published in *Meridian Magazine* on July 13, 2014, demonstrates this fact that occurs over and over in the lives of faithful missionaries.

A father shared this story with President Albright about his son's mission call.

John Eastin writes,

I want to tell you about my son's mission call. His name is Anthony, but his nickname is Frenchie. The reason for his nickname is because he speaks fluent French. He has dual citizenship, because his mother is a French citizen. When Anthony turned 19, we tried to guess where he would be called on a mission. Some said French Guyana, Madagascar, France and other French speaking countries in Africa. When he finally received his mission call letter, there was a crowd gathered in our home. As he was opening the letter, his brother Carl shouted out as a joke: "You're going to Boise, Idaho!" Anthony smiled and then opened his letter and found out that the Prophet had indeed called him to serve in Boise, Idaho. At first we all thought he was joking, like in the movie "Singles Ward." But we read the letter carefully and found it was true. After he had served in Idaho about 10 months, I received a discouraging letter from Anthony where he stated that he felt like his skills were not being utilized. He stated that he should have been called to Africa, and the Prophet must have made a mistake with his mission call.

Two months later I received a wonderful and faith-promoting letter from Anthony. He stated that he had been asked by the Spanish speaking missionaries to teach a group of five large families that they had located in their area. The Mission President gave him permission to go there since there were about 50 potential investigators. When he arrived he found that the families were refugees from Congo, Africa. They spoke only French. Anthony was the only missionary in the entire mission who spoke French. He asked one of the fathers if he believed in God. He replied, "I lived in a refugee camp for ten years that had terrible conditions that included murder. I prayed every day to get out of there and now I am here. I believe in God."

Anthony's last words in his letter were, "NOW I KNOW WHY THE LORD SENT ME TO BOISE, IDAHO!"[2]

Opening Your Missionary Call

Some parents put a big map on the wall of the world and all your family and friends put a pin on where they think you will be called to serve. Some of your friends may already have their calls to serve in a foreign country. You may be hoping for a foreign mission assignment; it sounds so exotic and fun. At this point you often don't think much about serving people. You may be consumed with the question of, "Where will I serve?" This is understandable, since you are caught up in the moment of opening your mission call. All of your friends and family gather for the big moment. You carefully open the large envelope to reveal the letter from the prophet, and it reads, "Dear Elder/Sister . . . , You are hereby called to serve as a missionary of The Church of Jesus Christ of Latter-day Saints. You are assigned to labor in the Utah Salt Lake City mission." And for a moment you might pause and wonder . . . Salt Lake City? Then it hits you. You have been called to serve the Lord Jesus Christ. It doesn't matter where you go. Your eyes may glisten, and you could shout, "Hurrah!" just like Heber C. Kimball and Brigham Young did when they left for England. Everyone will cheer for you and your call. You can be happy, wherever you are called. You are the Lord's missionary.

That night, you can read the letter carefully again and note the things the prophet has asked you to do. Remember, this is the prophet of God counseling you on what you need to do to be a worthy and a magnificent representative of the Lord Jesus Christ.

This is really important! Make a plan to do everything he has asked you to do. Here is what will be expected of you—

- Prepare to preach the gospel—Study *Preach My Gospel,* take a missionary preparation class, and study other good missionary preparation books.

- You have been recommended as one worthy to represent the Lord as a minister of the restored gospel of Jesus Christ— Repent of anything and everything that could prevent you from serving and preaching with the power of God.

- You are an official representative of the Church. You will be expected to live the highest standards of the Church by keeping the commandments, obeying the rules of missionary conduct, and following the counsel of your mission president—The highest standards! Seek to take upon you the divine nature of Christ (see 2 Peter 1:3–10).

- You will need to devote your time and attention to serve the Lord and leave behind all your personal affairs, and the Lord will bless you with increased knowledge and testimony of the Restoration and gospel truths—Start now, devoting a good share of your time to preparing. Learn to take care of yourself in every aspect of your life. Seek gospel knowledge and exercise faith to strengthen your testimony.

- Your purpose is to invite others to come unto Christ as they receive the gospel through faith in Jesus Christ and His Atonement and all the ordinances of the gospel and endure to the end—Seek to understand the Atonement and its enabling power in your life, as well as the covenants and ordinances you have entered into.

- Serve with all your heart, might, mind, and strength, and the Lord will lead you to those who seek the truth and will have a desire to be baptized—Be diligent in every aspect of preparation and service as a missionary.

- The Lord will reward you for all that you do as you humbly and prayerfully serve in this labor of love—Fast and pray to be strong in your humility and firm in your faith (see Helaman 3:35) for every soul is precious to the Lord, and to you (see D&C 18:10).

- Our prayers go with you and our confidence is in you to become an effective missionary—The Lord and the prophet not only have confidence in you, but their prayers and everyone's prayers are in behalf of the missionaries.

- Then, you are asked to write a letter of acceptance to the prophet endorsed by your bishop. Writing the letter of acceptance is an important part of making a covenant with the Lord to serve Him. This is your commitment to serve with all your heart, might, mind and strength.

Now, make a plan to do as our living prophet has counseled you!

Next, read the wonderful booklet, prepared just for you. In the booklet, there is a letter from the Quorum of the Twelve Apostles welcoming you to your mission, and reminding you that you are called to proclaim the gospel and help build up the kingdom of God. They counsel you to lose yourself in the work and to savor the honor and privilege of bringing souls to Christ. They encourage you to study the scriptures to increase in your knowledge and testimony of the gospel, that you may be led by the Holy Spirit, so you can teach and testify with power. And they remind you to "be obedient and work hard."

As you ponder the scripture they quoted about the worth of souls, you can think about your Savior and how He suffered for you. You will come to realize that you are encircled in the arms of His love. Think about the price your Savior paid for every living soul on the earth and how He did it out of love (see 2 Nephi 26:24). Offer a prayer of thanksgiving and gratitude, and surely your Heavenly Father and your Savior will be pleased. God has called you through the living prophet. Study carefully the entire booklet. It has a map of your mission and lists many things you need to do and bring on your mission.

In your letters and packet, you will find additional information that will help you prepare. The Missionary Department is amazing with all the help and programs they have for you as a missionary. In addition to the *Missionary Handbook,* you will find a wonderful course online on how to manage stress and how to use family history in missionary work, and for those speaking a foreign language, you will complete the online language study checklist. (These resources can be found on missionary.lds.org. They are only available after you receive your call, and your packet will include instructions for logging on to the website.) In addition, on lds.org there are missionary pamphlets, missionary preparation topics, frequently asked questions, and sharing the gospel online.

In addition to all the previous helps mentioned, the Missionary Department has produced a resource booklet entitled *Adjusting to Missionary Life.* This booklet is available at all the distribution centers or online. This is *vital* in your preparation to serve. It will help you understand and appreciate stress, and you will be better prepared to adjust to missionary life. This is in addition to the online course (How to Manage Stress) you will study online at missionary.lds.org.

The booklet *Adjusting to Missionary Life* contains material you simply must read and appreciate to help you deal with this dramatic change in your life as you get ready to serve a full-time mission. It helps you in the following ways:

- Understanding stress
- Assess your present feelings in regard to stress
- Principles to manage stress
- Resources for managing physical, emotional, social, intellectual, and spiritual demands

This book is absolutely crucial in assisting you to prepare. It will also help you as you serve your mission.

A few weeks after receiving your call, you will receive a letter from the Provo MTC (or another MTC) welcoming you and giving you your email address and some instructions regarding the MTC. The letter will provide the MTC website address (www.mtc.byu.

edu) that will give you all the information you need concerning your arrival at the MTC.

What preparations are necessary before entering the MTC?
What if I am fluent in or speak some of my mission second language?
What should I bring to the MTC?
Where should I report?
What supplies and services will the MTC provide?
How will my expenses be handled?
May my family come to the MTC?
May I have visitors at the MTC?
May my family deliver packages to the MTC?
Do I qualify as a student for my parents' health insurance policy?
What about travel from the MTC to the mission field?

As you ponder about all that has happened since your call, you will come to realize more fully the great trust that your Heavenly Father and your Savior have in you. Bruce R. McConkie taught the following concerning our mission call:

> I am called of God. My authority is above that of the kings of the earth. By revelation I have been selected as a personal representative of the Lord Jesus Christ. He is my Master and He has chosen me to represent Him. To stand in His place, to say and do what He himself would say and do if He personally were ministering to the very people to whom He has sent me. My voice is His voice, and my acts are His acts; my words are His words and my doctrine is His doctrine. My commission is to do what He wants done. To say what He wants said. To be a living modern witness in word and deed of the divinity of His great and marvelous latter-day work.[3]

For young men who have received their call and graduated from high school, now it is time to receive the Melchizedek Priesthood and be ordained an elder. Prepare well, and learn your duty (see D&C 107:99–100). (See also *Preparing for the Melchizedek Priesthood and my Mission* by Ed J. Pinegar.)

Remember

Remember you are called by God through a living prophet. You will be set apart as a minister of the Lord to be His Disciple and invite all to come unto Christ. This is a high and holy calling so go forward and "declare His word among his people, that they might have everlasting life" (3 Nephi 5:13).

CHAPTER 3

Realizing Your Divine Potential and Responsibility

"Go to, and Labor in the Vineyard"

You, young women and young men, are the fulfillment of prophecy: "And the Lord of the vineyard said unto them: Go to, and labor in the vineyard, with your might. For behold, this is the last time that I shall nourish my vineyard; for the end is nigh at hand, and the season speedily cometh; and if ye labor with your might with me ye shall have joy in the fruit which I shall lay up unto myself against the time which will soon come" (Jacob 5:71). You are the ones who have been called and chosen to prune the vineyard for the last time. You are among those of whom the Lord was speaking when he told of "choice spirits who were reserved to come forth in the fulness of times to take part in laying the foundations of the great latter-day work. . . . Even before they were born, they, with many others, received their first lessons in the world of spirits and were prepared to come forth in the due time of the Lord to labor in his vineyard for the salvation of the souls of men" (D&C 138:53, 56).

Yes, *you* have been saved for this day and this work. Do you realize how needed you are? The Lord trusts you! And He asks you to help Him in hastening His work:

Behold, I will hasten my work in its time.

33

And I give unto you, who are the first laborers in this last kingdom, a commandment that you assemble yourselves together, and organize yourselves, and prepare yourselves, and sanctify yourselves; yea, purify your hearts, and cleanse your hands and your feet before me, that I may make you clean;

That I may testify unto your Father, and your God, and my God, that you are clean from the blood of this wicked generation. (D&C 88:73–75)

When you understand how vital you are to this great latter-day work, you will understand the importance of preparing to become an instrument in the hands of God. As Alma stated, "I know that which the Lord hath commanded me, and I glory in it. I do not glory of myself, but I glory in that which the Lord hath commanded me; yea, and this is my glory, that perhaps I may be an instrument in the hands of God to bring some soul to repentance; and this is my joy" (Alma 29:9). You must prepare well. You will be blessed as you prepare—because you can do anything in the strength of the Lord (see Alma 26:11–12).

The Lord motivates and inspires us because He loves us and we love, trust, and respect Him. He can help us most effectively when we approach him after the pattern of spiritual growth discussed in chapter 1, as we first recognize our weaknesses and imperfections: "And if men come unto me I will show unto them their weakness. I give unto men weakness that they may be humble; and my grace is sufficient for all men that humble themselves before me; for if they humble themselves before me, and have faith in me, then will I make weak things become strong unto them" (Ether 12:27). He will guide and teach us with all the tenderness and love of a parent for a child, for we are literally His sons and His daughters (see Mosiah 5:7). Our values are His values. His work is our work. We have made covenants to serve Him and build up the kingdom of God on earth. As our commitment to these covenants deepen, our desire to do good increases. Remember that God has covenanted to bless us with all things if we are faithful and obedient to our covenants and commandments.

We must ask ourselves the following questions as we ponder

our motivation to serve the Lord: How converted are we to Christ and His gospel? How deep is our gratitude for His atoning sacrifice? When the answers to these questions fill our hearts with gratitude and understanding of who we are, we will echo the sentiments of one missionary who said, "It's the least I could do to be a good missionary after all my Savior has done for me."

Bringing souls to Christ is both the goal and the reward of missionary work. Nothing will bring you greater happiness. A missionary who was serving in Germany wrote me, "Oh, Brother Ed, it's so great. A sister is committed for February 8th to be baptized. It's like you said, I've never been so happy." And then he added some beautiful words: "I am continually being strengthened by the Atonement of the Lord Jesus Christ. There are elders and sisters who understand why we do what we do. And when we set a baptismal goal, or any other worthy goals, it's because we love Heavenly Father's children." Surely we should seek to have this love as our motive in missionary work. For this love is the motive for Heavenly Father and our Savior in all that They do for us (see John 3:16; 2 Nephi 26:24).

Our Responsibility to Proclaim the Gospel

The Lord, through the Holy Scriptures, has spoken. We are to proclaim His gospel to all people in all lands. Consider the following scriptures:

1. "Go ye therefore, and teach all nations, baptizing them in the name of the Father, and of the Son, and of the Holy Ghost: Teaching them to observe all things whatsoever I have commanded you: and, lo, I am with you always, even unto the end of the world. Amen" (Matthew 28:19–20).
2. "Go ye into all the world, and preach the gospel to every creature" (Mark 16:15). "That repentance and remission of sins should be preached in his name among all nations, beginning at Jerusalem" (Luke 24:47).
3. "For behold, thus said Jesus Christ, the Son of God, unto his disciples who should tarry, yea, and also to all his disciples,

in the hearing of the multitude: Go ye into all the world, and preach the gospel to every creature" (Mormon 9:22. See also D&C 1:2, 4; 133:8).

The Savior has made it abundantly clear that we are to take His gospel and proclaim it to every nation, every land, every people, every tongue, every soul, and every creature—all the world. We are to preach His word and "stand as witnesses at all times and in all things and in all places" (Mosiah 18:9). Prophets have taught us this concept through the ages as well.

The Lord also emphasizes the importance of missionary work time and again through His modern prophets. To catch a vision of the work, ponder the following quotes from our prophets:

Thomas S. Monson declared,

> Young men, I admonish you to prepare for service as a missionary. Keep yourselves clean and pure and worthy to represent the Lord. Maintain your health and strength. Study the scriptures. Where such is available, participate in seminary or institute. Familiarize yourself with the missionary handbook Preach My Gospel.
>
> A word to you young sisters: while you do not have the same priesthood responsibility as do the young men to serve as full-time missionaries, you also make a valuable contribution as missionaries, and we welcome your service.[1]

President Monson reminds us, "Remember that this is the Lord's work, and when we are on the Lord's errand, we are entitled to the Lord's help. The Lord will shape the back to bear the burden placed upon it."[2]

Gordon B. Hinckley admonished:

> I wish I could awaken in the heart of every man, woman, boy, and girl here this morning the great consuming desire to share the gospel with others. If you do that you live better, you try to make your lives more exemplary because you know that those you teach will not believe unless you back up what you say by the goodness of your lives. Nobody can foretell the consequences of that which you do when you teach the gospel to another. Missionary work is a work of love and trust, and it has to be done on that basis. Be a part of this great process, which constantly adds to the vitality of the Church.

Every time a new member comes into the Church, something happens. There is an infusion of strength and faith and testimony that is wonderful. Think of what this Church would be without the missionary program. Think of it! I think this is the greatest age in the history of the world. I think this is the greatest time in the history of the Church. I believe that. I think there will be greater times in the future. We are growing ever and ever stronger. . . . What a responsibility we have. The whole fate of the world depends on us, according to the revelations of the Almighty. We cannot waste time. We cannot be unrighteous in our living. We cannot let our thoughts dwell on immoral things. We have to be the very best that we can be, you and I, because the very relationship of God our Eternal Father to His children on the earth depends on their accepting what we have come to teach according to His magnificent word.[3]

Joseph Smith declared, "After all that has been said, the greatest and most important duty is to preach the Gospel."[4]

The Prophet Joseph Smith prophesied of the latter days in which the gospel would be taken to all corners of the globe:

Our missionaries are going forth to different nations, and in Germany, Palestine, New Holland, Australia, the East Indies, and other places, the Standard of Truth has been erected; no unhallowed hand can stop the work from progressing; persecutions may rage, mobs may combine, armies may assemble, calumny may defame, but the truth of God will go forth boldly, nobly, and independent, till it has penetrated every continent, visited every clime, swept every country, and sounded in every ear, till the purposes of God shall be accomplished, and the Great Jehovah shall say the work is done.[5]

Do these words still apply? In the Doctrine and Covenants, the Lord confirms that they do.

What I the Lord have spoken, I have spoken, and I excuse not myself; and though the heavens and the earth pass away, *my word shall not pass away, but shall all be fulfilled, whether by mine own voice or by the voice of my servants, it is the same.* (D&C 1:38; emphasis added)

The Lord Will Assist You

We are to proclaim the gospel of Jesus Christ, but the Lord is able to do His own work. Two elders were proclaiming the gospel with all their hearts, might, minds, and souls. They were praying with hope that someone, anyone, might come unto Christ. They were working in an area outside of London, in a city called Croydon. A sweet sister (we will call her Sally) was progressing nicely and was committed for baptism. As they were reviewing the baptismal service, she started to have some doubts. They struggled to resolve her concerns to no avail. They had worked diligently over the last six weeks in bringing her to the knowledge of the truth. She knew, but she was scared and doubt began to consume her heart. She finally said that she just couldn't be baptized. The elders were devastated. They pleaded to no avail.

Now remember, they had been called of God to proclaim the gospel to every nation, kindred, tongue, and people, and they were saddened beyond belief. The phone rang at the mission home, and a weeping missionary who could hardly talk cried out, "Oh, President, Sally is not going to be baptized." They were beside themselves. I had had this experience many times with the missionaries who had investigators call off their discussions, and it really was hard on them because they loved their investigators so much it hurt. They cared for their souls.

Then, as always, the Lord heard the cries of His missionaries and answered their prayers. I said with great confidence, because it was given me what to say, "Elders, everything will be okay." They doubted for a moment, but I said, "Just give me her phone number and she will be prepared for Sunday to be baptized." "How can you be sure?" the elder asked. I merely said, "The Lord is in charge, and everything will be fine." Finally, they felt consoled enough to say good-bye.

I remember the following morning as if it were yesterday. Sally picked up the phone after just a couple of rings. I mentioned who I was and she thanked me for my letter congratulating her on her upcoming baptism, and then we talked together about her testimony and knowledge of the Lord, and her desire to please Him and come into the waters of baptism and follow Him. She told me how nervous she had been the night before, and I mentioned that I was going to be at the baptism. A little sparkle came into her voice. I told her that

I would call the elders, and they would make all the arrangements, so she should be at peace. I reminded her that they would call and make sure everything was okay. The following Sunday was a glorious evening as we pulled up to the Croydon chapel. There was this beautiful sister, Sally, standing by the front door of the chapel with the missionaries to greet us. The baptism was a spiritual feast and everyone was edified and uplifted. Everyone was happy and life was good.

Remember

As we read the words of the prophets and search the scriptures, our duty becomes clear—invite all mankind to come unto Christ that they too might enjoy the blessings of exaltation. We are to further the kingdom of God by proclaiming the gospel, perfecting the saints, redeeming the dead, and caring for the poor and needy. These four tasks are the purposes of the Church, which fulfills the great plan of happiness. This work is a grave and joyous responsibility, and the Lord needs those who accept the call to be better prepared by understanding their own divine worth and then accepting the call to serve. We need to be worthy, willing, and eager to do the Lord's work. It is our sacred calling as disciples of Jesus Christ to help our brothers and sisters come unto Him.

CHAPTER 4

Preparation in All Things

The Power of Preparation—Prepare Well and Early

When we prepare, we put ourselves in a condition of *readiness*. We make plans and set goals. We set things in order and organize every needful thing. The goals and plans we will discuss in this section are those that will prepare you to serve a mission and to receive your temple endowment. This will take both effort and determination. You will need to exercise faith, work with all diligence, and then be patient as you prepare to do every needful thing to become a servant of the Lord.

Preparing for your mission is more than getting new clothes and a missionary haircut. You need to be prepared in many aspects to serve a mission. You need to live having faith unto repentance before you can preach faith unto repentance. You need to be worthy to enter the temple in order to receive your temple blessings. President Howard W. Hunter has taught,

> To qualify for the blessings of the temple, each of us must ensure that our lives are in harmony with the teachings of the Church. Before going to the temple, you are interviewed by your bishop. In that interview you certify to him that you meet a standard of conduct relating to the holy temple. . . .
>
> You must believe in God the Eternal Father, in his Son Jesus Christ, and in the Holy Ghost. . . .

You must sustain the General Authorities and local authorities of the Church. . . .

You must be morally clean to enter into the holy temple. . . .

You must ensure that there is nothing in your relationship with family members that is out of harmony with the teachings of the Church. . . .

To enter the temple you must be honest in all of your dealings with others. . . .

To qualify for a temple recommend, you should strive to do your duty in the Church, attending your sacrament, priesthood, and other meetings. . . .

To enter the temple you must be a full–tithe payer and live the Word of Wisdom.[1]

There are spiritual, emotional, intellectual, social, and physical preparations you need to make. Sometimes future missionaries play until the last minute to get all the fun they can cram into their lives and then literally crash in the MTC from the shock of the lifestyle change. Missionary work is hard work. It drains you spiritually, emotionally, intellectually, and physically. If you fail to prepare, you are sowing the seeds of frustration and disappointment. Thank goodness the Lord is patient with us and helps us through these trying times. How much better it is when you pay the price of preparation and become a strength to others when you serve.

I have learned that this life on Earth is a time to learn and that you learn through your own experience. There are things you can learn vicariously through study. There are things you can learn through inspiration and revelation. And there are simply those things you have to live through, suffer through, and endure in order to understand and appreciate. The law of opposition, temptation, and agency are always in operation; therefore, you need to understand opposition, overcome and avoid temptation, and make good choices. Whether before your mission or on your mission, you will have to learn certain lessons:

- You have to learn to live through separation from family, friends, and special relationships.

- You have to learn to be on your own, away from home, and have some experience providing for yourself.
- You have to learn to do hard things.
- You have to learn to be self-reliant.
- You have to learn to act and not be acted upon.
- You have to learn to care about others and quit feeding your own wants. Learn to think of others instead of "me, me, me."
- You have to learn to help others.
- You have to learn how to pray and commune with Heavenly Father.
- You have to learn to understand and appreciate the Atonement of our Savior Jesus Christ.
- You have to learn to understand and appreciate the empowering nature of the temple endowment.

And all of this learning is *your* responsibility. Mom and Dad can't do it for you. You have to learn your duty. You have to fulfill the measure of your creation. You have to make the mighty change. You have to try with all you heart, might, mind, and strength. Yes, the Lord will help you. Yes, the Holy Spirit will guide and comfort you. In obtaining Their help, you have to love Heavenly Father and our Savior, exert faith in Jesus Christ, become clean and worthy, and seek to keep the commandments—then the promised blessings can come showering down upon you.

The Atonement was not easy for our beloved Savior Jesus Christ. He suffered in agony and sacrificed His very being to bring forth the infinite and eternal Atonement. You will also have to sacrifice and suffer within your own realm of responsibility. It will not require what the Savior had to do, but it will require you to sacrifice. So gird up your loins and take courage, for missionary work is work and it is worth it. You will feel the joy after you have paid the price! You will know when you are really converted when you start to care about your fellowmen.

I was a teachers quorum adviser with the legendary coach of BYU football, Lavell Edwards. He told the quorum that he held a meeting with the football team on the first day of practice, and he asked them if they wanted to win the conference championship. They all yelled and chanted, "Yes! Yes! Yes!" Then he paused and asked them, "How many of you are willing to pay the price of preparation to win the conference championship?" Silence. Then he continued, "When you want to prepare as badly as you want to win, then we can be champions." Preparation precedes power.

Spiritual Preparation

A missionary mentioned to me one day, "I remember when I was preparing to serve, I didn't even think about these five areas of preparation (spiritual, emotional, intellectual, social, and physical), let alone being spiritual. I just didn't think about the things I should have been thinking about." Being led by the Holy Spirit is the key to being spiritually in tune and becoming a successful missionary.

Spirituality can be defined in many ways. It is often referred to as living an inspired life, or enjoying the companionship and blessings of the Holy Spirit. It involves using self-mastery to become spiritually directed rather than carnally minded. As you increase in your spirituality, your spirit, by the power of the Holy Ghost, directs your life—your spirit governs your flesh. In this state, you can be shown by the Holy Ghost all things you should do (see 2 Nephi 32:5). By doing this, you have begun the process of sanctification to become clean and pure. You seek the will of Heavenly Father, yielding your heart to Him (see Helaman 3:35). The blessings of spirituality received from the Holy Spirit are many and varied, enumerated as the gifts of the Spirit (see Moroni 10:7–19; D&C 46:8–31), the fruits of the Spirit (see Galatians 5:22–23), and trust in the Spirit, which leads you to do good (see D&C 11:12–13), and many other blessings of the Spirit.

A spiritual foundation is an essential ingredient in being a well-adjusted and happy missionary. Jacob explained, "Remember, to be carnally-minded is death, and to be spiritually-minded is life eternal" (2 Nephi 9:39). Carnally minded refers to the things of the world. Self-aggrandizement and the natural man have a lot in common. "The natural man receiveth not the things of the Spirit of God: for they are foolishness unto him: neither can he know them, because they are spiritually discerned" (1 Corinthians 2:14). This is what King Benjamin was teaching his people when he said, "For the natural man is an enemy to God, and has been from the fall of Adam, and will be, forever and ever, unless he yields to the enticings of the Holy Spirit, and putteth off the natural man and becometh a saint through the atonement of Christ the Lord, and becometh as a child, submissive, meek, humble, patient, full of love, willing to submit to all things which the Lord seeth fit to inflict upon him, even as a child doth submit to his father" (Mosiah 3:19). The enticings and blessings of the Holy Ghost are simply magnificent and bear repeating, "And now, verily, verily, I say unto thee, put your trust in that Spirit which leadeth to do good—yea, to do justly, to walk humbly, to judge righteously; and this is my Spirit. Verily, verily, I say unto you, I will impart unto you of my Spirit, which shall enlighten your mind, which shall fill your soul with joy" (D&C 11:12–13).

You need spiritual power. You need to increase in your spirituality so that you can be in tune with the Holy Ghost, and so that He can be your companion. Your relationship with Heavenly Father and your Savior needs to be deepened. Here are some things you can consider as you increase in your spirituality and in receiving the power of the Holy Ghost in your life.

Increase your faith in Jesus Christ. After hearing the prophecies and teachings of his father, Nephi recorded, "I, Nephi, was desirous also that I might see, and hear, and know of these things, by the power of the Holy Ghost, which is the gift of God unto all those who diligently seek him, as well in times of old as in the time that he should manifest himself unto the children of men" (1 Nephi 10:17). To increase in faith, you need to hear and feast upon the word of God (see Romans 10:17; 2 Nephi 32:3–5) and fast and pray that you might become firm in your faith (see Helaman 3:35), which is the moving cause of all action. Remember Nephi: "And I was led by the Spirit, not knowing beforehand the things which I should do" (1 Nephi 4:6).

Love God and purify yourself. "But great and marvelous are the works of the Lord, and the mysteries of his kingdom which he showed unto us, which surpass all understanding in glory, and in might, and in dominion; . . . for they are only to be seen and understood by the power of the Holy Spirit, which God bestows on those who love him, and purify themselves before him" (D&C 76:114, 116). You express love to your Heavenly Father and Savior as you receive Their love through the infinite Atonement of our Savior by receiving the ordinances and covenants of the priesthood, being faithful and obedient, fasting and praying, expressing gratitude, worshiping in the temple, serving your fellowmen, and seeking to please your Heavenly Father and Savior at every opportunity. You purify yourself by applying the Atonement to your life through the grace of God, through the reception of the Holy Ghost, and by practicing individual righteousness. This is the process of sanctification. This is a process of becoming purged from your sins through the blood of Christ. This is applying the Atonement to your life through repentance. This is what the Lord commanded Adam to do. "Thou shalt repent and call upon God in the name of the Son forevermore" (Moses 5:8). This is what you do when you partake of the sacrament every Sabbath day.

Keep the commandments. "O God, the Eternal Father, we ask thee in the name of thy Son, Jesus Christ, to bless and sanctify this bread to the souls of all those who partake of it, that they may eat in remembrance of the body of thy Son, and witness unto thee, O God, the Eternal Father, that they are willing to take upon them the name of thy Son, and always remember him and keep his commandments which he has given them; that they may always have his Spirit to be with them. Amen" (D&C 20:77). Keeping the commandments is a demonstration of your love (see John 14:15, 21).

Make the mighty change in your hearts. "And now behold, I ask of you, my brethren of the church, have ye spiritually been born of God? Have ye received his image in your countenances? Have ye experienced this mighty change in your hearts?" (Alma 5:14). In this scripture, Alma exhorts Church members to be spiritually minded—to be born of the Spirit, to radiate the light of Christ (see 3 Nephi 12:16; 18:24; D&C 103:9–10).

When you have a change of heart, you will yield to the enticings of the Spirit (see Mosiah 3:19), you will yield your heart to God (see Helaman 3:35) and you will have "no more disposition to do evil" (Mosiah 5:2). You offer a broken heart and contrite spirit, which is to offer your will to the Lord in all humility and meekness. You hearken to His prophets (see 3 Nephi 12:1–2; 28:34–35) and then you will "abound in good works" (Alma 7:24) and "do good continually" (Mosiah 5:2).

President Hinckley counseled,

> If I were a bishop or stake president today, what would I do? I think that I would try to put my major efforts on building the spirituality of the people. I would work as hard as I knew how to work in building their faith in the Lord Jesus Christ, in God our Eternal Father, in the Prophet Joseph Smith and the restoration of this work and what it means and what it is all about. I would encourage my people to read the scriptures, to read the Book of Mormon, to read the New Testament. I would urge them with all the capacity I have to read quietly and thoughtfully and introspectively, if you please. I would urge them to read the teachings of the Prophet Joseph Smith.
>
> You need to build yourselves spiritually. You live in a world of rush and go, of running here and there and in every direction. You are very busy people. You have so much to do. You need to get off by yourselves once in awhile and think of the spiritual things and build yourselves spiritually. . . . Get by yourself and think of things of the Lord, of things of the Spirit. Let gratitude swell up in your hearts. Think of all the Lord has done for you. How blessed you are, how very blessed you are. Think of your duty and your responsibility. Think of your testimony. Think of the things of God. Just meditate and reflect for an hour about yourself and your relationship to your Heavenly Father and your Redeemer. It will do something for you.[2]

President Howard W. Hunter has taught us,

Developing spirituality and attuning ourselves to the highest influences of godliness is not an easy matter. It takes time and frequently involves a struggle. It will not happen by chance, but is accomplished only through deliberate effort and by calling upon God and keeping his commandments. . . . We must take time to prepare our minds for spiritual things. The development of spiritual capacity does not come with the conferral of authority. There must be desire, effort, and personal preparation. As you already know, this requires fasting, prayer, searching the scriptures, experience, meditation, and a hungering and thirsting after the righteous life.[3]

President Hunter went on to say,

I find it helpful to review these admonitions from Almighty God:

"If thou shalt ask, thou shalt receive revelation upon revelation, knowledge upon knowledge, that thou mayest know the mysteries and peaceable things—that which bringeth joy, that which bringeth life eternal" (D&C 42:61).

"Ask the Father in my name in faith, believing that you shall receive, and you shall have the Holy Ghost, which manifesteth all things which are expedient unto the children of men" (D&C 18:18).

"Let the solemnities of eternity rest upon your minds" (D&C 43:34).

"God shall give unto you knowledge by his Holy Spirit, yea, by the unspeakable gift of the Holy Ghost" (D&C 121:26).

These are promises that the Lord will surely fulfill if we prepare ourselves. Take time to meditate, ponder, and pray on spiritual matters.[4]

Remember, your spirit needs nourishment—and it doesn't eat proteins, carbohydrates, or fats. It only metabolizes the word of God. The Lord has commanded you,

And I now give unto you a commandment to beware concerning yourselves, to give diligent heed to the words of eternal life.

For you shall live by every word that proceedeth forth from the mouth of God.

For the word of the Lord is truth, and whatsoever is truth is light, and whatsoever is light is Spirit, even the Spirit of Jesus Christ.

And the Spirit giveth light to every man that cometh into the world; and the Spirit enlighteneth every man through the world, that hearkeneth to the voice of the Spirit. (D&C 84:43–46)

Living by the word of God increases our spirituality. This is why you hearken to your prophets, feast upon the word of God, and listen for promptings of the Holy Spirit and answers to your prayers, for they all contain the word of God. Here is some additional counsel for increasing our spirituality:

> We seek spirituality through faith, repentance, and baptism; through forgiveness of one another; through fasting and prayer; through righteous desires and pure thoughts and actions. We seek spirituality through service to our fellowmen; through worship; through feasting on the word of God, in the scriptures and in the teachings of the living prophets. We attain spirituality through making and keeping covenants with the Lord, through conscientiously trying to keep all the commandments of God. Spirituality is not acquired suddenly. It is the consequence of a succession of right choices. It is the harvest of a righteous life.[5]

Wow! Becoming spiritual is no easy task. I am still growing, still becoming, and I know it is a life-long process. Don't be discouraged and don't compare yourself to *anyone*. In the strength of the Lord, you can do all things.

Emotional Preparation

When you enter the MTC, there is a great change in what you are accustomed to and in your lifestyle in general. Change can be hard to deal with, especially when coupled with increased stress. I remember some missionaries struggling with almost everything they faced at the MTC because they were not prepared emotionally to handle this major change in their lives, especially when they were not expecting it. Unrealized expectations often bring negative feelings. It simply is not getting what you expected. They asked, "Where is all this happiness I am supposed to feel? Why isn't it fun? Why can't we . . . ?" And the questions continued, since they were *not* prepared emotionally. You have to learn to do hard things. Here are some things that can help you to be self-reliant and emotionally strong.

Learn to Work—Learn to work hard. Learn to manage your time and money. Learn to do hard things. There is no joy without effort, and that effort is based upon your ability to diligently and faithfully work in building up the kingdom of God. President Benson reminds us,

> One of the greatest secrets of missionary work, is work. If missionaries work we will get the Spirit; if we get the Spirit, we will teach by the Spirit; and if we teach by the Spirit, we will touch the hearts of the people; and we will be happy. There will be no homesickness and no worrying about families, for all time and talents and interests are centered on the work of the ministry. That's the secret—work, work, work. There is no satisfactory substitute, especially in missionary work.[6]

Gain Self-Mastery and Become Self-Reliant—This requires you to do things on your own. You have to have experiences away from home if at all possible. Prepare your own meals. Do your own laundry. Iron your own clothes. Become responsible and accountable for every aspect of your life. Don't just know how to do it but practice doing it for several weeks. Take control of your environment so you are not being acted upon. You are in charge of yourself.

Have a Physical and an Emotional Checkup—When someone suffers from any medical concern, it is magnified when coping with stress. People are often unaware of underlying medical concerns because they have never been tested. This is why people undergo a stress test, to see if their heart really is functioning properly, even though they have no symptoms. I was feeling fine and didn't know I had a problem until I took the stress test. Bingo! Bypass surgery and now I am doing fine.

Treat Medical and Emotional Conditions—Everyone has different medical conditions, and people often need to be medicated for them. This is part of life. So if there is a need for medication in regards to your emotional well-being, it is surely okay. Many missionaries fulfilling a full-time mission are medicated for some emotional concerns, just as some are medicated for physical ailments. In the MTC, I would often speak with missionaries who had medical conditions that required medication. They would come to me and explain that they were tired of taking the medication, and they knew that their faith would be strong enough. Some missionaries would stop their medication and fall apart. I would plead with them to keep taking their medication and would often reach in my drawer and take out my "puffer" for my asthma. I would explain how the Lord inspired people to develop these wonderful drugs for our benefit. If I didn't use my "puffer," I couldn't breathe well. I exercised my faith by doing everything I could to help my medical condition. There are medications for emotional, mental, and physical needs that can help us be strong and be able to serve a full-time mission. Be obedient to your physician and you will be healthier as you serve.

Separate Yourself from Time with Electronic Devices—your video games, social media, and so on—the sooner, the better!

Learn to Set Goals and Make Plans—Learn to live by a schedule because in the mission field you will have a set schedule to accomplish everything you need to do. Learn to organize every needful thing, or else you will easily become frustrated and feel overwhelmed. Heavenly Father made a perfect plan for us to live by. You need a plan to be successful in the work. And whatever you do, be sure to follow up on yourself just like you follow up with your investigators in their reading assignments and commitments.

Learn the Virtue of Patience—Be patient with yourself in the process of becoming a good missionary. This takes time. In your weakness, you can be made strong as you humble yourself before the Lord (see Ether 12:27). Do *not* beat yourself up because things are not perfect or because you didn't have the success you expected. Just do your best and be positive in the work.

Express Gratitude and Keep a Gratitude Journal—Gratitude is an empowering virtue. It is the catalyst for change. It is a cardinal virtue for life. Life is better in every aspect when you look for the good and record your grateful feelings in your journal. You will please God when you live in thanksgiving daily and you will feel better too.

Take Care of Your Health—Exercise. Get proper rest. Eat well. All these things can help you reduce stress in your life.

Remember There Is Opposition in All Things—Every day you will be faced with trials and adversity. This is part of life. Be prepared for setbacks. Don't take personally the decisions of others to reject you or the message of the Restoration. In opposition, you will be made stronger, and as you grow, you will be able to help other missionaries who are struggling just as you struggled earlier in your mission.

Live with Hope and Optimism—Looking on the bright side and having hope in our Savior Jesus Christ keeps you in a state of emotional well-being. Sooner or later things will be better.

Build Strong Relationships with Your Companion and Other Missionaries—You strengthen one another and support each other in your time of need (see D&C 108:7). Reach out to others with love and kindness. Look for ways to serve and help and life will be sweet.

Remember Who You Are—You are a child of God and you have a purpose in life. You are to love and serve others. When you forget yourself, you will find that everything is better because your trials are swallowed up with the pure love of Christ, for charity never fails. If your love fails to embrace God, a tragedy will occur just as in the days of Adam: "And Satan came among them, saying: I am also a son of God; and he commanded them, saying: Believe it not; and they believed it not, and they loved Satan more than God. And men began from that time forth to be carnal, sensual, and devilish" (Moses 5:13).

Social Preparation

There are many social skills you need to learn and practice in order to be a better missionary. Going out with the full-time missionaries can help you develop many of these skills.

- Learn how to talk to people. Practice going into stores and striking up a conversation.
- Learn early and practice teaching the lessons in *Preach My Gospel*. Practice giving talks and leading discussions in your family home evening (FHE).
- Learn to follow your leaders.

- Learn how to give directions clearly.
- Learn how to get acquainted with new people. This can be a roadblock you have to overcome if you wait until you are on your mission.
- Learn to meet new people. Learn to listen.
- Learn to love people with the pure love of Christ.
- Learn how to disagree on a subject and still be friends and get along.
- Learn how to express your concerns without complaining.
- Learn to communicate face-to-face without reliance on texting and electronic devices. Discuss a topic around the dinner table.

Social skills are absolutely vital in building relationships of trust. These relationships provide a stable platform for you and your companion to learn to live together and to work in unity and love. You will be better able to understand and appreciate another's concerns. You will be more compassionate and be able to express your love towards others. You will be able to work in harmony with the members in inviting all to come unto Christ.

Intellectual Preparation

There are many things you need to know and do to prepare and feel at peace while getting ready for your mission. Go to lds.org and click on Resources and then click on Missionary. Under the missionary tab is a plethora of resources that will help you prepare every needful thing.

To become a good missionary you need to have knowledge of what a missionary "Is" and what a missionary "Does." *Preach My Gospel* is your missionary guide. Read it. Study it. Underline it. Write notes in the margin. You will come to realize that this knowledge found in *Preach My Gospel* is what you need to prepare and to serve well. *Preach My Gospel* contains knowledge that you need to obtain. It teaches you the "hows" and the "whats" of every phase of missionary work. Knowing what to teach and how to recognize the Holy Spirit are crucial to your preparation.

You need gospel knowledge, as found in the scriptures and words of our living prophets and leaders. Your Sunday School, Young Women, and Priesthood lessons are geared to help you understand and learn the gospel of Jesus Christ and be able teach it to others.

There is no royal road to gospel knowledge; it comes as *you* study and pray concerning this life-saving and exalting knowledge. This is the knowledge that leads you to know your Heavenly Father and your Savior Jesus Christ. "And this is life eternal, that they might know thee the only true God, and Jesus Christ, whom thou hast sent" (John 17:3). This is the knowledge that leads to conversion.

> And thousands were brought to *the knowledge of the Lord*, yea, thousands were brought to believe in the traditions of the Nephites; and they were taught the records and prophecies which were handed down even to the present time.
>
> And as sure as the Lord liveth, so sure as many as believed, or as many as *were brought to the knowledge of the truth*, through the preaching of Ammon and his brethren, according to the spirit of revelation and of prophecy, and the power of God working miracles in them—yea, I say unto you, as the Lord liveth, as many of the Lamanites as believed in their preaching, and were converted unto the Lord, never did fall away. (Alma 23:5–6; emphasis added)

This is the knowledge that empowers you just as it did the sons of Mosiah and their Lamanite converts. "They had waxed strong in the knowledge of the truth; for they were men of a sound understanding and they had searched the scriptures diligently, that they might know the word of God. But this is not all; they had given themselves to much prayer, and fasting; therefore they had the spirit of prophecy, and the spirit of revelation, and when they taught, they taught with power and authority of God" (Alma 17:2–3).

Time is your ally. Study daily and surely you will come to know all the things you need to do as a missionary. Set a time, a place, and a way so that your time to study is regular and effective.

Physical Preparation

I testify to you that when you are healthy, and physically and mentally alert, you will feel better and perform better in every aspect of your life.

Nutrition and Weight—Eat well. Cut out junk food. Eat fruits, vegetables, and lean proteins, and keep your weight under control. You will feel better.

Exercise—Exercise is critical to keep your body in its best operating condition. Exercise also burns calories. Calories can burn adipose tissue (fat). Weight gain is often a problem on your mission. If you eat less and exercise more, with a difference of between 2,800 and 3,700 calories a day you can lose one pound a week. This simple math can help you eat properly and exercise more. The big plus about good eating habits and exercise is that you feel so much better, and it reduces stress too.

Cleanliness and Personal Hygiene—Develop habits of cleanliness. You are a temple of God (see 1 Corinthians 3:16) and you have a responsibility to make sure you are clean and pure inside and out.

Rest—Always get eight hours of sleep and you will be at your best.

Be wise and always report any health concerns before they become life threatening. If you are taking *any* medication, be sure that you adhere to the prescribed medication and the directions given by your physician.

Remember

Remember, doing these things prior to your mission will not only help you establish the skills but also create habits that will strengthen you for the huge change you will have as you enter the MTC and the mission field.

1. Keep the commandments—Live having faith unto repentance so you can preach faith unto repentance. You can't expect to teach the commandments with power if you are not living them. Make a commitment to live *ALL* the

mission rules. This includes the *Missionary Handbook* that you will receive in the MTC and things specified by your mission president. They will keep you safe, and through your obedience, you will qualify for the companionship of the Holy Ghost.

2. Establish a time, a place, and a way to search and feast upon the scriptures and pray mightily to our Heavenly Father.
3. Gain a testimony of the gospel truths and bear it often.
4. Work with your local full-time missionaries and your ward mission leader whenever possible.
5. Save your money before your mission and be frugal on your mission, because the money you use related to your mission is for a sacred purpose: saving souls.

"If ye are prepared ye shall not fear" (D&C 38:30). When I served as a mission president and as president of the Provo MTC, I could always recognize those who had paid the price of preparation for their mission. They radiated the light of the Lord (see 3 Nephi 18:24). When I spoke with them, I could feel the presence of the Holy Spirit. They were enthusiastic and confident, yet meek and humble (see Alma 7:23–24). They were easily entreated, or easy to approach about any matter, knowing full well the great opportunity that lay ahead of them. They were eager and even anxious to do the work. They were excited to learn. By their demeanor and the Spirit that surrounded them, it was clear that their hearts were right before the Lord (see D&C 39:8). I could feel their love of God and sense the charity that welled up from their very souls (see 4 Nephi 1:15–16; Moroni 7:44–48).

You may be wondering, how could this be? How could someone so young—still a teenager—be so prepared? It was possible because they had yielded their hearts to God (see Helaman 3:35) and were enticed by the Holy Ghost (see Mosiah 3:19). They had become humble and firm in their faith. They had become saints through the Atonement of Christ the Lord. They had started their quest to be an instrument in the hands of the Lord (see Alma 29:9–10). No, they were not perfect. They were nervous, and they were human. Yet they were in a state of readiness to serve the Lord, "the Lord requireth the heart and a willing mind" (D&C 64:34). They had prepared to serve!

When you allow the Spirit to teach and direct you in all things, you will find yourself willing to work with a disposition of faith, diligence, and patience. The Spirit will strengthen your faith, which will help you be diligent—meaning you will learn to work with all your heart, might, mind, and soul.

Remember what President Benson said about work. You must learn how to work. In my experience, missionaries who took extra time and effort to do well in school or with a job had usually learned how to work—and were always that much better as missionaries. Those who knew how to work were successful. If they had not learned how to work hard before the mission, they had to be taught how to work in the mission field.

When I was a mission president, all the missionaries knew that I loved them, but if they didn't want to work, it saddened me. I remember I would call them in to my office individually at times and say, "I don't feel so good. I don't know if we are working as hard as the Lord would want us to work." Then we would discuss the Atonement at great length. By and by, these missionaries' gratitude for their beloved Savior, Jesus Christ, would increase and their hearts would be touched. The Spirit would testify of truth, we would discuss a commitment to change, and then these missionaries' lives would then proceed to change. I understood that each of these missionaries wanted to do good but just needed the strength of the Lord to be at his or her best. And I knew that the missionaries would work harder and find greater joy after we had talked because there is nothing more joyous than working for the Lord.

When you find yourself struggling to find the energy to work harder, I encourage you to think about what the Savior has done for you. Gratitude will fill your soul. It is difficult to imagine the pain and suffering the Lord endured as He worked out His infinite sacrifice and Atonement. The price was high, but it was worth it. Likewise, the price of missionary work is high. And very, very worth it! We too are required to sacrifice—not in the same manner as the Savior but for the same cause: the welfare of the souls of all mankind.

You will see the law of the harvest in effect in every moment of your mission. What we sow, we can then reap! When you have a hard day, you must get up and do it again. Never quit, never give up, never give in, and never give out. In order to reap the rewards of the harvest, we must be valiant in serving and helping others, in doing the Lord's work. Life will be sweet as you learn and live these precious truths. The Lord has admonished us:

> Therefore, O ye that embark in the service of God, see that ye serve him with all your heart, might, mind and strength, that ye may stand blameless before God at the last day.
>
> Therefore, if ye have desires to serve God ye are called to the work;
>
> For behold the field is white already to harvest; and lo, he that thrusteth in his sickle with his might, the same layeth up in store that he perisheth not, but bringeth salvation to his soul;
>
> And faith, hope, charity and love, with an eye single to the glory of God, qualify him for the work.
>
> Remember faith, virtue, knowledge, temperance, patience, brotherly kindness, godliness, charity, humility, diligence.
>
> Ask, and ye shall receive; knock, and it shall be opened unto you. (D&C 4:2–7)

This scripture is the creed of all missionaries and disciples of the Lord Jesus Christ. It must be your motto and your standard of behavior—both what you *do* and who you *are*. And though it may seem an impressive task, you *can* be prepared to be that kind of missionary. The Lord will help you.

As future missionaries, take courage from the examples of Moroni, Ammon and his brothers, Alma and his sons, Helaman, and all the great missionaries of the Book of Mormon. Look to Peter, Paul, and all the great missionaries of the New Testament. Think of Ruth, Esther, and Mary, and their bravery and courage in doing the work of the Lord. Know that Peter prophesied of your day concerning you: "And it shall come to pass in the last days, saith God, I will pour out of my Spirit upon all flesh: and your sons and your daughters shall prophesy, and your young men shall see visions, and your old men shall dream dreams: And on my servants and on my handmaidens I will pour out in those days of my Spirit; and they shall prophesy" (Acts 2:17–18). Likewise remember the words of Mormon: "Doubt not, but be believing, and begin as in times of old, and come unto the Lord with all your heart, and work out your own salvation with fear and trembling before him" (Mormon 9:27). Believe in yourselves. You can do this . . . if you prepare well. Preparation is power!

You will gain wisdom and understanding as you set goals and make plans in preparing to serve the Lord. As you feel the desire to prepare then act upon this desire, you will truly set in motion the process of becoming a true disciple for the Lord.

Now that young men and young women have the option of leaving earlier on their missions, it is all the more critical for you to prepare more diligently. More is expected of you. The Lord is hastening His work. Read carefully what the Lord expects of this chosen generation, which has been called to hasten the work. Now is the time to reap and sow with more diligence than ever. You are the one who will put your hands to the plow. The Lord says,

> I give unto you a commandment that you shall teach one another the doctrine of the kingdom. . . .
>
> That ye may be prepared in all things when I shall send you again to magnify the calling whereunto I have called you, and the mission with which I have commissioned you.
>
> Behold, I sent you out to testify and warn the people, and it becometh every man who hath been warned to warn his neighbor. (D&C 88:77, 80–81)

In many ways, these scriptures are astounding. It is humbling to think that this generation has been called to serve at this time, for this great work. As you remember this, your doubts will be calmed and your fears will be lessened.

As you prepare every needful thing for your mission, remember the following: "If ye are prepared ye shall not fear" (D&C 38:30). Paul spoke about this important truth as well, saying,

> Wherefore I put thee in remembrance that thou stir up the gift of God [the gift of the Holy Ghost], which is in thee by the putting on of my hands.
>
> *For God hath not given us the spirit of fear; but of power, and of love, and of a sound mind.*
>
> Be not thou therefore ashamed of the testimony of our Lord, nor of me his prisoner: but be thou partaker of the afflictions of the gospel according to the power of God;
>
> Who hath saved us, and called us with an holy calling [to preach His gospel], not according to our works, but according to his own purpose and grace, which was given us in Christ Jesus before the world began. (2 Timothy 1:6–9; emphasis added)

Yes, you are young. But you are becoming a disciple of Jesus Christ. You are learning the gospel line upon line. You are striving to become like Christ. You have a growing testimony and knowledge of the gospel. That is all you need to begin. Each person will start at a different level. You may have fears and other concerns, but please do not allow them to bring you down into despair. If you put your life in the hands of the Lord, you will be able to accomplish everything we discuss in this book. You will be able to prepare well in the strength of the Lord. Go forward with faith. You will be magnificent missionary!

Discipleship is a sacred trust given to each of us when we choose to follow Christ. We covenant that we are willing to stand as witnesses of God at all times and in all things and in all places (see Mosiah 18:8–9). We make this promise because we are His friends, His disciples, His witnesses, and His servants.

As we reflect on this sacred calling, we must consider whether we are truly fulfilling this covenant of standing as a witness of God: Does your demeanor radiate love? Do you inspire trust? Are you always exemplary in your behavior? Do you feel genuine love for those around you? Have you determined to *always* be a "light," to *always* live up to the standard of the gospel, and to *always* do as Jesus would do? As you ponder these questions, the Lord will reveal to you by the power of the Holy Ghost the things you need to do.

Elder Ballard counseled us to raise the bar in our preparation when he said,

1. Do you search the scriptures regularly?
2. Do you kneel in prayer to talk with your Heavenly Father each morning and each night?
3. Do you fast and donate a fast offering each month—even if you are a poor, struggling student who can't afford to donate much?
4. Do you think deeply about the Savior and His atoning sacrifice for you when you are asked to prepare, bless, pass, or partake of the sacrament?
5. Do you attend your meetings and strive to keep the Sabbath day holy?
6. Are you honest at home, school, church, and work?
7. Are you mentally and spiritually clean? Do you avoid viewing pornography or looking at websites, magazines, movies, or apps, including Tinder and Snapchat photos, that would embarrass you if your parents, Church leaders, or the Savior Himself saw you?
8. Are you careful with your time—avoiding inappropriate technology and social media, including video games, which can dull your spiritual sensitivity?
9. Is there anything in your life you need to change and fix, beginning tonight?[7]

Prayerfully ponder these questions from a prophet. They will bless your life.

CHAPTER 5

Catching the Vision of the
Lord's Servants—What You Need to Be

Ambassadors and Disciples of Christ

As missionaries and mission leaders, we talk of Christ, we preach of Christ, and we testify of Christ (see 2 Nephi 25:26). All those who serve the Lord, whether within or without the mission field, are His disciples and ambassadors. We must make ourselves worthy to be called such. We must recognize that the light we hold up is the Lord Jesus Christ Himself. "Therefore, hold up your light that it may shine unto the world. Behold I am the light which ye shall hold up" (3 Nephi 18:24). As Elder Hans B. Ringger explains,

> The foundation and guiding light for all our decisions is the gospel of Jesus Christ and His message to the world. The teachings of Christ must be embedded in our desire to choose the right and in our wish to find happiness. His righteous life must be reflected in our own actions. The Lord not only teaches love, He *is* love. He not only preached the importance of faith, repentance, baptism, and the gift of the Holy Ghost, He *lived* accordingly. His life reflected the gospel that He preached. There was and is total harmony between His thoughts and His actions.[1]

You cannot bear testimony of this Church and this kingdom without first knowing Jesus Christ, the Savior, light, and life of the world (see John 8:12). When you know Christ, you can hold up His light.

And when you hold up that light, then you truly become His disciples.

In 3 Nephi, Jesus Christ tells His disciples that they are "the light of this people" (3 Nephi 12:14), and He explains that they will bless all of Heavenly Father's children. Christ also instructs the Nephites not to put their light under a bushel, but to put it "on a candlestick, and it giveth light to all that are in the house" (3 Nephi 12:15). That same instruction applies to you: when you possess the light of Jesus Christ, you must not put it under a bushel. That light must be held up for others to see and draw near to. And then—and only then—will you be true and worthy representatives of our Savior, Jesus Christ.

We choose, like Alma the Younger, to be instruments in the hands of God—to find and help save the children of God. You will be given strength and abilities beyond your own as you embark in this endeavor. All of the knowledge and skills you learn will be magnified by the power of God, by the attributes of Christ, by the Spirit of the Lord, and by the mind and will of the Lord.

What a glorious concept. You will find these words to be true as you prepare to serve faithfully. And you will find that, when you are ready to return home, you will be like the missionary in the following story told by David Bryan Viser:

> As I jumped on board my flight from Miami to Salt Lake City, I paused a moment to catch my breath. Seated near the front of the plane was an excited young man, probably nineteen, sitting with his parents. His hair was short and his clothes new and sharp. His suit was fitted perfectly, and his black shoes still retained that store-bought shine. His body was in good shape, his face clear, and his hands clean. In his eyes I could see a nervous look, and his movements were that of an actor on opening night.
>
> He was obviously flying to Utah to become a missionary for the Mormon Church. I smiled as I walked by and took pride in belonging to this same Church where these young men and women voluntarily serve the Savior for two years. With this special feeling, I continued to the back where my seat was located.
>
> As I sat in my seat, I looked to the right and to my surprise saw another missionary sleeping in the window seat. His hair was also short, but that was the only similarity between the two. This one was

obviously returning home, and I could tell at a glance what type of missionary he had been. The fact that he was already asleep told me a lot. His entire body seemed to let out a big sigh. It looked as if this was the first time in two years he had even slept, and I wouldn't be surprised if it was.

As I looked at his face, I could see the heavy bags under his eyes, the chapped lips, and the scarred and sunburned face caused by the fierce Florida sun.

His suit was tattered and worn. A few of the seams were coming apart, and I noticed that there were a couple of tears that had been hand sewn with a very sloppy stitch.

I saw the name tag, crooked, scratched and bearing the name of the Church he represented, the engraving of which was almost all worn away. I saw the knee of his pants, worn and white, the result of many hours of humble prayer. A tear came to my eye as I saw the things that really told me what kind of missionary he had been. I saw the marks that made this boy a man.

His feet—the two that had carried him from house to house— now lay swollen and tired. They were covered by a pair of worn-out shoes. Many of the large scrapes and gouges had been filled in by the countless number of polishings.

His books—lying across his lap—were his scriptures, the word of God. Once new, these books, which testify of Jesus Christ and His mission, were now torn, bent, and ragged from use.

His hands—those big, strong hands which had been used to bless and teach—were now scarred and cut from knocking at doors.

Those were indeed the marks of that man. And as I looked at him, I saw the marks of another man, the Savior, as he was hanging on the cross for the sins of the world.

His feet—those that had once carried Him throughout the land during His ministry—were now nailed to the cross.

His side now pierced with a spear, sealing His gospel, His testimony, with His life.

His hands—the hands that had been used to ordain His servants and bless the sick—were also scarred with the nails that were pounded to hang Him on the cross.

Those were the marks of that great man.

As my mind returned to the missionary, my whole body seemed to swell with pride and joy, because I knew, by looking at him, that he had served his Master well.

My joy was so great. I felt like running to the front of the plane, grabbing that new, young missionary, and bringing him back to see what he could become, what he could do.

But would he see the things that I saw, could anyone see the things I saw? Or would he just see the outward appearance of that mighty elder, tired and worn out, almost dead.

As we landed, I reached over and tapped him to wake him up. As he awoke, it seemed like new life was entering his body. His whole frame just seemed to fill as he stood up, tall and proud. As he turned his face towards mine, I saw a light about his face that I had never seen before. I looked into his eyes. Those eyes. I will never forget those eyes. They were the eyes of a prophet, a leader, a follower, and a servant. They were the eyes of the Savior. No words were spoken. No words were needed.

As we unloaded, I stepped aside to let him go first. I watched as he walked, slow but steady, tired but strong. I followed him and found myself walking the way that he did.

When I came through the doors, I saw this young man in the arms of his parents, and I couldn't hold it in any longer. With tears streaming down my face, I watched these loving parents greet their son who had been away for a short time. And I wondered if our parents in heaven would greet you the same way. Will they wrap their arms around us and welcome us home from our journey on earth? I believe they will. I just hope that I can be worthy enough to receive such praise, as I'm sure this missionary will.

I said a silent prayer, thanking the Lord for missionaries like this young man. I don't think I will ever forget the joy and happiness he brought me that day.

When you prepare to serve, you will live up to this portrayal of a magnificent missionary. You will come home carrying in your bearing a very real similarity to the Savior. This will happen because you have served with faith, hope, and charity with an eye single to the glory of God. You will have caught the vision of your role in preaching the gospel.

Catching the Vision of the Lord's Servants—Doctrine and Covenants 4

Perhaps the best scriptural summary of what the Lord's servants should be, and do, is found in Doctrine and Covenants Section 4.

This revelation is both inspirational and instructional. Never have seven short verses had such a profound effect on hundreds of thousands of missionaries. I have watched missionaries as they have read, recited, and pondered those precious words, and then prayed to have the strength to live them. Surely Mormon was correct in declaring, "The preaching of the word had a great tendency to lead the people to do that which was just—yea, it had had more powerful effect upon the minds of the people than the sword, or anything else, which had happened unto them—therefore Alma thought it was expedient that they should try the virtue of the word of God" (Alma 31:5). There is virtue and power in the word of God; we see this happen as Section 4 brings motivation and strength to serve into the lives of the Lord's disciples every day throughout the world. I have seen missionaries with testimonies in their souls and tears in their eyes, because this scripture had become a fundamental part of their lives.

This section applies to *all* aspects of service that help build up the kingdom of God. It is the standard by which all saints should live. As we seek to qualify ourselves for the work (by working to bring souls to Christ) we must also take upon ourselves the divine nature of Christ (see 2 Peter 1:3–12). These divine attributes will both qualify us for the work and transform our hearts, bringing us closer to our goal of becoming like the Lord Jesus Christ (see Moroni 7:48; 3 Nephi 27:27).

I encourage you to read and reread and even feast on Section 4 of the Doctrine and Covenants. This will cultivate your desire to serve and help you to become the missionary the Lord wants you to be. As we discuss each impactful verse of Section 4, let the Holy Spirit fill your heart and give you an understanding of the great work in which you are an important part:

D&C 4:1—A Marvelous Work

Take a moment to think of the wording the Lord uses here—a *marvelous* work. The Book of Mormon was the introduction to this marvelous work of the restoration and the gathering of Israel. It, in itself, is a marvelous work and a wonder. But it was merely the beginning of the full restoration in the fulness of times. Everything about the restoration is marvelous: the gospel was restored through the Book of Mormon; the priesthood was restored through John the Baptist, Peter, James, and John; the Church itself was then restored, and with that came all the blessings of the temple and priesthood keys that would allow the Lord's kingdom to be present again upon the earth. Through this restoration, we understand who we are, where we came from, and what we can become. We know we have heavenly parents that love us. Is not this amazing, awe inspiring, and *marvelous*? Indeed, this is a marvelous work and a wonder that has come forth. As we begin to understand—to see and marvel at the gospel for what it is—we become aware of what a privilege it is to share it with all of God's children.

D&C 4:2—Serve God with All Your Heart, Might, Mind, and Strength

I'd like you to ponder those words: *with all your heart*. What do they mean? When we serve with all our heart, it means we love God—we love our fellowmen. Our affection for the Lord and His work will be evident through our actions. We will *want* to do His will because we have yielded our hearts unto Him (see Helaman 3:35). When we serve God with our whole hearts, we feel a love for God and His children so deep and pure that we will want to spread the gospel.

With all our might means with all of our will power, our desire, and our efforts. We use this might to concentrate on the things of the Lord. We become completely invested in what the Lord would have us do. We give it our all.

With all our mind means with all our mental capacities, our reasoning abilities, our understanding, and our intellectual powers. Our mind stays on the things of the Lord. We truly focus our thoughts on the work of the Lord—with an eye single to the glory of God.

With all our strength means we give our energy to the Lord. We literally funnel all of our physical powers and our mental, emotional, and spiritual strength into all things the Lord would have us do. Every fiber of our being is focused on His work.

Yes, to be the missionary the Lord expects you to be, you must serve Him with *all* your heart, might, mind, and strength. With this complete and unwavering devotion to God, you will serve well. Your mission will become something you anticipate and love, not merely wait out. When you turn your full capacity over to the Lord, He will do greater things with you than you could ever do alone.

It makes all the difference when we surrender our will to the will of God. It is humility that says "Thy will be done," and trusts that He can empower us. President Benson taught, "Men and women who turn their lives over to God will find out that he can make a lot more out of their lives than they can. He will deepen their joys, expand their vision, quicken their minds, strengthen their muscles, lift their spirits, multiply their blessings, increase their opportunities, comfort their souls, raise up friends, and pour out peace."[2]

Joseph Fielding Smith reminds us, "Every missionary who goes forth is under the solemn obligation and pledge to bear testimony of the restoration of the Gospel, and witness of its truth. In doing this, he leaves all who hear him without excuse and their sins are on their own heads. If he fails to do this then he will not 'stand blameless before God at the last day.' "[3]

D&C 4:3—If You Have Desires to Serve God Ye Are Called

Desire surely is the beginning point of all missionary work. These desires can be inspired by many different sources: You may have the desire to serve because you love God; because you love your fellowmen; because you are grateful for the Atonement of your Savior Jesus Christ; because you have a desire to help people be happy; because you understand the nature of the eternal plan of God—the plan of happiness; because you have come to understand the depth of the gospel of Jesus Christ as it is centered in the Atonement. As you come to understand each of the principles and doctrines of the gospel, your desire to share them with others will increase. Notice how the sons of Mosiah felt in regards to this matter: "Now they were desirous that salvation should be declared to every creature, for they could not bear that any human soul should perish; yea, even the very thoughts that any soul should endure endless torment did cause them to quake and tremble" (Mosiah 28:3).

D&C 4:4—The Field Is White Already to Harvest

There was a long, dark time on the planet Earth prior to the Restoration of the gospel of Jesus Christ; however, gratefully, times have changed. The field is now white and ready to harvest. There are so many people who want and need the gospel, so many you can reach through your efforts. You are called to declare God's word throughout the earth after the manner of Mormon: "Behold, I am a disciple of Jesus Christ, the Son of God. I have been called of him to declare his word among his people, that they might have everlasting life" (3 Nephi 5:13).

The elect will hear the word of God: "And ye are called to bring to pass the gathering of mine elect; for mine elect hear my voice and harden not their hearts" (D&C 29:7). Trust that there *will* be, and are, elect sons and daughters of God who will hear His voice and will not harden their hearts. They will come unto Christ as you love them and teach them by the Spirit, bringing them to a knowledge of the truth (see Alma 23:6).

D&C 4:4—Bring Salvation to Your Soul

As you serve the Lord in building the kingdom, not only do you become free from others' sins, but you also become blameless, or free from your own sins. We read, "Your sins are forgiven you, and you shall be laden with sheaves upon your back, for the laborer is worthy of his hire" (D&C 31:5). Part of repentance is dedicating your life to the Lord. It is not merely forsaking wrong behavior, it's *doing* good. When you confess and forsake your sins, you must then move forward in righteousness. For example, when Enos was praying for forgiveness and his guilt was swept away, it is significant that his heart then turned to the welfare of his brethren, the Nephites, and then to his people's enemies, the Lamanites, and then to a future people who would live upon the American continent—who would receive the gospel and the record of Enos's people. As you see from this example, when you are free from sin, the Spirit is able to rest upon you, and you have an overwhelming desire to do good. You seek to do the Lord's will by blessing and serving others. Similarly, when you seek to serve and bless, Satan's hold on you is diminished, and so you repent more and you become more pure in heart.

As you thrust in your sickle and work with all your heart, might, mind, and soul, working hard and smart, your sins will be forgiven. It is interesting to note that in James 5:20 the Lord says, "Let him know, that he which converteth the sinner from the error of his way shall save a soul from death, and shall hide a multitude of sins." As you help people come into the kingdom, you too become purified. You become a true disciple of the Lord Jesus Christ and are free from sin. We read in the Doctrine and Covenants, "And now, concerning the residue, let them journey and declare the word among the congregations of the wicked, inasmuch as it is given; And inasmuch as they do this they shall rid their garments, and they shall be spotless before me" (D&C 61:33–34). It is interesting to note that being clean and forgiven is likened to having spotless garments. This process of repentance and forgiveness is dependent upon both the grace of God and your works: "And may God grant, in his great fulness, that men might be brought unto repentance and good works, that they might be restored unto grace for grace, according to their works" (Helaman 12:24). After all you can do (see 2 Nephi 25:23) you are made clean and saved through the blood of the Lamb (see Moroni 9:6).

As your conversion deepens, your faith in and love of God will fuel the desire within you to serve. You will want everyone to feel what you feel and know what you know.

D&C 4:5—Qualifying for the Work

The Lord expects you to try to have a heart full of faith, hope, charity, and love, with an eye single to the glory of God. This is what qualifies you for the work. Through your faith you develop a relationship with the Lord and desire to serve Him. You can gain hope in eternal life as you embrace the vision of what you are doing here on earth. Finally, you will develop a Christlike love that prompts you to want to share these things with all of God's children. Let's now discuss in greater detail how you will qualify for the work. To do this you will need to obtain the following:

Faith—Faith is the first principle of the gospel of Jesus Christ and the governing principle in applying the Atonement to your life. You will learn that it is impossible to please God, except by exercising faith (see Hebrews 11:6). Faith, then, becomes an attribute you must possess not only to gain eternal life but also to do the will of God while you are on the earth. In Hebrews 11 and Alma 32, you will learn that faith is something you hope for, yet do not see. However, too often we end our definition of faith with this hopeful and believing stage. The Prophet Joseph Smith describes the three degrees of faith in the *Lectures on Faith*. He taught that the first degree is the substance of things hoped for (see *Lectures on Faith* 1:7–8). Of the second degree, the Prophet Joseph said, "Faith is the moving cause of all action in intelligent beings."[4] He then stated that the third degree of faith is a principle and source of power (see *Lectures on Faith* 1:15). When all three degrees are applied, faith is exercised to its fullest. The prophet went on to say, "Faith, then, is the first great governing principle which has power, dominion, and authority over all things; by it they exist, by it they are upheld, by it they are changed or by it they remain agreeable to the will of God."[5]

Ask yourself the following question: Is your faith sufficient now? In Luke we read, "And the apostles said unto the Lord, Increase our faith" (Luke 17:5). If the apostles of the Lord needed an increase in faith, how much more do we need greater faith in our lives, especially if we are to be missionaries!

Faith can accomplish all things according to the will of God, including and perhaps most significantly the repentance process, which will bring you into harmony with the Savior. The most important thing you will ever do is to repent and come unto Christ with full purpose of heart. And the thing that will be of most worth to you—and will bring you true joy—is to help others repent (see D&C

15:6; 18:10–16; Alma 29:9–10). Amulek taught,

> And thus he shall bring salvation to all those who shall believe on his name; this being the intent of this last sacrifice, to bring about the bowels of mercy, which overpowereth justice, and bringeth about means unto men that they may have faith unto repentance.
>
> And thus mercy can satisfy the demands of justice, and encircles them in the arms of safety, while he that exercises no faith unto repentance is exposed to the whole law of the demands of justice; therefore only unto him that has faith unto repentance is brought about the great and eternal plan of redemption.
>
> Therefore may God grant unto you, my brethren, that ye may begin to exercise your faith unto repentance, that ye begin to call upon his holy name, that he would have mercy upon you. (Alma 34:15–17)

Modern prophets have likewise made it clear that we must exercise faith in the Lord Jesus Christ, and they have explained what this means in our daily lives. President Benson said, "Now let me describe to you what faith in Jesus Christ means. Faith in Him is more than mere acknowledgment that He lives. It is more than professing belief. Faith in Jesus Christ consists of complete reliance on Him. As God, He has infinite power, intelligence, and love. There is no human problem beyond His capacity to solve. Because He descended below all things, He knows how to help us rise above our daily difficulties."[6]

President Hinckley taught, "If there is any one thing you and I need in this world it is faith, that dynamic, powerful, marvelous element by which, as Paul declared, the very worlds were framed (Hebrews 11:3). . . . Faith—the kind of faith that moves one to get on his knees and plead with the Lord and then get on his feet and go to work—is an asset beyond compare, even in the acquisition of secular knowledge."[7]

I would encourage you to ponder and remember these words concerning faith. It is significant that faith is a doctrine and principle of power. The following are examples from scripture and revelation that will deepen your understanding of this principle:

Faith is the power of God:

1. The earth was created by the power of faith (see Hebrews 11:3). Look at the marvelous things faith can do! It is impossible to truly serve God without faith.

2. The power of the priesthood relies on faith (see Ether 12) and can be worked only through the principles of righteousness (see D&C 121:36).

3. Faith is the foundation of all righteousness (see *Lectures on Faith* 1, 10).

4. Faith is an attribute of God and dwells independently within Him (see *Lectures on Faith* 2:2).

Righteous men and women likewise live by faith (see Habakkuk 2:4; Galatians 3:11; and Romans 1:16). We can look to the following examples from scripture:

1. Just men are made perfect by faith in Jesus Christ (see D&C 76:69).

2. You are justified by your faith through the grace of your Savior Jesus Christ and His atoning sacrifice (see Romans 3:28, 5:1).

Faith is a blessing in your life. Here are more examples from scripture:

1. Faith is the shield of protection from the fiery darts of the wicked (see Ephesians 6:16).

2. Faith is evidenced by your works (see James 2:18).

3. Enos, the great prophet, exercised faith in Christ unto repentance, and his guilt was swept away (see Enos 1:6–8).

4. By faith the prophet Lehi received the blessing and the gift of the Holy Ghost (see 1 Nephi 10:17).

5. Healing blessings and other miracles occur by the power of faith (see James 5:15; 2 Nephi 26:13).

6. The Liahona worked by faith, diligence, and heed given to the word of God (see 1 Nephi 16:28).

7. Receiving direction for your life depends on the faith you exercise (see 1 Nephi 16:28).

8. Faith will give you strength; by it you can do all things (see Alma 2:30; 14:26).

9. You are alive in Christ through faith (see 2 Nephi 25:25).

10. You become mighty in word and are able to preach the word

through faith in the Lord Jesus Christ (see Ether 12:23).

11. Miracles are wrought through faith; angels appear through faith in the Lord Jesus Christ (see Moroni 7:37).

12. You learn through faith (see D&C 88:118).

13. By faith you can do all things that are expedient in the Lord (see 2 Nephi 1:10; Moroni 7:33).

14. As parents pray, exercising faith with real intent for help with struggling children, the Lord will send angels (see Mosiah 27:13–14), be they mortal or celestial.

15. It was by faith that Nephi and Lehi (the sons of Helaman) helped bring about the great change among the Lamanites (see Ether 12:14).

16. Faith is necessary for the Lord to work through us; He is only able to work through those who exercise faith (see Ether 12:30).

17. Faith is the principle that moves you to do good (see Alma 29:4).

Are you convinced? I would like to share with you a couplet by my dear friend Cyril Figuerres:

Faith is the Power
Love is the Motive
Obedience is the Price
The Spirit is the Key
And Christ is the Reason

When the first elders were taught in the School of the Prophets, they were given seven lectures on faith. This was their preparation to serve as missionaries—the Prophet knew they would best prepare to serve by increasing their faith. You can likewise increase your faith.

Do not expect to move all the mountains today. Start by simply having the faith to follow the prophet and prepare yourself to be a servant of the Lord Jesus Christ by becoming a missionary to match the message. Start by building enough faith to build up the kingdom of God through love and service to your fellow beings. By small and simple things, great things come to pass (see D&C 64:33). Start by committing to a few simple goals and make a plan to increase your faith by searching the scriptures, fasting and praying, and cultivating a spirit of humility that will allow you to teach your brothers and sisters to increase their own faith in coming unto Christ.

Hope—Hope is the next principle you should explore in your effort to qualify for the work. Hope is the anticipation and expectation that the Lord will bless you with every needful thing and that your life will improve. Your hope must be based upon the Lord Jesus Christ, the plan of happiness, and eternal life—which God promised to the faithful before the world began (see Titus 1:2). Hope will provide you with a sense of confidence as you live a righteous life. When we lose hope, life becomes difficult in every sense. If we lose hope, life loses its purpose and even the future does not seem to hold any promise. A life without hope is empty; but a life filled with hope is a life filled with light and meaning. Hope will fill your life as you have faith in Jesus Christ and the gospel plan and cultivate an attitude of being realistically optimistic.

True hope is always centered in Christ. For example, through Christ we can obtain hope of forgiveness for our sins through repentance. The hope of resurrection likewise resides in Christ. Christ is your rock upon whom you can build and not fall (see Helaman 5:12). "Blessed is the man that trusteth in the Lord, and whose hope the Lord is" (Jeremiah 17:7).

Basing your life around your faith in the Savior Jesus Christ will give you hope—in fact, a *perfect brightness* of hope. You will then be filled with light and proceed to do good because of your hope. As you perfect an attitude of hope you will gain power and motivation to move forward. Nephi said, "Wherefore, ye must press forward with a steadfastness in Christ, having a perfect brightness of hope, and a love of God and of all men. Wherefore, if ye shall press forward, feasting upon the word of Christ, and endure to the end, behold, thus saith the Father: Ye shall have eternal life" (2 Nephi 31:20).

In order for your life to have true meaning, and in order for you to gain power to cope with adversity, your life must be riveted to hope. Hope becomes, in essence, an anchor for your soul. Hope is not some platitude of a mere positive attitude; hope is an expectation rooted in Christ. It must be sought after through understanding the gospel plan. "Wherefore, whoso believeth in God might with surety hope for a better world, yea, even a place at the right hand of God, which hope cometh of faith, maketh an anchor to the souls of men, which would make them sure and steadfast, always abounding in good works, being led to glorify God" (Ether 12:4).

Hope can be obtained through the Spirit as you draw closer to God by repenting and becoming meek and lowly. We read the following: "And the remission of sins bringeth meekness, and lowliness of heart; and because of meekness and lowliness of heart cometh the visitation of the Holy Ghost, which Comforter filleth with hope and perfect love, which love endureth by diligence unto prayer, until the end shall come, when all the saints shall dwell with God" (Moroni 8:26).

President Hinckley taught that the missionary message is a message of hope for all mankind. He said, "Ours is truly a message of hope and reconciliation. It is a word of hope for all mankind, a beacon of eternal truth to which men may look as they lift their eyes and souls to their Creator and in the process come to recognize their common brotherhood."[8]

Since hope is such an important part of qualifying to serve, it is critical that you exert sincere effort in obtaining it—through and in the Lord Jesus Christ. I encourage you to seek to understand and apply the following:

- Hope is centered in Jesus Christ. The opportunity to repent and gain eternal life is made possible through your Savior, who wrought the magnificent Atonement and Resurrection.
- Hope is connected to faith. The power of faith is increased as you cultivate an attitude of hope.
- Hope gets things done. Hope, like faith, is a self-perpetuating principle, for it brings about the conditions to realize the vision that it sees for the future. Therefore, hope is an indispensable ally.
- Hope can be your guide for life. Through the eyes of hope,

you will see opportunities that would otherwise be invisible—and therefore lost. Look at life from the perspective of hope.

- Count your blessings. In particular, take inventory of the blessings of the gospel and all those associated with eternal life. They will fill you with hope. Look at the bright and optimistic side of life. It's a choice you can make.

- Plan your schedule around hope. You can create a feeling of hope in life as you take the initiative to plan and carry out things that are enjoyable and uplifting to you.

- Be a problem solver. If you start to feel dejected or hopeless, study the situation and make decisions to solve the problem. Focus on hope instead of despair.

- Work on long-range goals. Hope is a partner with action—the more you do the right kinds of things to attain your goals, the more hope you will have.

- Ask for hope. Look to God for help and comfort. The highest form of hope is based on deep spiritual awakenings. Therefore, pray for hope each day.

- Be a leader of hope. A leader shares his or her vision of the future, and then helps generate the hope-filled actions that bring it about. Without hope, there can be no righteous leadership; with hope, leaders are empowered to lift and inspire.

It is your hope that will make the work of the Lord worthwhile. It will sustain you in trials. It will give you purpose and direction in life as you strive to be found worthy to return to your Father in Heaven. This is the pattern the Lord wants His missionaries to emulate.

Charity—Charity is the ultimate attribute of godliness that qualifies you for the work. Charity is found by obtaining the divine nature of Christ through faith, virtue, knowledge, temperance, patience, brotherly kindness, and godliness with all humility and diligence (see D&C 4:6; 2 Peter 1:3–8). This pure love of Christ is total, complete, enduring, and Godlike. When you are possessed of this love, your desires will mirror your Savior's—you will earnestly want to bless and serve mankind. You will have such compassion, love, and respect for others that you strive to serve them—not because you are *supposed* to, but because it is part of *who you are.*

Charity never fails. Christ did not fail His Father, nor did He fail us; His pure love motivated His great sacrifice—the eternal, infinite, vicarious Atonement. When you possess that kind of love, you act in accordance with the principles of the Atonement. When you possess this love, you will likewise never fail. Through the Atonement of Christ, you can begin to acquire this unconditional, Godly love— this divine nature of Christ.

Do you see why charity ultimately qualifies you for the work? When you love God and His children that much, you will want nothing more or less than to serve them.

Let charity be your ultimate goal as you seek to become like the Savior. You are nothing without Christ, and you will be nothing without charity. The qualities of charity indicate the Christlike character that is involved in obtaining this magnificent virtue. You will find great joy as you master each of these qualities of charity. Surely this is a most worthwhile goal. As Moroni taught us, "And charity suffereth long, and is kind, and envieth not, and is not puffed up, seeketh not her own, is not easily provoked, thinketh no evil, and rejoiceth not in iniquity but rejoiceth in the truth, beareth all things, believeth all things, hopeth all things, endureth all things" (Moroni 7:45).

Why will it be "well with you" to have charity? As we discussed earlier, Peter, that magnificent Apostle of the Lord, taught us that when we have charity we take upon ourselves the Savior's divine nature. By pursuing this path of righteousness, our calling and election will be made sure (see 2 Peter 1:3–12). As true followers of Christ, we must seek to be like Him (see 3 Nephi 27:27), will keep His commandments, and in all things seek to follow Christ and please our Heavenly Father. Then we will be made pure and be worthy of Their presence.

Seeking charity takes effort: "Wherefore, my beloved brethren, pray unto the Father with all the energy of heart, that ye may be filled with this love, which he hath bestowed upon all who are true followers of his Son, Jesus Christ; that ye may become the sons of God; that when he shall appear we shall be like him, for we shall see him as he is; that we may have this hope; that we may be purified even as he is pure" (Moroni 7:48).

President Benson has taught concerning charity:

> The final and crowning virtue of the divine character is charity, or the pure love of Christ (see Moroni 7:47). If we would truly seek to be more like our Savior and Master, learning to love as He loves should be our highest goal. Mormon called charity "the greatest of all" (Moroni 7:46). . . . Charity never seeks selfish gratification. The pure love of Christ seeks only the eternal growth and joy of others.
>
> The Lord Jesus Christ liberated man from the world by the pure gospel of love. He demonstrated that man, through the love of God and through kindness and charity to His fellows, could achieve His highest potential. He lived the plain and sure doctrine of service, of doing good to all men—friends and enemies alike.[9]

Here are just a few things to keep in mind as you seek to obtain charity.

- Pray with all your heart to possess charity (see Moroni 7:48).
- Make a plan to increase your faith and follow the steps outlined in D&C 4:6.
- Remember your Savior in all things (see D&C 20:77, 79).
- Apply the following motto to your attitude and behavior: Do as Jesus would do (see 3 Nephi 27:27).
- Be qualified by charity to assist in the Lord's work (see D&C 12:8).
- Clothe yourself in all of the qualities of charity (see D&C 88:125).

Christ's love for you will endure forever. When you possess this love, you have the capacity to bless others. Take a few moments to think about the benefits and the blessings of exercising charity in your life. You can seek to have charity with all the energy of your heart, with your whole soul, with all your might, mind, and strength in all that you do. You will come to see life as a beautiful experience, and you will find peace, as only the Lord can give (see D&C 19:23). Most important, you will be a pure disciple of the Lord Jesus Christ (see John 13:34–35).

Remember the counsel the prophet Mormon gave to his son, Moroni: "[We] must needs have charity; for if [we] have not charity [we are] nothing; wherefore [we] must needs have charity" (Moroni 7:44).

As you seek to build up the kingdom of God, remember that faith, hope, and charity indeed qualify you for the work. In fact, the work going forward hinges on whether or not you possess them. These three attributes are so closely connected that they cannot be separated: "And no one can assist in this work except he shall be humble and full of love, having faith, hope, and charity, being temperate in all things, whatsoever shall be entrusted to his care" (D&C 12:8). When you depend upon God and exhibit the fruits of humility (being submissive, easily entreated, a broken heart and contrite spirit, teachable, and so on), become full of love (concern for your fellowmen that brings about righteous service), exercise your faith (belief and hope, the impetus for all action, and the power to do all things), have an attitude of hope (an optimistic attitude toward the future due to the infinite Atonement of our Savior), and are filled with charity (love that never fails), you will be able to help the Lord in His glorious work. See how wonderful you will become.

An Eye Single to the Glory of God—Having an eye single to the glory of God, or having pure motives, will likewise qualify you to work for the Lord. Your motive is to build up His kingdom. Your motive is to bless lives. Your motive is to help people come unto Christ and partake of the goodness of God. There is no room for self-aggrandizement; there is simply a desire to help people be happy, keep the commandments, and be free from sin. Helping people come unto Christ is the most important thing. Why? The Lord has said, "For behold, this is my work and my glory—to bring to pass the immortality and eternal life of man" (Moses 1:39). We will look "forward with an eye of faith" (Alma 32:40).

D&C 4:6—The Divine Nature of Christ

"Remember faith, virtue, knowledge, temperance, patience, brotherly kindness, godliness, charity, humility, diligence" (D&C 4:6). Note the parallel attributes that can be found in the second epistle of Peter 1:3–12. Peter includes most of the same virtues listed here, which gives us a sense of how important they are. These qualities, along with faith and hope, will help you become a true disciple, serve with honor, and emulate Christ.

It is important to realize that the attributes found in Doctrine and Covenants 4:6 are not given in random order. They provide a blueprint for being endowed with charity (see 2 Peter 1:3–7). The importance of these virtues is reiterated throughout the scriptures.

Faith—A belief and confidence in things not seen. The moving cause of all action and power to do all things. Notice how the Lord emphasizes once again the principle of faith as part of the divine nature of Christ.

Virtue—This is the power that stems from the priesthood and righteous living.

Gospel Knowledge—You must treasure up the words of the scriptures and the prophets before you can teach these words. We will discuss this principle in depth later on.

Temperance and Patience—These attributes are integral aspects of charity. Gaining self-control and seeking to understand and being long-suffering are integral in having charity and expressing love for others.

Brotherly Kindness—Compassion and caring for others is essential if you are to teach them the gospel.

Godliness—When we deny ourselves of all ungodliness—worldliness, selfishness, and so on—we become more Christlike (see Moroni 7:48; 10:32–33) and full of charity.

Humility—As we have discussed previously, humility is the initiating virtue of exaltation. It is knowing your relationship with God and dependence upon Him. You will then obtain the fruits of humility: submissiveness, being easily entreated, and being teachable so that you can be an instrument in the hands of the Lord Jesus Christ.

Diligence—This is the ethic of work. How diligent will you be as a missionary? Will you give it your all? Will you work hard and smart? Diligence is critical to success in the mission field. Review chapter 6 in *Preach My Gospel.*

Determine now that you will do every needful thing to prepare to be a pure disciple of Christ. Learn and acquire the attributes that you must possess; this is the standard for the servants of the Lord.

We have discussed many principles that are critical to success in the mission field; it may feel like an overwhelming task to embrace all of them. How do you catch the vision of the brilliance and beauty of the Lord's plan? It all comes down to one question: Are you willing to prepare? So many people want to win, but as BYU coach Lavell Edwards said, "Maybe they don't want to prepare to win." Preparation precedes the power to become a pure disciple of Christ. The principles we have discussed will help you prepare for this most important battle.

D&C 4:7—Ask, and Ye Shall Receive

You must never forget the eternal verity that requires you to ask (see James 1:5–6). Mighty prayer is an important part of being a disciple of Jesus Christ, because it will help you to become a mighty instrument in His hands. Once you come to understand and appreciate the mighty words in Section 4 and your role in bringing the Lord's work about, you must seek the Lord in prayer and ask for His help in becoming the missionary He wants you to be. He will give you a vision of the work as a revelation to your soul, and He will strengthen you to do all things (see Alma 26:11–12).

Increase Your Desire

As you gain a vision of the importance of the work of the Lord discussed in Section 4, you will gain a better understanding and appreciation for the work. Then, as you feel a sense of gratitude stemming from this understanding, you will desire to work. You want to be a missionary. You want to share the gospel. You want to prepare. You want to be an instrument in the hands of the Lord. This desire, when it swells within you, will cause you to work harder. When Alma the Younger and the sons of Mosiah were converted, they couldn't wait to share the gospel. Enos, after praying all day and into the night, received a forgiveness of his sins, and his guilt was swept away. He then began to pray for the Nephites, then the Lamanites, and then he implored Heavenly Father to save the written record of the prophets and his people, for it was so good and so precious that it would inspire future generations. Do you see the pattern here? When your conversion to Christ is real, your desire begins to increase. You *want* to share the gospel of Jesus Christ. When you have a clear vision of the importance of the work, you will have a desire, and then you will become a worthy disciple of Jesus Christ.

A Worthy Instrument

Earlier in my life, I was a practicing dentist. I performed oral surgeries in the hospital to remove the third molars (wisdom teeth). I can still remember preparing for surgery with the nurses around me, the anesthesiologist sedating the patient, and my instruments and equipment ready to go for the operation. Surgery is delicate work, and the instruments I used performed their duty correctly because I had them in my hand and I was in control. I knew what I was supposed to do.

You may be surprised to realize that this experience is an analogy for missionary work. To begin, note that the instruments I used were clean, pure, and sharp, and so performed the surgery well and efficiently.

Thus, each instrument could meet its intended purpose in my hand. I knew how to use each instrument, for I was the doctor and I was in charge. And that's what your relationship should be with our Savior. He is our master, and we are instruments in His hands—submissive to His will—provided we are clean and pure and know our purpose. As we come to better understand missionary work and the need for this marvelous gospel to be spread, we will want nothing more than to be worthy servants of our Savior—before, during, and after our missions.

Obedient Disciples

In the mission field there is a great law you will hear spoken of often—it is called obedience. In our mission it was called immediate, exact, and courageous obedience. The principle of obedience is built upon love, faith, and trust in God. When you live the principle of obedience, you will be more diligent in all that you do.

Let me share the following story my wife told in General Conference in October 1999: I know of a young boy who wanted to fly a kite. He and his father purchased a kite along with two spools of string, which they combined into one big spool. They fixed it all up and went out to fly their kite. The kite started taking off. "Dad, look at it go, look at it go!" the boy cried. Soon, the kite soared higher and higher. They let all the string out. The boy pulled on the string and said, "Dad, the string is holding the kite down. Look how tight it is. It's really tight. Let's cut it so the kite can fly up higher."

The dad said, "No, you don't understand, son. The string is what holds the kite up. It needs the string."

The boy said, "No, Dad, look!" And he pulled on the string. "See, it's holding it down."

The dad shook his head and answered, "No, son, the string helps the kite fly."

"No, it doesn't," insisted the boy, growing impatient.

"So you want to cut the string?" asked the father.

"Yes. I want to let it fly up all the way, all the way to the clouds," replied the boy.

The father considered a moment, then agreed. He took out his pocketknife and let the boy cut the string.

Well, you know what happened next. The kite came crashing down to the ground. The boy looked at his father in confusion and asked, "Why didn't it go higher?"

The father replied, "Son, the string was part of the law by which the kite could fly."[10] This boy learned a lesson about following temporal laws that day. And just as physical laws govern the world around us, spiritual laws govern the principles, ordinances, and other unseen forces at work in our lives. "There is a law, irrevocably decreed in heaven before the foundations of this world, upon which all blessings are predicated—And when we obtain any blessing from God, it is by obedience to that law upon which it is predicated" (D&C 130: 20–21).

I imagine that boy was grateful for the string the next time he flew a kite. Likewise, when you understand the purpose of commandments, you will want to keep them. You will understand that blessings are bestowed in connection with the law on which that blessing is based. If you eat properly, you feel good. If you study, you learn.

So what is the blessing you receive when you are obedient? When you are obedient, you receive the greatest gift in the entire world—the gift of the Spirit. Every Sunday when you go to Church and partake of the sacrament, you hear the words at the end of the sacramental prayer that say, "and keep His commandments which He hath given [you]," (or in other words, be obedient) "that [you] may always have His Spirit to be with [you]." If we are obedient, we are given the marvelous gift of the Spirit's companionship. Obedience allows you to have the companionship of the Holy Spirit (see D&C 20:77), and the Holy Spirit is the key to your missionary work (see D&C 42:14). The Spirit will guide you, it will testify to you, it will lead you, it will correct you, it will comfort you, and it will show you all things that you should do (see 2 Nephi 32:5). You cannot accomplish anything in the mission field without having the Spirit, and you can't have the Spirit unless you choose to be obedient.

This is difficult for many missionaries to understand and do. If you are exactly, immediately, and courageously obedient in all things, the Lord will bless you. Your desire to serve God and His children will increase as you desire to be more obedient. This life is a test to see whether you will obey. The Lord reminds us of this important principle through Abraham: "And we will prove them herewith, to see if they will do all things whatsoever the Lord their God shall command them" (Abraham 3:25).

When obedience becomes our quest, we will be happy and we will grow spiritually. Our obedience will increase our desire to serve. This is why obedience brings such happiness in our lives. Along these lines, King Benjamin promised, "I would desire that ye should consider on the blessed and happy state of those that keep the commandments of God. For behold, they are blessed in all things, both temporal and spiritual; and if they hold out faithful to the end they are received into heaven, that thereby they may dwell with God in a state of never-ending happiness. O remember, remember that these things are true; for the Lord God hath spoken it" (Mosiah 2:41).

Spirituality and righteousness is the fruit of the mighty change obedience brings, along with becoming like Christ. It is who you are and what you do. You are directed by the Spirit. You have yielded to the enticing of the Holy Ghost. Obedience becomes the fruit of who you are. You are Christlike. You are kind. You no longer have to think about obeying the rules, because the rules are part of your soul. You love the law and you obey.

Diligence and Work

When you allow the Spirit to direct your path in all things, you will work smarter and harder. You will undertake each effort presented you with greater faith, diligence, and patience. Think of how good you feel when you work hard for something and accomplish it. Now imagine how much more amazing that feeling will be when you spend your time doing the most important work—spreading the gospel and bringing souls unto Christ.

Understanding spiritual truths will give you the power to keep the commandments and the motivation to work with all of your heart. This understanding provides a sense of purpose for your obedience. Our Savior and His prophets have counseled us to gain this understanding by searching the scriptures, fasting and praying, and living by the Spirit.

Remember

Preparation precedes power—the power to do good and the power to bless lives. Remember that preparation is the first key to success as a missionary. You cannot be the kind of missionary the Lord expects you to be without it. As you go forth, prayerfully prepare to serve. Organize every needful thing. Evaluate where you are and what you need to do.

As we close this section, I would like to share with you a lesson my sweetheart taught me about preparation. She recorded in her journal:

> When our children were young and many (we had eight children), at times I felt overwhelmed with all I had to do. And, yes, at times I felt a little discouraged.
>
> Still, Ed was doing wonderfully well teaching and practicing dentistry, and we lived in our dream home; I remember tidying up the family room and kitchen area before he came home in the evening so there would be some sense of order. On one particular afternoon, I was vacuuming up the graham cracker crumbs and other debris on the carpet and Ed walked in, much earlier than I expected. He came over to me, I turned off the vacuum, and he gave me a wonderful hug. He whispered in my ear that he loved me, and then he said something that gave me cause to think and take action. He said, "I know what you're going to be doing in the eternities." I eagerly asked, "What?" He replied, "You are going to be the chief vacuumer."
>
> That statement is funny to me now, but back then, it was devastating. That is not what I wanted to be doing in the eternities. Being a woman of action, that evening I got on the phone and called a babysitter to come the next day, for the entire day.
>
> I was blessed that my parents owned a small A-frame cabin up at Sundance that was not being used, so the next day—I remember it as a beautiful fall day—I drove up to Sundance with stacks of paper, pens, my scriptures, a calendar, and in the attitude of fasting. I began my experience with prayer, asking for help and guidance. Then I started to write. I made lists of everything that I needed to do—everything from cleaning our home and teaching our children to preparing to live with my sweetheart forever.
>
> I remember writing things such as, "Clean out the refrigerator with the moldy vegetables in the drawer, mend the children's clothes

before they grow out of them, clean out the bathroom drawers where the toothpaste is mixed in with the combs and yucky hair," etc. I wrote them in no special order, also including things of an eternal nature as they came to my mind, such as, "Read the scriptures more regularly, live in the eternities as a forever family, go to the temple more regularly, have better family home evenings, tell my children I love them more often."

I worked on my list all morning; I had pages. Then I stopped and went for a lovely walk and enjoyed the beautiful colored leaves, and thought, *What do I really want?*

I returned to the cabin. I suddenly knew what I wanted. I knew what was most important. I wanted to live my life so I would be worthy to live with Ed in the eternities and have a "forever" family. It was interesting because I had known that before, but the little exercise of writing down all of the things that were distracting me was very enlightening.

I went back to my lists and put a number one by what was most important and a number two and on down my list. I never did put a number by that yucky bathroom drawer.

I went to my scriptures and read a few of my favorites. "Trust in the Lord with all thine heart and lean not unto thy own understanding. In all thy ways acknowledge Him and He will direct thy paths" (Proverbs 3:5–6).

My next step was to draw up a calendar with the hours of the day. I began to put onto my calendar the things I needed to do and when. I scheduled a temple day, I scheduled when I was going to read my scriptures and family home evening. I felt so at peace.

I drove home that fall afternoon with such gratitude to my Heavenly Father for the direction I had been given. I felt such peace. When I got home and had a chance to visit with Ed about my experience and share with him how wonderful it was, I asked him if he felt it was something we could do together. He readily agreed, and that became the beginning of our weekly, monthly, and yearly planning sessions.

Those planning times drew us closer together than we had ever been. We attended the temple weekly, then had lunch together in the cafeteria and did our planning. We talked about our individual goals and how we were doing. We talked about each of our children and what their current needs were and what we could do to encourage them and bless their lives. We talked about future goals and plans, family plans, and outings. We talked about current conference talks and the direction we had received and planned how to implement that direction. We planned how we would change.

Yearly, Ed and I would go on a little overnighter and make a plan for the entire year. What a blessing this was in our lives. What a wonderful way to stay on track and work together toward what mattered most in both our lives.

I echo my eternal companion's words in saying that these were magnificent moments in our lives. We became better prepared as a husband and wife. We became better parents. We changed. We improved. Planning brought joy to our lives, and never again did we think, "We are just fine the way we are." You will likewise find that as you evaluate, plan, prepare, and then act upon your goals and plans, remembering always to root your focus in the Atonement and after the pattern of the endowment, you will succeed.

CHAPTER 6

Preparing for the Temple

The Spirit helped me recognize something very important related to missionary work and building up the kingdom of God: the power of the Atonement of Christ and of the endowment received in the holy temple. When I was a mission president, I reviewed some of the missionaries and their behaviors over a period of time. Following zone conference they were on fire. The Spirit had enlightened their minds. I remember the letters that I would receive weekly from the missionaries, and the scenario would go like this:

First week's letter: President, Zone conference was super! We are committed! Things are going great!

Second week's letter: Things are going pretty well. We are mostly on track, and so on.

Third week's letter: We have hit a few snags and we are struggling, but . . .

Fourth week's letter: President, we need help. I will explain during our interview, and so on.

I watched this pattern repeat itself many times. Why was there no staying power in their motivation to work? They had been trained. The Holy Ghost had inspired them. What was holding them back? Where had their motivation gone? Where was their strength?

Rooted to Christ the Lord through the Atonement and the Temple Endowments

After lengthy prayer and interviews, the Lord helped me understand something important. The missionaries were devoted and excited to do the work, but they had not fully rooted themselves in Christ. Their conversion level and application of the Atonement to their lives was not solidified. They did not fully understand the Atonement and its enabling power to strengthen them. Their temple covenants had not empowered them from on high because they did not remember them, let alone understand and appreciate them so as to faithfully keep them. The Lord had done His part. It was time for the missionaries to do theirs.

We all struggle at different levels. We all need to change. For the missionaries, it was necessary for them to learn how to be spiritually sufficient in the Lord by understanding and appreciating the important and foundational doctrines and covenants of the Atonement and the temple. Needless to say, we spent many hours and taught many lessons before they received sufficient knowledge, understood key truths, and integrated the doctrine of the Atonement into their very souls. At last I began to see that they were converted to the Lord. They understood! When they committed themselves, the results were phenomenal. They were the instruments in the hands of the Lord like Ammon and the other sons of King Mosiah.

Why do we sometimes live lives of mercurial, or shifting, behavior? It is because we do not understand or fully appreciate the Atonement. Like these missionaries, we have not received it into our souls. And why not? Because our gratitude is not deep enough—which makes it difficult to change and apply the Atonement to our lives.

The word *atonement* means "to cover, or to become at one." That is, to be reconciled to God, to be in harmony with God, to return into the presence of the Father. The endowment is a symbolic representation of this process. In the temple we receive ordinances and covenants and keep them faithfully so we can return to the presence of the Father and our Savior. In the temple we see that the Atonement and the endowment are inseparably connected. The Atonement is literally the enabling power of the endowment. Indeed, we are empowered by Christ through His infinite Atonement to do all things in His name, all in the strength of our Savior, Jesus Christ.

Through the endowment and the Atonement, we become rooted in Christ. He becomes our rock. He becomes our salvation. We learn to see as He sees, do as He did, and live as He lived. We learn to look for the good. We learn to live with hope through Christ the Lord. Discouragement and despair begin to flee from our minds and have no place in our hearts and souls, and we will live after the manner of happiness through the Atonement (see 1 Nephi 8:10; 4 Nephi 1:15–16). We learn to keep the commandments and be happy (see Mosiah 2:41; Alma 50:23). We change. We become.

The lessons I learned with these missionaries apply in each of our lives. We learn that the doctrine of the plan of exaltation is transcending and powerful when we come to truly understand and appreciate it. We are filled with hope as we come to understand the plan of redemption. As you apply yourself to knowledge and understanding in these matters, the enabling power of the Atonement will give you strength to carry on. When you grasp it and appreciate this knowledge, it will fill you with gratitude. You will then be able to receive it into your heart and soul and embrace it as a loving child of God. Your thoughts and actions will then reflect that gratitude with an overwhelming desire to do good. You will be motivated to work hard. You will be diligent and faithful. You will be a mighty missionary for the Lord Jesus Christ.

Missionaries who are prepared (and you *will* be prepared!) with every needful thing will reap the blessings of the Lord in all things. You will find that you are always at work in one way or another, doing the Lord's work. This is what it means to serve with all of your heart, might, mind, and strength. This is the type of person you will desire to become, and you will be happy in the service of your God.

My dear friends, the enabling power of the Atonement and being endowed with power from on high in the Lord's holy house is the heart of the gospel (see Acts 10:38; Luke 24:49; Alma 7:11–12; 26:11–12; D&C 105:10–12). This is what we seek to understand and live. We can be the missionaries we envision. We can be worthy, obedient, diligent servants who live by the Spirit. It all depends on how willing you are to become such. The gospel is glorious, and so many are waiting for it, aching for it. The field is white. It is now our opportunity to qualify ourselves to bring souls unto Christ.

Receiving the Melchizedek Priesthood and Being Ordained an Elder

You young men may not realize the magnificence and power of the priesthood, or of being ordained an elder, until you have an experience that has a profound effect upon you. Many men have told me that they felt bad because they didn't understand and appreciate the privilege of exercising the power and authority that they had been given by God to act for Him here upon the earth. I hope that this section will help open your eyes to this wonderful blessing, opportunity, and responsibility that you have to bless and serve others with the authority and power of the priesthood.

I came to realize that it was my *responsibility* to learn the doctrine of the priesthood and my duty when I read, "Let every man learn his duty, and to act in the office in which he is appointed, in all diligence. He that is slothful shall not be counted worthy to stand, and he that learns not his duty and shows himself not approved shall not be counted worthy to stand" (D&C 107:99–100).

I came to understand that priesthood power governs the kingdom of God here upon the earth. You witnessed this as you saw the prophet, Thomas S. Monson, declare the age change for serving missions. Can you imagine the rippling effect upon the world? Hundreds of thousands of God's children will come unto Christ because of this magnificent change. This will bless lives! That is the purpose of the priesthood.

So why would God entrust this awesome power to young men such as yourself? It is inherently a call to service, a commitment to be a force for good. One of the most important ways that you will come to understand and use the powers of the priesthood will be through serving a full-time mission, where you *practice* the priesthood on a continual, focused basis. When you receive the Melchizedek Priesthood, go forth to use it! Go forth to serve. Like Alma and the sons of Mosiah, you will break every worldly stereotype, perform mighty miracles, and assist in the great work of salvation.

As I studied, I came to understand this miraculous gift and privilege to act with priesthood power and realized that there were some foundational doctrines that would help me better understand and appreciate the priesthood.

Knowing and understanding doctrine is key to coming to the understanding of the truth of all things. The word *doctrine* means the rules, guidelines, teachings, and principles that are accepted as the canon—or in other words, as the laws, tenets, and beliefs of a religion. The doctrine of the priesthood includes the following:

- The holy priesthood is the authority and power of God delegated to worthy men in The Church of Jesus Christ of Latter-day Saints.
- A man's priesthood is empowered through his righteousness and faith in God and His Beloved Son Jesus Christ.
- The rights of the priesthood are connected to heaven and controlled only by the principles of righteousness.
- Brethren and sisters can be called to positions within the Church only under the direction of and by virtue of the Melchizedek Priesthood, held by those in authority.
- The priesthood is eternal, and the greater priesthood administers the gospel and all its ordinances, including the exalting ordinances of the temple.
- The priesthood encompasses covenants and ordinances for men and women that lead to exaltation and eternal life.
- The keys of the priesthood are necessary for the great work of the Restoration, including the key of the gathering of Israel, as restored by Moses; the key of the dispensation of the gospel of Abraham, as restored by Elias, "that in us and our

seed all generations after us should be blessed"; and the key of turning "the hearts of the fathers to the children, and the children to the fathers, lest the whole earth be smitten with a curse," as restored by Elijah (D&C 110:12, 15 [11–15]).

- In essence, everything operates in the Church and kingdom of God by and through the holy priesthood.

Never forget the pathway to learning the doctrine of the priesthood: "Let thy bowels also be full of charity towards all men, and to the household of faith, and let virtue garnish thy thoughts unceasingly; then shall thy confidence wax strong in the presence of God; and the doctrine of the priesthood shall distil upon thy soul as the dews from heaven" (D&C 121:45). Remember also "that the rights of the priesthood are inseparably connected with the powers of heaven, and that the powers of heaven cannot be controlled nor handled only upon the principles of righteousness" (D&C 121:36).

It is by the authority of this greater priesthood that men and women officiate in the Lord's holy house, and because priesthood keys are here upon the earth, you can receive your temple blessings and thus be empowered to go forth to bless Heavenly Father's children.

Elder Dallin H. Oaks has stated, "Priesthood power blesses all of us. Priesthood keys direct women as well as men, and priesthood ordinances and priesthood authority pertain to women as well as men." He further explained,

> We are not accustomed to speaking of women having the authority of the priesthood in their Church callings, but what other authority can it be? When a woman—young or old—is set apart to preach the gospel as a full-time missionary, she is given priesthood authority to perform a priesthood function. The same is true when a woman is set apart to function as an officer or teacher in a Church organization under the direction of one who holds the keys of the priesthood. Whoever functions in an office or calling received from one who holds priesthood keys exercises priesthood authority in performing her or his assigned duties.[1]

Sisters, remember that in your setting apart you are acting under the direction of priesthood power and that you will be endowed with power and the Holy Ghost when you receive your own endowments just as the Lord did (see Acts 10:38). The Lord is mindful of you, and you will bring many souls to Christ as you teach and serve by the power of the Holy Ghost.

An Invitation to Come to the Lord's Holy House

The Lord does not assign us to come to His holy house—He *invites* us to come so that He may endow us with power and the Holy Ghost and so that we may redeem the dead and be refreshed in our knowledge of God. He invites us to partake in the power of godliness and the mysteries of the kingdom through His ordinances, covenants, and the word of God. It is significant to note that no one will ever ask you how many times you have been to the temple or require you to account for the number of ordinances completed. Temple worship is sacred, personal, and between the Lord and each individual.

It is our choice whether we accept God's invitation and receive of His love. When you choose to come to the temple, you choose to separate yourself from the world. You will even change your street clothes for white clothing, a symbol of cleanliness and purity. In the Lord's house, all are alike. We are simply His children; He loves us all, and He is no respecter of persons. All may receive the same blessings through individual faithfulness.

Your Heavenly Father will never violate your agency. Agency gives you the right to choose to come and worship in the temple. You alone are responsible and accountable for every choice and decision you will make or fail to make. As you make choices about when and how often to attend the temple, follow the promptings of the Spirit.

President Gordon B. Hinckley asked us to consider the following regarding worship in the temple:

> I hope that everyone gets to the temple on a regular basis. I hope your children over 12 years of age have the opportunity of going to the temple to be baptized for the dead. If we are a temple-going people, we will be a better people, we will be better fathers and husbands, we

will be better wives and mothers. I know your lives are busy. I know that you have much to do. But I make you a promise that if you will go to the House of the Lord, you will be blessed; life will be better for you. Now, please, please, my beloved brethren and sisters, avail yourselves of the great opportunity to go to the Lord's house and thereby partake of all of the marvelous blessings that are yours to be received.[2]

President Howard W. Hunter likewise made this eloquent statement, urging the members of the Church to attend the temple:

Truly, the Lord desires that His people be a temple-motivated people. It would be the deepest desire of my heart to have every member of the Church be temple worthy. I would hope that every adult member would be worthy of—and carry—a current temple recommend, even if proximity to a temple does not allow immediate or frequent use of it. Let us be a temple-attending and a temple-loving people. Let us hasten to the temple as frequently as time and means and personal circumstances allow. Let us go not only for our kindred dead, but let us also go for the personal blessing of temple worship, for the sanctity and safety which is provided within those hallowed and consecrated walls. The temple is a place of beauty, it is a place of revelation, it is a place of peace. It is the house of the Lord. It is holy unto the Lord. It should be holy unto us.[3]

Ponder on these statements and the blessings promised you as you prepare to attend the temple, and think of the many wonderful truths that you will learn as you are endowed with knowledge and power. Within the temple walls, you will gain perspectives and knowledge you had not previously imagined.

Your Temple Recommend

To help you prepare to enter the temple prior to receiving your endowment, you will likely be interviewed by your bishop and receive a limited use recommend, which will allow you to participate in baptisms for the dead. The following are some of the key issues covered in the temple recommend interview mentioned by President Hunter:

- You must believe in God the Eternal Father, His Son Jesus Christ, and the Holy Ghost.

- You must sustain the general authorities and local authorities of the Church.
- You must be morally clean.
- You must ensure that nothing in your relationships with family members is out of harmony with the teachings of the Church.
- You must be honest in all of your dealings with others.
- You must strive to do fulfill your duties in the Church, and attend your sacrament, priesthood, and other meetings.
- You must be a full-tithe payer and live the Word of Wisdom.[4]

President Howard W. Hunter also made the following statement along these lines: "Our hearts and hands must be clean and pure and our thoughts must be focused on things of an eternal nature when you go to the temple. We hope you will feel that entering the temple is a privilege given to worthy Church members and not a right that automatically comes with Church membership."[5]

In preparing to enter the temple of the Lord, whether initially or upon any subsequent visit, it will be an exercise in taking upon yourself what Peter called the "divine nature" of Christ (2 Peter 1:4)—consisting of those spiritual qualities such as diligence, faith, virtue, knowledge, temperance, patience, godliness, brotherly kindness, and charity (see 2 Peter 1:5–8). In purifying our thoughts, actions, and desires to enter the temple, we ensure that we will "neither be barren nor unfruitful in the knowledge of our Lord Jesus Christ" (2 Peter 1:8). This same sentiment is echoed in the thirteenth article of faith: "We believe in being honest, true, chaste, benevolent, virtuous, and in doing good to all men; indeed, we may say that we follow the admonition of Paul—We believe all things, we hope all things, we have endured many things, and hope to be able to endure all things. If there is anything virtuous, lovely, or of good report or praiseworthy, we seek after these things" (Articles of Faith 1:13). These attributes are essential to discipleship, and as we discussed earlier, they culminate in charity, the pure love of Christ. Above all things, strive to cultivate charity as you prepare to enter the Lord's house. It is this love that will qualify you to come into the presence of the Savior, as Mormon explained: "Wherefore, my beloved brethren, pray unto the Father with all the energy of heart, that ye may be filled with this love, which he hath bestowed upon all who are true followers of his Son, Jesus Christ; that ye may become the sons of God; that when he shall appear we shall be like him, for we shall see him as he is; that we may have this hope; that we may be purified even as he is pure. Amen" (Moroni 7:48).

Symbolism in the Gospel and Temple Ordinances

As you prepare to enter the temple, and as you attend the temple, seek to understand and appreciate symbolism. Symbolism and figurative language are used in the scriptures and in the Lord's holy house. Symbols are simply objects, words, or gestures that represent something else. All of these things can carry symbolic meanings in addition to their literal meanings. Symbols have the ability to teach deep, and often hidden, truths that add greater dimension to our understanding. Symbolism stimulates and arouses the thought process and is the language of the Lord in ritual ceremonies. We see this in all of the ordinances of the gospel. Symbolism brings rich meaning and a greater depth to the doctrines and covenants being taught and entered into. One excellent example of symbolism is the parables found in the scriptures. These parables are rich in metaphoric language and symbolic representation. For example, consider the vision of the tree of life, the allegory of the olive tree, and Alma's description of faith as a seed. The scriptures also contain many symbolic representations of our Lord and Savior Jesus Christ, including His many names, titles and descriptions.

All ordinances and covenants have within them elements of symbolism, which can expand our understanding of them. The sacrament, for example, is highly symbolic: we place the emblems of the Lord Jesus Christ on the altar of God, which we call the sacrament table, and then symbolically partake of the body and blood of Christ while we promise to remember Him and keep His commandments. As you come to better understand the symbols found in the gospel, you will feel greater appreciation for them, and greater motivation to serve and love others.

I challenge you to seek greater understanding of both the symbols themselves and the reason why the Lord uses symbolism in teaching us. Seek to understand, rather than set aside, the beautiful symbolic meanings found within the gospel of Jesus Christ. Sometimes individuals are counseled not to worry about symbolism, and rightfully so, but we need to seek to understand the symbols as best we can. With time, they need to be understood to fully understand the things of God. Indeed, there is symbolism in every aspect of the gospel, so seek the Holy Spirit to literally wash over you with light and truth. Surely, God will reveal the truth of all things as you prepare diligently to understand them (see Moroni 10:5).

Ours is a church rich in symbolism, a fact that we must embrace rather than shy away from. I, like you, have at times been tentative about rituals and ceremonies and have not always studied them as I should. This is because I was lacking in knowledge and understanding of their significance. Understanding symbolism is not a matter of simply asking and receiving the revelation of the meaning; we must follow the Lord's counsel when He says, "Behold, you have not understood; you have supposed that I would give it unto you, when you took no thought save it was to ask me. But, behold, I say unto you, that you must study it out in your mind; then you must ask me if it be right, and if it is right I will cause that your bosom shall burn within you; therefore, you shall feel that it is right" (D&C 9:7–8). We must study and ponder the scriptures, which often explain the doctrines as well as the meaning of the symbols. We must also be cautious about declaring the meaning of a particular symbol, as many symbols have a multitude of potential meanings. The ordinance of baptism is a perfect example. Most of us participated in this ordinance at the age of eight. We were expected to understand as best we could the ordinance of baptism and the subsequent accountability. The scriptures teach us that baptism can also be symbolic of the following:

1. Baptism is in similitude of and is symbolic of Christ's death, burial, and resurrection (see Romans 6).
2. Baptism is symbolically putting on Christ (see Galatians 3:27).
3. Baptism symbolizes the washing away and remission of sins (see Acts 22:16; D&C 19:31).
4. Baptism is symbolic of being born again (see John 3:3–5; Moses 6:59).
5. Baptism symbolizes our willingness to take the name of the Lord Jesus Christ upon us (see D&C 20:37).
6. Baptism symbolizes the fact that we become the sons and daughters of Christ (see Mosiah 5:7).
7. Baptism symbolizes the concept that we are changed from our carnal and fallen state (see Mosiah 27:25).
8. Baptism symbolizes the recipient's willingness through humility to be obedient to the commandments of God (see Matthew 3:15–16).

Surely, there are even more symbolic meanings of baptism. A prayerful study of symbolism in the gospel will enable you to understand and appreciate the doctrines and covenants of the gospel more completely, and thus be filled with *gratitude*, which, as we have learned, is the ultimate catalyst for change and spiritual growth. As time passes, your understanding of the gospel, and especially of the ordinances of the temple, will mature, and your desire for further light and knowledge will increase. That has been my own delightful experience.

Yes, the gospel of Jesus Christ is rich in symbolism, and you will need to study as much as you can to fully understand and appreciate its doctrines and be filled with gratitude. Know that you will come to understand more as time goes by, as your maturity in the gospel grows, and as your desire to know increases.

The parables are just one example that stand as magnificent teaching tools of the Lord, which are loaded with symbolism to better portray their meaning and give deep understanding to the doctrine taught. Jesus explained to his chosen disciples that he used parables, which are by definition symbolic stories, "Because it is given unto you to know the mysteries of the kingdom of heaven, but to them [the multitudes] it is not given" (Matthew 13:11). In other words, the Savior often cloaked his meaning in such stories so that only a certain number of His followers, or even his enemies, would grasp the true meaning of those stories. Indeed, as the Book of Mormon prophet Nephi taught, "All things which have been given of God from the beginning of the world, unto man, are the typifying of him" (that is, all things *prefigure* or *represent* Christ) (2 Nephi 11:4).

The examples of uses of symbolic language could go on and on; my purpose here is simply to show that the gospel is rich in symbolism, and we should seek to understand it, rather than shy away from it, especially as it pertains to worship in the holy temples. Having served as a temple president, sealer, and ordinance worker, I find great joy in the study of gospel symbolism and its applications to my life. The depth of my understanding has increased. I have gained an overwhelming feeling of gratitude to my Heavenly Father and my Savior Jesus Christ.

The Hymns of the Temple

In the Old Testament, there are several sections (in Psalms 15:1–5, Isaiah 33:14–17, and Psalms 24:3–5) that are known as "temple hymns." These hymns are songs of praise that speak of Deity and coming to His holy house.

The hymn I have chosen for an example speaks of who will come to the temple and what is required to enter the temple. It also describes the blessings bestowed on those who are worthy to come to the temple. I would also encourage you to study and ponder the other temple hymns:

The Psalm of David—Psalm 24:3–5

The Question: "Who shall ascend into the hill of the Lord? or who shall stand in his holy place?"

The Answer: "He that hath clean hands, and a pure heart; who hath not lifted up his soul unto vanity, nor sworn deceitfully."

The Promised Blessings: "He shall receive the blessing from the Lord, and righteousness from the God of his salvation."

The Symbols:

- Clean Hands: Be clean in all that you do. Be free from sin. Repent. Be morally pure, unpolluted, and upright.
- Pure Heart: The motive for your actions is the will of God. You have real intent, with no guile or deceit. You do not have ulterior motives. You seek the welfare of others, and your heart has worthy motives, affections, desires, and decisions. As Proverbs 23:7 states, "For as he thinketh in his heart, so is he."
- No Vanity: You are not prideful, showy, and you do not seek to esteem yourself above another, or feel conceited in anything.
- Swear Deceitfully: You do not make a promise to God or your fellowman with the intention to deceive and mislead. Lying is the worst kind of deceit.[6]

When we come to understand what the Lord expects of us in order to come to His holy house, we recognize that this is not a social event. Attending the temple is one of the most sacred things you will do on this earth. Here, you receive blessings from a perfect and loving Heavenly Father—even all that He has if we are faithful (see D&C 84:38). He is the God of our salvation, for we are saved by His grace after all we can do (see 2 Nephi 25:23). As you attend the temple, you will come to recognize that the Lord seeks to bless you in every moment of your life. This is why He seeks to gather all of us to His temple, so that we can be endowed with power to go about doing good. So let us be worthy to receive the blessings Heavenly Father and our Savior desire to give us in Their holy house.

Remember

Just as preparation is critical to becoming an effective missionary, preparation is also imperative to understanding the holy endowment. Prepare to receive your own endowment, first and foremost, by living worthily and righteously. Other ways to prepare include taking a temple preparation class and studying the pamphlet *Preparing to Enter the Holy Temple.* Another great way to prepare for your endowment is to read the scriptures, using the topical guide as a reference, and study topics such as endowment, atonement, garments, robes of righteousness, temples, Christ, perfection, exaltation, priesthood, and the oath and covenant of the priesthood. You will also find many helpful articles and talks when you search lds.org for articles on the temple.

Always remember that it is *your* responsibility to personally prepare to enter the house of the Lord. No one can prepare for you. My dear friend Truman G. Madsen told of an experience with President McKay that illustrates this point. He said,

> Well, on the occasion in Los Angeles, President McKay stopped everyone by saying: "This young lady came to me. She had had both experiences (entering the temple and joining a sorority), but said she had been far more impressed with her sorority." We gasped. President McKay was a master of the pause. He let that wait for several seconds and then said: "Brothers and sisters, she was disappointed in the temple. Brothers and sisters, I was disappointed in the temple." Then he finished his sentence: "And so were you." Then no one gasped. He had us. "Why were we?" he asked. And then he named some of the things. We were not prepared. How could we be, fully? We had stereotypes in our minds, faulty expectations. We were unable to distinguish the symbol from the symbolized. We were not worthy enough. We were too inclined quickly to respond negatively, critically. And we had not yet seasoned spiritually. Those are my words, but they cover approximately what he said. I will give you the quotation verbatim. This was a man, at that time eighty years of age, who had been in the temple every week for some fifty years, which gave him, I thought, some right to speak. He said: "I believe there are few, even temple workers, who comprehend the full meaning and power of the temple endowment. Seen for what it is, it is the step-by-step ascent into the Eternal Presence. If our young people could but glimpse it, it would be the most powerful spiritual motivation of their lives."[7]

Read that paragraph again. Few people understand and comprehend the temple endowment, and if we "could get a glimpse of it, it would be the most powerful spiritual motivation of [our] lives." Now you see the importance and the reason for giving your best effort to understand and appreciate the temple ordinances and covenants.

Study and seek Heavenly Father in mighty prayer, so that you may learn these supernal truths.

Later in the story, Truman noted the following, as applied to his own experience in preparing for the temple:

> There were three things amiss in me, and I dare to suppose these may apply to some others. First, I hadn't even carefully read the scriptures about the temple. It had not occurred to me that there are over three hundred verses, by my count, in the Doctrine and Covenants alone that talk about the temple and the "hows," if you will, of preparation. I had not read what the Brethren had said to help us—I was unaware of those statements.
>
> Second, I was, I am afraid, afflicted with various kinds of unworthiness and not too anxious to change all that. Oh, we talk of it and we aspire. We want change, but we don't want it enough. We are (and I don't laugh at poor Augustine for saying this) like Augustine, who said in a prayer, "Oh God, make me chaste, but not yet." We talk of sacrifice. The one the Lord asks of *us now* is the sacrifice of your sins—the hardest thing in the world to give up. There's still a certain bittersweet enjoyment. But His promise is crystal clear. "If you will purify yourselves, sanctify yourselves, I will bless you" (see D&C 88:74). And I'm afraid the postscript is: "And if you don't, I can't."
>
> The third point is that I had a built-in hostility to ritual and to symbolism. I was taught by people both in and out of the Church—with good intention, I have no doubt—that we don't believe in pagan ceremony; we don't believe in all these procedures and routines; that's what they did in the ancient apostate church: we've outgrown all that. Well, that in effect is throwing out the baby with the bath water. We're not against ordinances. God has revealed them anew. And I suspect they are as eternal as are what we often call eternal laws. There are certain patterns or programs, certain chains of transmission, which are eternal. Ordinances tie in with those, if they are not identical with them. God has so decreed, but that decree is based upon the very ultimate nature of reality. You *cannot* receive the powers of godliness, says the scripture, except through the ordinances (see D&C 84:20). Well, that hadn't ever entered my soul. I thought our sacraments were a bit of an embarrassment and that sometime we could do away with them. One day it suddenly became clear to me—this is the Lord's pattern of our nourishment. We need spiritual transformation. We can eat, if you will, receive, drink (the Lord uses all those images) the Living Fountain through ordinances.

Well, I pray that we will reach out for what is written, reach out for repentance, and reach out in the recognition that the ordinances are channels of living power.[8]

The temple is the only way to return to the presence of God—through Christ the Lord. All the blessings of exaltation can be yours if you are faithful in all things. Obedience is the price of such great rewards. The more you come to understand and appreciate these principles, the greater your gratitude will be—and the more you will change, grow, and progress toward your ultimate goal. The love of God will fill your soul and you will have an overwhelming desire to do good. This is what the temple is all about: the empowerment to become like Christ, to do as He would do, to love as He has loved. Seeking always to "succor the weak, lift up the hands which hang down, and strengthen the feeble knees" (D&C 81:5). The Apostles of old were instructed to tarry in Jerusalem so they might receive the great blessing of the temple endowment (see Luke 24:49), and likewise you, and all those in this generation are invited to "tarry" and receive of the blessings of the temple: "And this cannot be brought to pass until mine elders are endowed with power from on high. For behold, I have prepared a great endowment and blessing to be poured out upon them, inasmuch as they are faithful and continue in humility before me" (D&C 105:11–12). This holy endowment and these temple sealings have been given as a sublime blessing in this, the dispensation of the fulness of times.

Be sure you are prepared for your temple blessings by taking the temple preparation class, and by studying books written concerning the temple. I encourage you to read carefully *The Temple: Gaining Knowledge and Power in the House of the Lord* by Ed J. Pinegar. The temple is sacred, but there are many things you can learn to help you understand and appreciate the doctrines and principles taught in the temple. Following your interview with your bishop and stake president for your temple recommend, you may receive your own temple endowment. The greater the preparation the grander the temple experience.

CHAPTER 7

Gaining Knowledge and
Power in the House of the Lord

Redemption of the Dead

You may be thinking to yourself, "I am preparing to serve a mission. My work is among the living." This is true. However, it is also essential for you to understand and appreciate the doctrine of redeeming the dead. This, too, is missionary work, but on the other side of the veil. The temple is critical to the redemption of the dead because the ordinances must be done vicariously here upon the earth.

This dispensation—*your* dispensation—has been charged with the responsibility of redeeming the dead as you serve as a savior on Mount Zion. This is a principle you will teach your investigators, and you will testify of its truthfulness. It is of significant note that new converts who are introduced to family history and temple work are much more likely to remain active in the Church. Why? Because they are involved in saving souls! They are actively engaged in the work of the Lord.

The great Redeemer, Jesus Christ, makes possible the redemptive work for the dead. He brought about the resurrection (see Mosiah 15:19–20) and has ensured that all who die without a knowledge of the gospel will be taught in the spirit world (see D&C 138). These spirits await the vicarious work we begin as we participate in baptisms for the dead and other ordinances. The work of redeeming the dead is critical, for they must all be baptized. Please read and ponder Doctrine and Covenants 128:18–24. Through these verses we come to understand that the work and glory of the Father and the Son (see Moses 1:39) literally becomes our work. Those spirits on the other side of the veil are alive, though we often call them dead. They stand waiting to receive their long promised blessings. They consider themselves in bondage due to the long absence from their bodies (see D&C 138:50). The gospel of repentance was and is being preached to them (see 1 Peter 4:6; D&C 138:18–19, 31–37, 57–60).

As you come to understand the great vision of the redemption of the dead and your important role in bringing this great work to fruition, take the time to reread Doctrine and Covenants 138. You will gain further understanding as you follow the same process as President Joseph F. Smith, who received this magnificent revelation: You must study the Atonement, search the scriptures, and prayerfully ponder. As you do this, you will better come to know and understand the doctrine of the redemption of the dead. As your vision of the work expands, you will come to better understand and appreciate it.

The work of the Lord is enormous. Each year, millions and millions of temple ordinances are completed for the dead, which bring the blessings of the gospel to our brothers and sisters in the spirit world. This great work brings the family of God together; without the sealing ordinances, the whole earth would be, "utterly wasted at his coming" (D&C 2:3). The work you do in the temple, whether baptisms for the dead, endowments, initiatories, or sealings, is life-exalting. All of it involves saving God's children. Through all of it, you become a savior on Mount Zion.

The Endowment—A Review and Summary

In the *Encyclopedia of Mormonism,* Alma Burton states, "An Endowment generally is a gift, but in a specialized sense it is a course of instruction, ordinances, and covenants given only in dedicated temples of The Church of Jesus Christ of Latter-day Saints. The words 'to endow' (from the Greek *enduein*), as used in the New Testament, mean to dress, clothe, put on garments, put on attributes, or receive virtue. . . . The prophet Joseph Smith taught that these were 'of things spiritual, and to be received only by the spiritual minded.'"[1]

The endowment was designed to give men and women an overarching understanding of their relationship with God and His plan of redemption and to receive the ordinances and covenants of the priesthood, including the mysteries of the kingdom, knowledge of God, and the power of godliness.

Brother Burton continues in his explanation, "The endowment of 'power from on high' in modern temples has four main aspects. The first is the preparatory ordinance known as the initiatory. It is a ceremonial washing and anointing, after which the temple patron dons the sacred clothing of the temple. The second aspect of the endowment is a course of instruction through dramatic representations. It includes the Creation, a figurative coming forth of Adam and Eve and coming into the Garden of Eden, and the Fall. In mortality they receive the plan of salvation from heavenly messengers.

The third aspect involves making covenants. The temple endowment is the unfolding or culmination of the covenants made at baptism. Temple covenants are, in a very real sense, 'Tests by which one's willingness and fitness for righteousness may be known.'[2] They include covenants to observe the law of chastity and have virtue; to have charity; to consecrate one's time, means, and talents to the work of the Lord; and to endure to the end and remain true to the faith in preparing for the Second Coming. In the endowment you will also promise to keep these covenants sacred and to 'trifle not with sacred things' (D&C 6:12). The fourth aspect of the endowment is a sense of divine presence. In the dedicatory prayer of the temple at Kirtland, Ohio, the Prophet Joseph Smith pleaded, 'That all people who shall enter upon the threshold of the Lord's house may feel thy power, and feel constrained to acknowledge that thou hast sanctified it, and that it is thy house, a place of thy holiness' (D&C 109:13). In holy temples, which have been built by sacrifice to the name of the Lord Jesus Christ, dedicated by His authority, and reverenced in his Spirit, the following promise is given: 'My name shall be here; and I will manifest myself to my people in mercy in this holy house' (D&C 110:7). In the temples, there is an 'aura of deity' manifest to the worthy.[3] As you attend the temple, you will in a very real sense stand in the presence of God and learn at His feet. Through the temple endowment, you may receive 'a fulness of the Holy Ghost' (D&C 109:15)."[4]

The Endowment Is a Gift from God

Brigham Young stated, "Your endowment is, to receive all those ordinances in the House of the Lord, which are necessary for you, after you have departed this life, to enable you to walk back to the presence of the Father."[5] In the simplest sense, the endowment is a presentation showing how, through ordinances and covenants, you can return to the presence of your Heavenly Father.

It is important to note that the giver of the gift—God—does not and indeed cannot demand reception of the gift of the endowment. Father will force no man to heaven. The gift bestowed must be received freely and without reservation. We must embrace the gift. And, because it is given with sacredness and holiness, we must receive it with holiness of heart. As you enter the temple and partake of the goodness of God, seek to understand and appreciate this magnificent gift.

What are some of the indicators that will show you whether or not you have truly received the gift of the endowment? The following questions will point the way: Are you seeking to change and become? Are your prayers reflective of your commitment to your covenants? Do you understand what it means to be endowed by being clothed? Are you taking upon yourself the divine nature of Jesus Christ? Do you prayerfully and diligently return to the Lord's holy house to refresh in your mind the covenants you have made? Is your heart turned to your Father and your own immediate family? Do you set time aside to ponder the goodness of God? Do you express gratitude to your Father for His goodness in providing the holy endowment, enabled and empowered by His Beloved Son? Do you feel the fulness of the Holy Ghost, which will lead you to do good? Oh, how I wish I had thought of these questions as a young man. So now, let us go forward with good cheer and gladness of heart toward the blessings of the holy endowment. The following ideas will help you prepare to understand the endowment:

A Spiritual Mind-Set—We read in 2 Nephi 9:39 that "to be spiritually-minded is life eternal." Spirituality refers to one's heart and its nature or condition. Is it any wonder that Alma would query, "Have ye spiritually been born of God? Have ye received his image in your countenances? Have ye experienced this mighty change in your hearts?" (Alma 5:14). Being spiritually minded is one of the most important preparations you can make to prepare for the endowment and to understand symbolism. I encourage you to seek for and embrace the following qualities, attributes, and capacities:

1. Be sensitive to the promptings of the Spirit. Seek the comfort and power of the Holy Spirit through prayer (see 3 Nephi 19:9).

2. Let your heart be "soft" and not past feeling (see 1 Nephi 17:45). Yield to the enticings of the Holy Spirit (see Mosiah 3:19).

3. Receive and understand the things of the Spirit (see D&C 50:21–22).

4. Seek to take upon yourself the divine nature of Christ (see 2 Peter 1:3–10). Your nature then becomes like your Savior's (see Moroni 7:48), full of love, even the love of God. When you have this love, you will know it from your fruits and blessings of the Holy Ghost (see 4 Nephi 1:15–16; D&C 11;12–13; Galatians 5:22–23).

5. Be like King Benjamin's people when they expressed that the Spirit of Lord had wrought a mighty change in their hearts and only wanted to do good continually (see Mosiah 5:2). All those who are spiritually minded are led to do good by the Holy Spirit (see D&C 11:12).

And thus we see that, most of all, a spiritually minded person is one who is worthy to be led and guided by the Holy Ghost. It is this spirit that will change your very heart and lead you to understanding and good works.

A Restoration of All Things—It was imperative that the Lord provide a way for us to return to His presence. The endowment is the only way. It is critical that you understand that the endowment is the way back to God and that it is a very important part of the restoration of all things. It was in February 1831, just ten months after the Church was organized, that the prophet Joseph received instructions to go to Ohio so the Lord could endow them with power from on high. Through the endowment, God gives His laws to His people by covenant, thereby endowing us with power from on high: "Wherefore, for this cause I gave unto you the commandment that ye should go to the Ohio; and there I will give unto you my law; and there you shall be endowed with power from on high" (D&C 38:32). The endowment allows us to know the goodness of God and our relationship to Him. It helps us recognize that all things are done for the blessing of God's children, and that we may return to His presence. The power He bestows upon us will also protect us against evil and temptation.

As you are spiritually minded and recognize the restorative nature of the endowment, it will truly lead you back to God, and help you grow and progress on the trajectory your Father intended for you.

Washings, Anointings, and the Holy Garment

We learn from the *Encyclopedia of Mormonism* that

> washings and anointings are preparatory or initiatory ordinances in the temple. They signify the cleansing and sanctifying power of Jesus Christ applied to the attributes of the person and to the hallowing of all life. They have biblical precedents. . . . Latter-day Saints look forward to receiving these inspired and inspiring promises with the same fervent anticipation they bring to baptism. They come in the spirit of a scriptural command: "Cleanse your hands and your feet before me."[6] (D&C 88:74; 1 John 2:27)

The *Encyclopedia of Mormonism* continues by saying, "In many respects similar in purpose to ancient Israelite practice and to the washing of feet by Jesus among his disciples, these modern LDS rites are performed only in temples set apart and dedicated for sacred purposes"[7] (see D&C 124:37–38).

As you read the scriptures and ponder the meaning found in the words and symbols present in the initiatory, you will notice striking parallels between other instances of washing and anointing found in the scriptures. I encourage you to search the topical guide and the scriptures with an eye to words such as *washing, anointing, ointment,* and *consecration.* As you search the word of God with an eye to symbolism, you will gain greater insight into the initiatory, both when you go to the temple for your own initiatory and when you return to do proxy work for the dead.

Consider also the following quote from the Guide to the Scriptures: "Symbolically, a repentant person may be cleansed from a life burdened with sin and its consequences through the atoning sacrifice of Jesus Christ. Certain washings performed under proper priesthood authority serve as sacred ordinances."[8]

The following scriptures will give you additional insight as you prepare to receive your endowment. I encourage you to study them and search for others:

1. "And Aaron and his sons thou shalt bring unto the door of the tabernacle of the congregation, and shalt wash them with water." (Exodus 29:4) "And thou shalt bring Aaron and his sons unto the door of the tabernacle of the congregation, and wash them with water." (Exodus 40:12)

2. "Wash me thoroughly from mine iniquity, and cleanse me from my sin." (Psalm 51:2)

3. "And such were some of you: but ye are washed, but ye are sanctified, but ye are justified in the name of the Lord Jesus, and by the Spirit of our God." (1 Corinthians 6:11)

4. "Not by works of righteousness, which we have done, but according to his mercy he saved us, by the washing of regeneration, and renewing of the Holy Ghost." (Titus 3:5)

5. "And from Jesus Christ, who is the faithful witness, and the first begotten of the dead, and the prince of the kings of the earth. Unto him that loved us, and washed us from our sins in his own blood." (Revelation 1:5)

The Lord's promised blessings will be clear as you remember your temple covenants within the initiatory ordinances. And as you remember them, you will be blessed.

It is important to understand that if we lay our covenants aside or treat them lightly, we will suffer the consequences of sin (see D&C 84:54–57). We receive the garment of the holy priesthood in the initiatory ordnances. It will remind you of and help you to remember your temple covenants. The garment has power to remind and strengthen us, only if we endow it with a symbolic meaning and then think about that meaning when we fold it, or put it on our bodies, or when we remove it.

Elder J. Richard Clark has said, "Sacred temple clothing is a shield and protection against Satan. As you receive your endowments in the temple, you receive the privilege of wearing the sacred temple clothing and the garments of the holy priesthood. The garments are a tangible reminder of your covenants with God. It has been said that modesty is the hallmark of a true Latter-day Saint. The temple garment reminds us that virtue sets us apart from the world and, in a special way, makes us one with God."[9]

The garment will be an outward expression of your inner commitment to follow your Savior Jesus Christ. It is a protection against temptation and evil. It truly is like unto armor, even the armor of God as expressed by Paul (see Ephesians 6:13–17). Isaiah reminds us, "I will greatly rejoice in the Lord, my soul shall be joyful in my God; for he hath clothed me with the garments of salvation, he hath covered me with the robe of righteousness" (Isaiah 61:10).

Wearing the garment is also part of becoming a Zion people. The Lord has declared, "For Zion must increase in beauty, and in holiness; her borders must be enlarged; her stakes must be strengthened;

yea, verily I say unto you, Zion must arise and put on her beautiful garments" (D&C 82:14).

To be pure before God, your garments must be cleansed through faith in the Lord and His sacrifice and Atonement (see 1 Nephi 12:10; Alma 5:21). Through properly honoring the garment and keeping it symbolically clean, you will be worthy to sit down with Abraham, Isaac, and Jacob, and the holy prophets in the kingdom of heaven someday (see Alma 7:25). Through the Atonement, our garments are symbolically washed clean, and we come to literally abhor sin (see Alma 13:10–12). This is critical, for we know from the scriptures that no unclean thing can enter into the rest of our Father, save their garments are washed clean through the blood of Christ. For our garments to be symbolically cleansed as we access the Atonement, we must be full of faith, repent, and endure to the end (see 3 Nephi 27:19).

When the Lord comes again, we need to be ready with oil in our lamps, which signifies our personal righteousness and worthiness through the blood of Christ. If we watch and are ready in this manner, we shall sit down with the bridegroom, even the Lord and Savior Jesus Christ (see the parable of the ten virgins in Matthew 25:1–13). Our garments are washed clean and white through the blood of the Lamb (see Alma 13:11). For as we learn earlier in Matthew, "And he saith unto him, Friend, how camest thou in hither not having a wedding garment? And he was speechless" (see Matthew 22:12–13, the parable of the king's son as compared to the kingdom of heaven). Receiving and keeping temple covenants is not a casual thing, it is a matter of eternal life. Being clothed in our temple garment covers our nakedness, our sinful and fallen state (see 2 Nephi 9:14; Isaiah 61:10; Revelation 3:18). The garment is a form of protection for us in a world of temptation and sin (see 2 Nephi 4:33; Revelation 3:18; 16:15).

Regarding keeping our garments symbolically clean, President Joseph Fielding Smith said,

"Save yourselves from this untoward generation, and come forth out of the fire, hating even the garments spotted with the flesh." (D&C 36:6) This expression is also found in Jude (23), and in Revelation, where the Lord says to John, "Thou hast a few names even in Sardis which have not defiled their garments; and they shall walk with me in white; for they are worthy" (Revelation 3:4). This is symbolic language, yet is plain to understand. Many in this generation walk in spiritual darkness, and the punishment for sin is spoken of as punishment by fire. Garments "spotted with flesh" are garments defiled by the practices of carnal desires and disobedience to the commandments of the Lord. We are commanded to keep our garments unspotted from all sin, and from every practice that defiles. We are therefore commanded to come out of the world of wickedness and forsake the things of this world.[10]

Our garments are made clean through the blood of the Lamb and by our faithfulness, especially as we seek to bring souls unto Christ (see D&C 88:85; 4:2; 31:5; 135:5; Ether 12:37).

Each of us has a divine responsibility as disciples of Jesus Christ: "That ye may be prepared in all things when I shall send you again to magnify the calling whereunto I have called you, and the mission with which I have commissioned you. Behold, I sent you out to testify and warn the people, and it becometh every man who hath been warned to warn his neighbor" (D&C 88:80–81). This is part of the covenants we make in the temple—promising to testify of Christ and in the process becoming clean from the blood and sins of this generation. We learn from the prophet Wilford Woodruff,

> Can we fold our arms in peace and cry "all is peace in Zion," when, so far as we have the power of the priesthood resting upon us, we can see the condition of the world? Can we imagine that our garments will be clean without lifting our voices before our fellow men and warning them of the things that are at their doors? No, we cannot. There never was a set of men since God made the world under a stronger responsibility to warn this generation, to lift up our voices long and loud, day and night so far as we have the opportunity and declare the words of God unto this generation. We are required to do this. This is our calling. It is our duty.[11]

Preaching about Christ and His gospel has everything to do with keeping our garments clean and without spot and also being clean from the blood and sins of this generation, Jacob states that blood of this generation is upon us if we do not teach and testify in the same manner as he did: "O, my beloved brethren, remember my words. Behold, I take off my garments, and I shake them before you; I pray the God of my salvation that he view me with his all-searching eye; wherefore, ye shall know at the last day, when all men shall be judged of their works, that the God of Israel did witness that I shook your iniquities from my soul, and that I stand with brightness before him, and am rid of your blood" (2 Nephi 9:44).

Remember, as you participate in the washing and anointing of the initiatory ordinances, that all things are given and done in the wisdom of that God who knoweth all things (see 2 Nephi 2:24). Always remember the counsel found in Isaiah, "For my thoughts are not your thoughts, neither are your ways my ways, saith the Lord. For as the heavens are higher than the earth, so are my ways higher than your ways, and my thoughts than your thoughts" (Isaiah 55:8–9). It may take some time before you begin to understand all of the symbolism present, but have faith that you will.

Spiritual Power and the Holy Ghost

In the endowment we learn that because of our faithfulness, we can actually draw upon the literal powers of Heaven. This power is the fulness of the Holy Ghost (see D&C 109:15). The power of God is activated by our faith in Jesus Christ. For example, we read in the scriptures that as the Savior went about healing, He often said, "Thy faith hath made thee whole" (Matthew 15:28; Mark 5:34; 10:52; Luke 8:48; 17:19). From this we learn that according to our faithful obedience and righteousness, we too may be endowed with power and go about doing good. The endowment is all about becoming worthy to enter into our Father's presence through the spiritual power we gain through our temple endowment.

It is possible, through this spiritual power, to bring about mighty changes in your life. It is possible to receive the image of Christ in your countenance. It is possible to be spiritually born of God. All of these things are possible through the ordinances and covenants of the gospel of Jesus Christ. When we give our will over to God's will through the covenants we make and keep, He can then empower us. President Benson taught, "Men and women who turn their lives over to God will find out that he can make a lot more out of their lives than they can. He will deepen their joys, expand their vision, quicken their minds, strengthen their muscles, lift their spirits, multiply their blessings, increase their opportunities, comfort their souls, raise up friends, and pour out peace."[12]

The endowment is, in the end, about being empowered (see D&C 38:32, 38; 43:16; 105:11; 110:9; 132:59). We understand that the Savior was empowered by God, because the last phrase in Acts 10:38 reads, "For God was with Him." Heavenly Father will likewise be with you by the power of His Holy Spirit. He will empower you with the ability to do good, the power to live justly, the power to walk humbly, the power to judge righteously, the power to be enlightened, and the power to literally have your soul filled with joy. Do these ideas sound familiar? These are also the blessings of the Holy Spirit (see D&C 11:12–13). This empowerment is centered in good works, being righteous and holy, being sanctified, and being justified through your Savior by the power of the Holy Ghost. It is through the power of God that you will enjoy the fruits of the Holy Spirit: "Love, joy, peace, longsuffering, gentleness, goodness, faith, meekness, temperance: against such there is no law" (Galatians 5:22–23).

Our constant goal should be to live by the Spirit so that we can have this power in our lives. We must seek to be directed by the Spirit and live worthy of the Spirit. And we must accept the empowerment of God by regularly worshipping in His holy house. As we attend the temple often, we will see and understand the blessings of God. I urge you to remember that it is one thing to have the potential to receive the Holy Ghost, and it is quite another to always have the Holy Ghost with you. This will happen as you have faith in Jesus Christ, love God, keep your heart pure, and above all keep the commandments, including your temple covenants.

The following key points, related to harnessing the spiritual power of the endowment and the Holy Ghost, will help you have the best experience possible as you receive your own endowment and then return to the temple to do work for the dead and continue to learn:

1. The endowment is a gift from God that endows us with power to return to Him. Our beloved Father in Heaven gave us the supernal and infinite gift of His Only Begotten Son, our Savior Jesus Christ (see John 3:16). It is only through our Savior that we are provided a way to return to the presence of the Father (see John 14:6), which is symbolized in the culmination of the endowment.

2. We are clothed or covered when we are endowed. In the initiatory, we are clothed in the garment of the holy priesthood, even the robes of righteousness. We are clothed and encircled in the arms of our Savior's love, and given spiritual power and protection. We are protected and watched over as we are faithful to our covenants. We are given power to resist temptation and evil. Our garments are washed clean through the blood of the Lamb—our Beloved Savior. We become prepared to meet our Heavenly Father and our Savior. Always remember that the proper wearing of your garments is an outward expression of an inner commitment to follow your Savior Jesus Christ.

3. The Atonement is the enabling power through which God's work is accomplished. Through the Atonement, the veil between heaven and earth is rent. The great High Priest has provided a way for us to return home through the infinite Atonement and the power of the resurrection. Christ, the Anointed One, has made all things possible, and His Atonement is continuous and everlasting in its scope and operation. The Savior reaches out to nurture us every day and in every way. He makes possible repentance and forgiveness and perfection. His Atonement, like the endowment, brings us back into the presence of the Father. The Atonement and endowment are integrally connected. The endowment symbolically brings us back into the presence of God, while the Atonement is the enabling power that literally brings us back into the presence of God. Without the endowment, we could not fully receive and accept the Atonement. It is through the holy priesthood and power of the ordinances and covenants that enable us, through our obedience, to return to the Father and the Son.

4. *The endowment empowers or endows us with power and the Holy Ghost.* Without this power, we are weak. In the strength of the Lord, we are strong. The Lord can make weak things strong, however, if we are humble and act with faith (see Ether 12:27). This divine power is given to men and women through the Holy Ghost. The Holy Ghost will give us power to know the truth, teach and testify, receive revelations, and lead us to do good (the very purpose for which the priesthood is used and for which the endowment is given). The Spirit will also help us to walk humbly, to do justly, and judge righteously. It will enlighten our minds and fill our souls with joy.

5. *We must keep our covenants to make the power and blessings of the temple effective in our lives.* We must receive these blessings with holiness of heart and then strive to keep the commandments to remain worthy of them. There is no other way.

The Oath and Covenant of the Priesthood

The word *endow* in its modern sense means to give something freely, and this is what the Lord does for us in the temple endowment: He provides instruction regarding the most profound doctrines of the gospel (those things that the scriptures often call *mysteries of godliness* (see Topical Guide); and immeasurable blessings through the endowment's ordinances and covenants.

It is the greater or Melchizedek Priesthood that holds the key to the doctrines and blessings of the temple. Of it we read, "This greater priesthood administereth the gospel and holdeth the key of the mysteries of the kingdom, even the key of the knowledge of God. Therefore, in the ordinances thereof, the power of godliness is manifest. And without the ordinances thereof, and the authority of the priesthood, the power of godliness is not manifest unto men in the flesh; For without this no man can see the face of God, even the Father, and live" (D&C 84:19–22).

Oh, the goodness of God in allowing His children to officiate in His Holy House, that all of His children may partake of the heavenly gifts available there. The prophet Joseph taught regarding the temple, "All men who become heirs of God and joint-heirs with Jesus Christ will have to receive the fulness of the ordinances of his kingdom; and those who will not receive all the ordinances will come short of the fulness of that glory, if they do not lose the whole."[13] The temple is the only way back home. Its ordinances and covenants enable us ultimately, if we are faithful, to literally to enter into the presence of our Father.

The same promises were made to the ancient Israelites, but they rejected them and suffered the consequences: "Now this Moses plainly taught to the children of Israel in the wilderness, and sought diligently to sanctify his people that they might behold the face of God; But they hardened their hearts and could not endure his presence; therefore, the Lord in his wrath, for his anger was kindled against them, swore that they should not enter into his rest while in the wilderness, which rest is the fulness of his glory. Therefore, he took Moses out of their midst, and the Holy Priesthood also" (D&C 84:23–25). The Israelites' lot was the lesser priesthood, and the law of Moses. But, through the higher priesthood, the covenants and ordinances of the temple have been made available in their fulness to the Saints in these latter days, as the Lord explains Doctrine and Covenants 84:

> For whoso is faithful unto the obtaining these two priesthoods of which I have spoken, and the magnifying their calling, are sanctified by the Spirit unto the renewing of their bodies.
>
> They become the sons of Moses and of Aaron and the seed of Abraham, and the church and kingdom, and the elect of God.
>
> And also all they who receive this priesthood receive me, saith the Lord;
>
> For he that receiveth my servants receiveth me;
>
> And he that receiveth me receiveth my Father;
>
> And he that receiveth my Father receiveth my Father's kingdom; therefore all that my Father hath shall be given unto him.
>
> And this is according to the oath and covenant which belongeth to the priesthood.

> Therefore, all those who receive the priesthood, receive this oath
> and covenant of my Father, which he cannot break, neither can it be
> moved. (D&C 84:33–40)

It is interesting to note that for men, receiving the Melchizedek Priesthood and being ordained an elder are not events that, in and of themselves, qualify them for exaltation and for entrance into the presence of the Lord. It is the temple ordinances that, for both men and women, promise exaltation in the highest degree of the celestial kingdom and allow them to receive all that our Father has, which includes eternal increase (D&C 131:1–4). Through the temple ordinances we learn that when the husband and wife are sealed together, they are each given specific responsibilities related to the priesthood and the temple covenants.

In Doctrine and Covenants 84:19–23, we learn that the greater priesthood administers the ordinances and covenants of the temple, for these are the ordinances that bring us back into the presence of God. Without these ordinances and the authority of the priesthood, no one could return home to see the face of God.

In verse 35 of this same section, the Savior states, "And also *all* they that receive this priesthood receive me." We come to understand throughout the rest of this chapter that if we receive Christ's servants, we receive the Savior himself; and when we receive the Savior completely by the priesthood and through His living prophets, we receive the Father. And when we receive the Father, we receive the Father's kingdom, even all that He has. We learn that this pattern is made possible by the oath and covenant of the priesthood. The oath and covenant of the priesthood comprises of the blessings and ordinances and promises of the temple, which the Father cannot and will not break, if we are faithful.

The scriptures refer to a multiplicity of blessings brought into our lives through the temple, specifically the oath and covenant of the priesthood. The Lord has said concerning these blessings, "they shall pass by the angels, and the gods, which are set there, to their exaltation and glory in all things, as hath been sealed upon their heads, which glory shall be a fulness and a continuation of the seeds forever and ever. Then shall they be gods, because they have no end; therefore shall they be from everlasting to everlasting, because they continue; then shall they be above all, because all things are subject unto them. Then shall they be gods, because they have all power, and the angels are subject unto them. Verily, verily, I say unto you, except ye abide my law ye cannot attain to this glory" (D&C 132:19–21).

The Doctrine of Receiving

One lesser understood doctrine related to the temple is the doctrine of receiving. To *receive* indicates acknowledgement and acceptance of knowledge, a gift, or a blessing from a giver. To receive the ordinances, covenants, and the word of God in the temple, you must accept them and act upon them, or else you have not truly received them. Receiving these things also means acknowledging that they are true. To *receive* the temple covenants and ordinances means taking them into your very soul. Further, it often entails having an experience with the Holy Spirit in regard to the gift or knowledge that you have accepted as true.

As you receive the blessings and ordinances of the temple, you should find that gratitude accompanies their reception. When it comes to the temple, if you do not receive with gratitude, you do not truly receive. Therefore, the power to change and grow (gratitude being the catalyst of spiritual growth and change) will lie dormant because the word of God, doctrine, principles, commandments, ordinances, covenants, gifts, blessings, and knowledge have not been truly received into your heart. We read, "For what doth it profit a man if a gift is bestowed upon him, and he receive not the gift? Behold, he rejoices not in that which is given unto him, neither rejoices in him who is the giver of the gift" (D&C 88:33).

As we noted chapter 1, ingratitude is one of the most grievous of sins. It follows that gratitude must be one of the cardinal virtues of life. Now we see why, when individuals do not receive the gospel, blessings may be withheld and difficult consequences follow. By contrast, when individuals receive and embrace the gift, they are blessed. Gratitude is one of the primary catalysts that activates receiving blessings from the Lord.

The blessing that accompanies our receiving the covenants and the ordinances of the priesthood, and hence the temple, is that we are able to become "sons [and daughters] of God." We read, "But verily, verily, I say unto you, that as many as receive me, to them will I give power to become the sons of God, even to them that believe on my name. Amen" (D&C 11:30). Further, we all receive the promise and blessing of full fellowship with the Father (see D&C 84:35–38). In mortality, we are also promised direction in our daily lives: "For behold, again I say unto you that if ye will enter in by the way, and receive the Holy Ghost, it will show unto you all things what ye should do" (2 Nephi 32:5).

Just as we are blessed for receiving the covenants and ordinances, we will find that consequences are serious for rejecting them: "And wo be unto him that will not hearken unto the words of Jesus, and also to them whom he hath chosen and sent among them; for whoso receiveth not the words of Jesus and the words of those whom he hath sent receiveth not him" (3 Nephi 28:34). Likewise we read, "For strait is the gate, and narrow the way that leadeth unto the exaltation and continuation of the lives, and few there be that find it, because ye receive me not in the world neither do ye know me." (D&C 132:22). When we receive knowledge and blessings of this magnitude, great gratitude and obedience to what we have received is the only response.

Keeping Our Covenants and Obeying the Commandments

Keeping your covenants is critical to your being worthy to receive the promised blessings of the temple. And the spirit in which you keep them will be what makes all the difference: "Verily I say unto you, all among them who know their hearts are honest, and are broken, and their spirits contrite, and are willing to observe their covenants by sacrifice—yea, every sacrifice which I, the Lord, shall command—they are accepted of me" (D&C 97:8). Ask yourself the following question regularly: Do you keep your covenants cheerfully or grudgingly?

We should never be casual or take lightly the sacred covenants we have made with the Lord. Many of the early Saints in Kirtland failed to realize the sacred nature of their promises. Of them the Lord said, "And your minds in times past have been darkened because of unbelief, and because you have treated lightly the things you have received—Which vanity and unbelief have brought the whole church under condemnation. And this condemnation resteth upon the children of Zion, even all. And they shall remain under this condemnation until they repent and remember the new covenant, even the Book of Mormon and the former commandments which I have given them, not only to say, but to do according to that which I have written" (D&C 84:54–57). Likewise, when we are casual about our covenants, we too stand in need of reprimand.

The quintessential promise, the ultimate promise, is extended to the faithful Saints by the Lord: "If your eye be single to my glory, your whole bodies shall be filled with light, and there shall be no darkness in you; and that body which is filled with light comprehendeth all things. Therefore, sanctify yourselves that your minds become single to God, and the days will come that you shall see him; for he will unveil his face unto you, and it shall be in his own time, and in his own way, and according to his own will. Remember the great and last promise which I have made unto you; cast away your idle thoughts and your excess of laughter far from you" (D&C 88:67–69).

The meaning of the phrase "to be filled with light" all but defies description, yet the results are clear: as we keep the commandments and our covenants, we will "comprehend all things." Let us press forward, that we may be sanctified in this incredible journey—seeing more clearly, feeling more deeply, and becoming more godlike—for these are the sources of hope and joy in mortality. This is why we came to this earth, and this is what the Father ordained for us, if only we will see.

The Importance of Prayer, Sacrifice, and the Word of God

The principle and act of prayer permeate the temple and the scriptures. It is through prayer that we draw upon the powers of heaven. The foundational principle of a loving Heavenly Father is that He invites His children to seek Him. This principle is taught with great clarity and by example in the temple, where we express gratitude; seek light, truth, wisdom, and understanding; plead for direction and help; and seek strength and confirmation.

We are taught to watch and pray always, so as not to be led away into temptation. Heavenly Father then answers our prayers by sending messengers, angels, prophets, leaders and teachers, and inspiration from the Holy Spirit. We learn that sometimes He answers swiftly and clearly. Other times, we need to wait patiently and do more work on our part. We learn that sometimes answers come through a stupor of thought, and that sometimes the Lord simply says no or points to alternatives. We learn that sometimes He sends a parent, neighbor, friend, or leader with the message. Sometimes an event occurs that answers our question or makes our problem solvable. But one point is made clear underlying all of these aspects of prayer: We must pray always, with real intent, having faith and coming before the Lord with a broken heart and contrite spirit. Then He will answer.

All of these principles and guidelines are taught clearly in the temple. While in the temple, do your "temple eyes" discern the doctrine of prayer and worship? Sometimes it is possible to miss the most elemental things. As you come to see and understand the goodness of God, your prayers of gratitude and need will echo daily in the presence of our Heavenly Father. Your home, as well as the temple, will become a sanctuary of your humble prayers.

In addition to the commandments to pray, we are admonished to read and study the scriptures—ancient, modern, and living. Scriptures are the revealed words of God through the power of the Holy Ghost, be they from prophets of the past or the present. We read of the word of God given by prophets: "This is the ensample unto them, that they shall speak as they are moved upon by the Holy Ghost. And whatsoever they shall speak when moved upon by the Holy Ghost shall be scripture, shall be the will of the Lord, shall be the mind of the Lord, shall be the word of the Lord, shall be the voice of the Lord, and the power of God unto salvation. Behold, this is the promise of the Lord unto you, O ye my servants" (D&C 68:3–5).

As you come to understand the principles of prayer, sacrifice, and studying the scriptures, the Spirit will beckon you to apply these truths to the temple, which will then truly become a *house of learning*. If you prepare prayerfully to go to the temple, being willing to sacrifice for this privilege if necessary, the Holy Ghost will become your instructor as you listen to and observe the "scripture" available there. When our sacrifice is within our soul, that of offering a broken heart and contrite spirit, we become the offering through which we are blessed because of what we receive. We literally offer our whole soul. When we lose our life through sacrifice we find it, even eternal life (see Matthew 19:29; 16:25; Mark 8:35; Luke 9:24; 17:33).

Remember

Preparing to receive your own endowment and worship in the temple is a personal matter and very private. I cannot dictate what you should or should not do to prepare most fully but rather share some principles of the gospel that will help you to be in tune with the Holy Spirit and silence some of the noise in this world. I encourage you to employ the following principles, which will bring you closer to God and greater sensitivity to the Spirit:

1. Prayerfully prepare. Seek to have "temple eyes," "temple ears," a "temple heart" and a "temple soul." Seek to see how symbolism is utilized throughout the temple ceremonies. As you search and feast upon the word of God, keeping your focus on the Atonement and the endowment, you will begin to see and appreciate the temple, the House of the Lord.
2. Remember the goodness of God your Father. Remember that the temple is integral in His perfect plan. The Lord always seeks

> to gather His people so He can endow them with power (see
> D&C 38:31–32; 95:8; 101:22, 65).
> 3. Ponder the tender mercies of the Lord and His infinite Atonement.
> 4. Recognize that the temple blessings are for both the living and
> the dead.
> 5. Seek to understand and appreciate the doctrines surrounding the
> temple. Be faithful in keeping the Lord's commandments, for
> this will allow you to always have the Holy Spirit to be with
> you.

I wish I had been encouraged to focus on these things, and do them, prior to receiving my own endowment. You are preparing to enter the Lord's house, so you must seek to be sanctified and holy in order to be taught His eternal verities. The Lord reminds us to become "sanctified by the reception of the Holy Ghost, that ye may stand spotless before me at the last day" (3 Nephi 27:20). When we are holy and sanctified, we become able to feel the glory and presence God. This requires great effort and takes time. I am beginning to see so much more as I get older, so be patient with yourself and you will grow line upon line and precept upon precept. It requires putting away our jealousies through charity and conquering our fears as we increase in faith, love, preparation, knowledge, and prayer. It requires us to humble ourselves. When we have done these things, the veil will be rent and we will see God, not with the natural or carnal mind but with the spiritual mind (see D&C 67:10). You may find yourself thinking that these standards are too high or that the price is too great. I testify that this is not the case. We are the divine children of God, and the scriptures have declared that we are temples of God. The very Spirit of God dwells in us (see 1 Corinthians 3:16–17; 6:19; D&C 130:22). As you prepare to attend and worship in the temple, you will become more holy, more pure, and more worthy to enter His holy house.

When you are worthy and ready, after receiving your mission call, you will be privileged to receive the holy endowment in the temple. You will be endowed with power from on high (see D&C 38: 32, 38;43:16; 105:11). The temple ordinances are the only way to receive a fulness of glory and exaltations. If you are faithful, these ordinances and covenants enable you to enter into the presence of our Heavenly Father. The temple is the only way.

CHAPTER 8

The Promised Blessings of the Temple

All of the covenants and ordinances of the gospel are tied to blessings, which hinge on our obedience to the laws upon which those blessings are predicated (see D&C 130:20–21). So it is the same with the blessings of temple worship. In the temple we receive knowledge and understanding related to eternal lives; in turn, our understanding of these doctrines, principles, commandments, covenants, and ordinances fill us with gratitude, for we see in them God's promised blessings. This gratitude draws us to the Lord and creates within us a desire to change—to change our hearts, our attitudes, and our behavior. As we change and become more like Christ, we reap blessing after blessing. The promised temple blessings truly underscore the power of temple worship. The purpose of this section will be to highlight the blessings we have alluded to throughout the previous chapter and to enlighten your mind with the goodness of God and the multiplicity of blessings found in His holy house.

Blessings of the Atonement

In the temple, we begin to see that all things and blessings typify Christ (see 2 Nephi 11:4). Joseph Smith said, "The fundamental principles of our religion are the testimony of the Apostles and Prophets, concerning Jesus Christ, that He died, was buried, and rose again on the third day, and ascended into heaven; and all other things which pertain to our religion are only appendages to it."[1] It is through the Atonement that we are cleansed. It is through the Atonement that we are ultimately brought into the presence of the Father. In sum, the Atonement is the enabling power of the endowment, not only for ourselves but for the salvation of all who did not receive these ordinances in this life. Constantly ask yourself the following question: What can I do to keep my mind and heart centered on my Savior, so that I can receive the blessings of the Atonement in my life?

Blessings of the Fulness of the Holy Ghost

It is only in the temple that we are able to "receive a fulness of the Holy Ghost, and be organized according to [His] laws, and be prepared to receive every needful thing" (D&C 109:15). One of the functions of the Holy Ghost is that it ratifies all temple blessings. We are able to preach, teach, and speak by the power of the Holy Ghost (see 2 Peter 1:21; D&C 68:3–7). We are also sanctified, or made holy, by the reception of the Holy Ghost (see 3 Nephi 27:20).

The prophet Wilford Woodruff confirmed all of these principles: "You may have the administration of angels, you may see many miracles; you may see many wonders in the earth; but I claim that the gift of the Holy Ghost is the greatest gift that can be bestowed upon man."[2]

Brigham Young also emphasized the blessing of the fulness of the Holy Ghost, when he said,

> If the Latter-day Saints will walk up to their privileges and exercise faith in the name of Jesus Christ and live in the enjoyment of the fullness of the Holy Ghost constantly day by day, there is nothing on the face of the earth that they could ask for that would not be given to them. The Lord is waiting to be very gracious unto this people and to pour out upon them riches, honor, glory, and power, even that they may possess all things according to the promises He has made through His apostles and prophets.[3]

The Holy Spirit is the key to becoming an instrument in the hand of the Lord.

Instruction, Edification, and Revelation

The house of the Lord is a place to be taught the doctrines, principles, ordinances, and covenants necessary to return to your Heavenly Father—if you go there in an attitude of humility and prayer. The Lord Himself describes His house as a house of learning in Doctrine and Covenants 109:8. Of this, Elder John A. Widtsoe stated:

> The temple ordinances encompass the whole plan of salvation, as taught from time to time by the leaders of the Church, and elucidate matters difficult of understanding. There is no warping or twisting in fitting the temple teachings into the great scheme of salvation. The philosophical completeness of the endowment is one of the great arguments for the veracity of the temple ordinances. Moreover, this completeness of survey and expounding of the Gospel plan, makes temple worship one of the most effective methods in refreshing the memory concerning the whole structure of the gospel. Another fact has always appealed to me as a strong internal evidence for the truth of temple work. The endowment and the temple work as revealed by the Lord to the Prophet Joseph Smith fall clearly into four distinct parts: The preparatory ordinances; the giving of instruction by lectures and representations; covenants; and, finally, tests of knowledge.[4]

The Lord answers the prayers of those who come to the temple seeking inspiration and direction in their lives. We may come to the temple seeking answers to any number of questions or problems in life—and we will find answers there as we learn at the feet of the Lord. The temple is one of the best places to listen to the still, small voice of the Holy Ghost and to clearly ponder questions and receive direction. If you have worries or troubles, come to the temple. If you have questions or concerns, come to the temple. You will find peace and guidance there.

Temple worship and work are also a wonderful opportunity to keep your spiritual knowledge and strength alive. There is great power in refreshing, renewing, and fortifying in the endowment. We come to better understand our place and role in the universe, our potential to become like God, and the nature of our divine spirit. In attending the temple, we leave the outside world behind and focus solely on our divine potential and the road home to our heavenly parents. The cares and trivial matters that might weight us down outside of the temple walls fall away. We begin to see ourselves as we truly are—and as we may become.

We Are Endowed with Power from on High

This dispensation is one of temple building so that the Lord can have a house in which to dwell. The temple allows Him to bless us with power, that we might go forth endowed (see D&C 38:38; 43:16). The Lord commanded His Apostles to tarry in Jerusalem until they were "endued with power from on high" (Luke 24:49). The Lord for the same reason instructed the Saints in this dispensation to tarry (see D&C 95:9). They received their endowment from on high. You will receive your own endowment prior to entering the MTC.

Qualified to Enter into the Presence of the Father

We make covenants and receive ordinances that qualify us to enter into the presence of the Father. As Brigham Young stated, "Your endowment is, to receive all those ordinances in the House of the Lord, which are necessary for you, after you have departed this life, *to enable you to walk back to the presence of the Father.*"[5]

Blessings of the Highest Order

President John Taylor stated,

The gospel, when introduced and preached to Adam after the fall, through the atonement of Jesus Christ, placed him in a position not only to have victory over death, but to have within his reach and to possess the perpetuity, not only of earthly, but of heavenly life; not only of earthly, but also of heavenly dominion; and through the law of that gospel enabled him (and not him alone, but all his posterity) to obtain, not only his first estate, but a higher exaltation on earth and in the heavens, than he could have enjoyed if he had not fallen; the powers and blessings associated with the atonement being altogether in advance of and superior to any enjoyment or privileges that he could have had in his first estate.[6]

One great blessings promised in the temple is the blessing of eternal increase. We read, "In the celestial glory there are three heavens or degrees; and in order to obtain the highest, a man must enter into this order of the priesthood [meaning the new and everlasting covenant of marriage]; and if he does not, he cannot obtain it. He may enter into the other, but that is the end of his kingdom; he cannot have an increase" (D&C 131:1–4). Another beautiful blessing is the knowledge that you can be "sealed up unto eternal life." The Doctrine and Covenants states, "The more sure word of prophecy means a man's knowing that he is sealed up unto eternal life, by revelation and the spirit of prophecy, through the power of the Holy Priesthood" (D&C 131:5). The Prophet Joseph Smith was likewise told, "And of as many as the Father shall bear record, to you shall be given power to seal them up unto eternal life" (D&C 68:12).

The keys to administer this sealing power of uniting families eternally is held by the president of the Church, and he alone administers those keys that bless and seal together the human family. Through revelation and by his authority, he confers this sealing power on other high priests in the Church. This authority and power reaches into the eternities:

> All covenants, contracts, bonds, obligations, oaths, vows, performances, connections, associations, or expectations, that are not made and entered into and sealed by the Holy Spirit of promise, of him who is anointed, both as well for time and for all eternity, and that too most holy, by revelation and commandment through the medium of mine anointed, whom I have appointed on the earth to hold this power (and I have appointed unto my servant Joseph to hold this power in the last days, and there is never but one on the earth at a time on whom this power and the keys of this priesthood are conferred), are of no efficacy, virtue, or force in and after the resurrection from the dead; for all contracts that are not made unto this end have an end when men are dead. (D&C 132:7)

The Garment: A Blessing of Protection

A booklet on preparing to enter the temple explains, "The garment represents sacred covenants. It fosters modesty and becomes a shield and protection to the wearer."[7] We learn much the same principle from the *Encyclopedia of Mormonism*:

> It is the special underclothing known as the temple garment, or garment of the holy priesthood, worn by members of The Church of Jesus Christ of Latter-day Saints who have received their temple endowment. This garment, worn day and night, serves three important purposes: it is a reminder of the sacred covenants made with the Lord in His holy house, a protective covering for the body, and a symbol of the modesty of dress and living that should characterize the lives of all the humble followers of Christ.[8]

The garment is highly symbolic. Its whiteness represents purity, and its covering reminds us of modesty and of the full armor of God. Its marks direct our thoughts to the Savior and to our covenants. By wearing this constant reminder of our covenants, we direct our actions toward principles of obedience, charity, chastity, truth, and godliness. Elder Carlos E. Asay, in his article concerning the garment, called attention to references of garments mentioned in the scriptures:

> Many references are found in the scriptures relating to garments and clothing. Enoch declared: "I beheld the heavens open, and I was clothed with glory" (Moses 7:3). Jacob spoke of a day of judgment when "we shall have a perfect knowledge of all our guilt, and our uncleanness, and our nakedness; and the righteous shall have a perfect knowledge of their enjoyment, and their righteousness, being clothed with purity, yea, even with the robe of righteousness" (2 Nephi 9:14). Isaiah rejoiced, saying, "God . . . hath clothed me with the garments of salvation, he hath covered me with the robe of righteousness" (Isaiah 61:10). Alma referred to "all the holy prophets, whose garments are cleansed and are spotless, pure and white" (Alma 5:24). These, and other prophetic statements, suggest not only a cleanliness and purity within one's soul, but also a spotless covering over one's soul, signifying a life of goodness and devotion to God.[9]

The garment also acts as a protection. The First Presidency has said, "The principles of modesty and keeping the body appropriately covered are implicit in the covenant and should govern the nature of all clothing worn. Endowed members of the Church wear the garment as a reminder of the sacred covenants they have made with the Lord, and also as a protection against temptation and evil. How it is worn is an outward expression of an inward commitment to follow the Savior."[10]

As you come to know and appreciate the garment of the holy priesthood, you will recognize the importance all these things and more. Ask yourself the following questions to gain further insight: What is it that protects me? Who is my great nurturer? What makes possible my forgiveness of sins? What enables me to do all things?

The garment is a robe of righteousness, as Nephi exclaimed: "O Lord, wilt thou encircle me around in the robe of thy righteousness! O Lord, wilt thou make a way for mine escape before mine enemies! Wilt thou make my path straight before me! Wilt thou not place a stumbling block in my way—but that thou wouldst clear my way before me, and hedge not up my way, but the ways of mine enemy" (2 Nephi 4:33; see also Isaiah 61:10).

Symbolically Enter the Presence of God

While still in mortality, we are blessed to symbolically come into the presence of God. We, being mortal and in a fallen state (a state of probation) are no longer in the presence of the Lord (see Alma 42:6–7, 9). However, we are able to return to His presence as we purify our hearts, receive the Holy Spirit, and keep His commandments. Experiencing God's presence may occur in several different types of manifestations:

1. We may literally see God face to face, as described by Moses (see Moses 1:2).
2. We may see God by the power of the quickening Spirit, through the spiritual mind (see D&C 67:10–12).
3. We may hear the voice of God audibly, as Nephi did (see 2 Nephi 31:15), or in the heart and mind, as Samuel the Lamanite did (see Helaman 13:5). Note that Adam and Eve, though cast out of the presence of God, still heard His voice as well (see Moses 5:4).

4. We may feel the presence of God by being in His temples, where He dwells (see D&C 94:8).

Those with pure hearts may see the Lord simply by attending the temple. The Lord, in His great condescension, said, "And inasmuch as my people build a house unto me in the name of the Lord, and do not suffer any unclean thing to come into it, that it be not defiled, my glory shall rest upon it; Yea, and my presence shall be there, for I will come into it, and all the pure in heart that shall come into it shall see God" (D&C 97:15–16). The Lord promised Joseph Smith and others that if they stripped themselves "from jealousies and fears" and humbled themselves before Him, "the veil shall be rent and you shall see me and know that I am," through spiritual eyes (D&C 67:10).

The same promise came to Joseph Smith when he and others were incarcerated in Liberty Jail: "Let thy bowels also be full of charity towards all men, and to the household of faith, and let virtue garnish thy thoughts unceasingly; then shall thy confidence wax strong in the presence of God; and the doctrine of the priesthood shall distil upon thy soul as the dews from heaven" (D&C 121:45). All these manifestations of the presence of the Lord are available to you as well and come through the Spirit, though we remain in the flesh. It is by the Spirit that we are able "to bear his presence in the world of glory" (D&C 76:118).

Perfected in Christ

The promised blessing of perfection through Jesus Christ is taught through the symbols, ordinances, and covenants of the temple. Moroni exhorted us to qualify for this blessing with these words: "deny yourselves of all ungodliness" (Moroni 10:32). To deny oneself of all ungodliness is to take upon oneself the attributes of godliness. These perfecting ordinances and covenants are received in the temple by the power of the priesthood.

As we assist in the work of saving our dead, we also bring about our own perfection: "For their salvation is necessary and essential to our salvation . . . that they without us cannot be made perfect—neither can we without our dead be made perfect" (D&C 128:15).

The Power of Godliness Is Manifest

Joseph Fielding Smith stated that "the power of godliness, or the power to become like God, is particularly manifest in the higher ordinances in the temple."[11] As we attend the temple, we will be able to harness and understand more fully this power. We read in the Doctrine and Covenants, "For if you keep my commandments you shall receive of his fulness" (D&C 93:20).

How and when do we manifest the power of godliness in our lives? Father's wonderful plan unfolds line up on line and precept upon precept, so a step at a time—a day at a time—we may find joy in the small and simple things. The power of godliness will be manifest in our lives to guide us to what matters most—faith unto repentance, which leads to good works: "And may God grant, in his great fulness, that men might be brought unto repentance and good works, that they might be restored unto grace for grace, according to their works" (Helaman 12:24).

The kingdom of God in heaven, and on earth, revolves around our relationship with other people, so when we help anyone we are contributing to the work of building up the kingdom of God. These people may be in our families or they may be our neighbors. They may be the people we are called to serve in our ward or branch, the poor, the ill, those otherwise in special need, the widow, or the orphan.

The concept of godliness should not overwhelm us. It means, most simply, becoming like our Savior, as He has commanded us to do (see 3 Nephi 12:48; 27:27). Opportunities to serve abound. We need only look around us through eyes that desire to do good.

The Mysteries of the Kingdom of God Are Unfolded to Us

In the temple we are taught the mysteries of God; they are unfolded to us as we seek wisdom through the Spirit (see D&C 6:7, 11; 11:7; Alma 12:10). To understand the mysteries (truth, light, doctrines, eternal verities), it is imperative that we give heed and diligence unto the word of God. The portion we receive is determined by the condition of our heart: Is it easily entreated? Does it, as King Benjamin asked his people, yield "to the enticings of Holy Spirit" (Mosiah 3:19)? According to Alma, the mysteries of God are imparted to "the children of men, according to the heed and diligence which they give unto [God]" (Alma 12:9).

Conversely, because Laman and Lemuel failed to inquire of the Lord (see 1 Nephi 15:8–9), they could not know the things of the Lord, and they thus were swift to do iniquity and slow to remember the Lord their God because their hearts were past feeling (see 1 Nephi 17:45). The mysteries of God can only be revealed to those who are truly humble and yield their hearts to God.

Listening is another key requirement to receiving the mysteries of God; King Benjamin counseled his people to *hearken*. He said, "Open your ears that ye may hear, your hearts that ye may understand, and your minds that the mysteries of God may be unfolded to your view" (Mosiah 2:9). He then gave one of the most profound sermons ever given, portions of which an angel of God had given to him; for instance, he spoke of the condescension of Christ, "who shall come down from heaven among the children of men, and shall dwell in a tabernacle of clay" (Mosiah 3:5). This message is likewise imbued in the temple endowment and is one of the "mysteries of godliness" (see Topical Guide "Mysteries of Godliness").

We Are Sealed as Eternal Families

Through the great sealing power restored by Elijah, hearts are turned to one another in love, and eternal families are created (see Malachi 4:5–6; D&C 110:13–15). Through the Atonement, we not only become sons and daughters of Christ, but we become organized and sealed as families of God, a foundational principle in the great plan of happiness and the measure of our creation.

Orson F. Whitney wrote these comforting words regarding the sealing power:

The Prophet Joseph Smith declared—and he never taught more comforting doctrine—that the eternal sealings of faithful parents, and the divine promises made to them for valiant service in the Cause of Truth, would save not only themselves, but likewise their posterity. Though some of the sheep may wander, the eye of the Shepherd is upon them, and sooner or later they will feel the tender hands of Divine Providence reaching out after them and drawing them back to the fold. Either in this life or the life to come, they will return. They will have to pay their debt to justice; they will suffer for their sins; and may tread a thorny path; but if it leads them at last, like the penitent Prodigal, to a loving and forgiving father's heart and home, the painful experience will not have been in vain.[12]

What could be of greater comfort than the sealings of eternal families? Where can there be greater hope? Where can the power of God be manifested in greater abundance? The answer: only in the Lord's holy house. The temple is the only way back to the presence of God. How blessed we are to have the opportunity to go there, to worship, and to receive ordinances and blessings there. The goodness and mercy of God is always present in the sealing power of temple ordinances.

Elder Richard Winkel of the Seventy brought this principle to the personal family level when he stated,

When you come to the temple you will love your family with a deeper love than you have ever felt before. The temple is about families. As my wife, Karen, and I have increased our temple service, our love for each other and for our children has increased. And it doesn't stop there. It extends to parents, brothers and sisters, aunts, uncles, cousins, forebears, and especially our grandchildren! This is the Spirit of Elijah, which is the spirit of family history work; and when inspired by the Holy Ghost, it prompts the turning of the hearts of the fathers to the children and the hearts of the children to the fathers. Because of the priesthood, husbands and wives are sealed together, children are sealed to their parents for eternity so the family is eternal and will not be separated at death.[13]

Elder Winkel continued stating,

Let's become a temple-attending and temple-loving people. I bear testimony that the temple is about families. I also testify that everything in the temple testifies of Jesus Christ. His example of love and service is felt there. The temple is His holy house. I know that He is the Son of God, our Savior, our Redeemer, our Mediator, and our Advocate with the Father. He loves us and wants our families to be happy and to be together forever. He wants all of us to be active in His temple.[14]

We Bless and Redeem Our Deceased Forbearers and Become Saviors on Mount Zion

According to the Prophet Joseph Smith, the greatest responsibility given to us in the dispensation of the fulness of times is to seek out and redeem our dead. This work is so important that the angel Moroni appeared to the boy prophet nearly seven years before the Church was organized and quoted the prophet Elijah, noting the fate of the earth if we failed to do this great work: "Behold, I will reveal unto you the Priesthood, by the hand of Elijah the prophet, before the coming of the great and dreadful day of the Lord. And he shall plant in the hearts of the children the promises made to the fathers, and the hearts of the children shall turn to their fathers. If it were not so, the whole earth would be utterly wasted at his coming" (D&C 2:1–3). Later, referring to the word *turn,* Joseph said that it should be translated as "bind" or "seal."[15] When the Savior visited the American continent approximately six hundred years after the Nephites had arrived, He also gave the Nephites those same words found in Malachi (see 3 Nephi 24–25). Surely the Lord has made clear the imperative nature of the salvation of all his children, living or dead.

The urgency of this work of redeeming the dead has become evident in the emphasis over the last few decades on the program of indexing existing family records, and especially in the engaging of the youth of the Church in that work. The program enables the Saints, old and young alike, to become "saviors on Mount Zion." We also see the hastening of the Lord's work in these latter days by the number of temples being built all across the world and the frequency with which they are being constructed.

The Prophet Joseph taught the Saints how they could become "saviors on Mount Zion." He stated, "How are they to become saviors on Mount Zion? By building their temples . . . and going forth and receiving all the ordinances . . . in behalf of all their progenitors who are dead . . . and herein is the chain that binds the hearts of the fathers to the children, and the children to the fathers, which fulfills the mission of Elijah."[16]

The Doctrine and Covenants states our responsibility to our ancestors: "And now, my dearly beloved brethren and sisters, let me assure you that these are principles in relation to the dead and the living that cannot be lightly passed over, as pertaining to our salvation. For their salvation is necessary and essential to our salvation, as Paul says concerning the fathers—that they without us cannot be made perfect—neither can we without our dead be made perfect" (D&C 128:15). Vicarious work in the temples, performed for those beyond the veil, is one of the most Christlike services we can perform.

We Are Blessed to Come to Know God and Jesus Christ

"And this is life eternal, that they might know thee the only true God" (John 17:3). Everything that transpires in the temple is a vivid reminder of the Atonement and a demonstration of Christ's love for us, "even that he layeth down his own life that he may draw all men unto him" (2 Nephi 26:24).

We Can Be Crowned with Glory, Immortality, and Eternal Life

The Lord, in defining the conditions of the new and everlasting covenant of marriage, spoke of the blessing of the sealing ordinances of the temple: "Ye shall come forth in the first resurrection; and if it be after the first resurrection, in the next resurrection; and shall inherit thrones, kingdoms, principalities, and powers, dominions, all heights and depths" (D&C 132:19).

Surely Alma also had in mind temple ordinances when he preached to the Saints in the city of Gideon: "May the Lord bless you, and keep your garments spotless, that ye may at last be brought to sit down with Abraham, Isaac, and Jacob, and the holy prophets who have been ever since the world began, having your garments spotless even as their garments are spotless, in the kingdom of heaven to go no more out" (Alma 7:25). We keep our garments clean through the blood of Christ by repenting, keeping our covenants, and (especially) seeking to build up the kingdom of God and bring souls unto Christ. "I say unto you, let those who are not the first elders continue in the vineyard until the mouth of the Lord shall call them, for their time is not yet come; their garments are not clean from the blood of this generation" (D&C 88:85).

All the scriptures that describe the multiplicity of blessings available in the temple make it clear that the temple is the only way to secure these blessings. Indeed, receiving the temple ordinances and keeping our temple covenants make available all the blessings of God.

Remember

Sometimes future missionaries get so excited about their mission calls that they forget about the greatest blessing that God has prepared for His faithful children—their temple blessings. These very blessings will help prepare you to be an effective missionary, for they will endow you with power and the Holy Ghost, which will lead you to do good.

When you enter the temple, you enter into the house of the Lord—and, as we read declared on the temple wall, "Holiness to the Lord." You will be asked to leave the world behind symbolically and literally as you cross the threshold into the Lord's house where He dwells. The counsel on this matter is clear: "All people who shall enter upon the threshold of the Lord's house may feel thy power, and feel constrained to acknowledge that thou hast sanctified it, and that it is thy house, a place of thy holiness" (D&C 109:13). When you recognize that His glory, power, and presence fill the temple, you will recognize that this holy place is not in or of the world. Doctrine and Covenants section 109, the glorious dedicatory pray of the Kirtland Temple, sheds a great deal of light and truth on the manner in which we should worship in the Lord's holy house. It deserves our careful study and pondering.

When you leave the temple, you will take it with you. You will have been endowed with power from on high. The Lord reminds us in His holy scriptures of how He wants to bless each of us with an endowment of power. However, He also states that we must accept His gift and receive it into our souls. Consider the following reminders of the goodness of God and the knowledge and power He seeks to give us. As you ponder these scriptures, they will help you prepare to receive your own endowment.

> That ye might escape the power of the enemy, and be gathered unto me a righteous people, without spot and blameless . . .
>
> There I will give unto you my law; and there you shall be endowed with *power from on high*." (D&C 38:31–32; emphasis added)

> Yea, verily I say unto you, I gave unto you a commandment that you should build a house, in the which house I design to endow those whom I have chosen with power from on high;
>
> For this is the promise of the Father unto you; therefore I command you to tarry, even as mine apostles at Jerusalem. (D&C 95:8–9)

> And ye are to be taught from on high. Sanctify yourselves and ye shall be endowed with power, that ye may give even as I have spoken. (D&C 43:16)

> That they themselves may be prepared, and that my people may be taught more perfectly, and have experience, and know more perfectly concerning their duty, and the things which I require at their hands.
>
> And this cannot be brought to pass until mine elders are endowed with power from on high.
>
> For behold, I have prepared a great endowment and blessing to be poured out upon them, inasmuch as they are faithful and continue in humility before me. (D&C 105:10–12)

> Yea the hearts of thousands and tens of thousands shall greatly rejoice in consequence of the blessings which shall be poured out, and the endowment with which my servants have been endowed in this house. (D&C 110:9)

These scriptures are a plea from Heavenly Father and Jesus Christ to Their beloved children to prepare to enter Their holy house. In

Their house, you will make sacred covenants and receive sacred ordinances that will empower you with knowledge, wisdom, protection, and an abundance of the Holy Spirit. All of these gifts will sanctify you on your journey here on earth, including your mission. With power from on high, you will be more able to do the Lord's work. The fulness of the Holy Spirit will be yours, as you remain faithfully obedient to your covenants.

In the temple, you will witness such love, kindness, concern, mercy, and grace. You will leave the temple walls with increased knowledge, which will give you great power to do good. You will leave refreshed by the eternal verities of the ordinances and covenants you have personally received in the temple, and you will feel edified again when you return to do vicarious work. You will leave clothed in the garment of the holy priesthood, even the robes of righteousness (see 2 Nephi 9:14; 4:33; Isaiah 61:10; Revelations 3:18—ponder these carefully), as a reminder to keep your covenants and to protect you against evil and temptation.

I urge you to spend time seriously contemplating the following question: What is your current level of preparation to enter the temple and serve the Lord as a missionary, being empowered from on high? Not perfection, but your heart and a willing mind. Let the answer to this question guide you as you prepare.

CHAPTER 9

To Be Set Apart as a
Missionary and Entering the MTC

Setting Apart

Just prior to entering the MTC, you will be set apart by your stake president. This could be the night before or the Sunday before. Your family, other special relatives, and friends can be in attendance. The stake president not only recommends you, but also sets you apart as a missionary. Sometimes this is done in your home or sometimes in the stake president's office. In addition to the setting apart, he will bestow upon you a blessing that will be a source of strength to you as you serve.

From that moment on, you are a full-time missionary who lives all the rules of being a missionary for the Lord. Obedience is the law upon which all blessings are predicated (see D&C 130:20–21). This kind of obedience is based upon love, and when you love the Lord deep enough (see John 14:15, 21), you will be exactly, immediately, and courageously obedient, and blessings will come now (see Mosiah 2:22, 24) and in the eternities (see Mosiah 2:41).

I'd like to relate to you the personal experience of a returned missionary who served in Italy:

> When I stepped into my stake president's office I didn't really have any idea what to expect. Maybe it would just feel like getting a calling, or getting a blessing, or like when I got the priesthood. It initially felt a little bit like all of those. I felt good, and it felt like the

words were coming from Heavenly Father. But there was something unique about this experience that stayed with me during my entire mission, something that I still remember today. My stake president said, "Your success will not be measured primarily with numbers, but by your dedicated service to God."

Now, I saw a lot of people get baptized during my mission. It was incredible how many miracles the Lord was pouring on the people of Italy. However, I never got hung up on the numbers. I never felt defeated when investigators couldn't, or wouldn't, commit to baptism. Because of my stake president's inspired words, I felt successful every single day of my mission because I tried to be obedient, and work hard. Every single day, the Lord helped me to feel His approval—the only kind of success I really needed to feel.

Remember as you serve:

> Faith is the Power
> Love is the Motive
> Obedience is the Price
> The Spirit is the Key
> And Christ is the Reason
> (*Cyril Figuerres*)

You are a disciple of Christ like Mormon, who said, "Behold, I am a disciple of Jesus Christ, the Son of God. I have been called of him to declare his word among his people, that they might have everlasting life" (3 Nephi 5:13).

Arriving at the MTC

Once you have been set apart, you will be ready to travel to the Missionary Training Center (MTC). The MTC is designed to help you understand and appreciate your purpose of inviting souls to come unto Christ, and to help you learn how to teach by the Holy Spirit. There are fifteen training centers worldwide, and there will be variability in each MTC from what you will read here, but the general principles will all be the same.

Arrival

You arrive with all your luggage at your designated time found on the MTC website. Sometimes you come to the Salt Lake City

International Airport and are transported to the Provo MTC, having already said your good-byes to your families. Sometimes parents and family members bring you to the MTC, and you have about five minutes to unload and say your good-byes.

Loving and kind volunteers will greet you, and everything is superbly organized to receive you. You will receive a special "colored sticker" that lets everyone know you are new and special, and you get the VIP treatment. After all, you are the Lord's missionary, just beginning your service as His servant.

You will have a guide to help you check in, and you will take your luggage to your room. Then you will go to the MTC bookstore and receive your training materials. In the early afternoon, you will meet your teachers and district members and participate in welcoming activities. After that, you will be privileged to hear from the MTC presidency prior to dinner. As the evening begins, you will be instructed about your purpose as a missionary and receive an orientation from your zone leaders. As you conclude your day, you will return to your room and unpack and record the first day of your mission in your missionary journal. Bedtime is 10:30 p.m., so you can rise early to begin your first full day of training.

Culture

The beautiful thing about the MTC is that you are surrounded by so many caring people who are anxious and willing to help in every way. Never be afraid to ask if you need help or don't understand something.

Your fellow missionaries have an immense desire to lift and help you succeed. I spoke with a missionary who recently returned home from a mission, who said,

> The MTC was such a special experience for me. It was a place where I could learn to let go of the world, and really give my heart to the Savior. I felt such a spirit of unity with the missionaries around me— we all had the same desires, and we were all headed in the same direction together. Some of us knew the scriptures better than others.

Some of us spoke the language better than others. But as soon as we stopped comparing ourselves to each other, we were able to reach out and serve each other, teach each other, and grow together in a spirit of love.

There are about 1,200 MTC instructors at the Provo Missionary Training Center, teaching fifty-five different languages. Typically, language-learning missionaries will be in the MTC for six weeks before going to their assigned missions; however, thirty-one of the languages require nine weeks of training.

Twenty-six of those thirty-one languages are Asian or Eastern bloc languages, such as Mandarin, Korean, Thai, and Russian. English-speaking missionaries will typically be in the MTC for two weeks prior to leaving for the mission field.

These instructors are returned missionaries who have an immense love for the gospel. Their primary desire is to help you to learn the essential skills that will assist you in succeeding as a missionary. A foreign-language instructor from the MTC once told me some of his experiences teaching missionaries:

Every six weeks, I get a new group of fresh faces and fresh hearts, some eager, some scared, some excited, some confused. Some missionaries struggle to know exactly why they are on a mission. Those first few days are crucial—what we want as teachers is to establish a relationship of love and trust with the missionaries, while also demonstrating to them our expectations as their teachers. Every missionary that comes into the MTC is precious to the Lord, and whether they know it yet or not, He has called them personally and specifically to their mission.

I often share these words on the first day with my missionaries: "Elders and Sisters! Welcome to the MTC! This place will be your home for the next weeks, a place of edification and preparation for your dedicated service to the Lord. He loves you. As your teacher, I am here to help you learn how to be a missionary, and how to learn the language He has called you to learn. I want you to know that I love all of you. I promise you that the Spirit will guide these classes. We will see miracles together, especially the miracle of the gift of tongues. The Lord is going to be working on you for the next 18 to 24 months, and you will be molded by the hand of your Savior. Trust in Him who created you. He loves you. He knows you by name. Let's get to work!"

I love returning to those words throughout my time with each district of missionaries. I like to ask them to reflect upon their growth every time I can—they often are surprised to see that truly the Lord is working miracles with them. It is *incredible*. The gift of tongues is real.

In addition to the support of the instructors at the MTC, every missionary is a part of a branch, with inspired leaders seeking to support the missionaries and their spiritual progress. Every branch president is sincerely invested in the emotional, physical, and spiritual well-being of the missionaries under his stewardship. I recall one missionary who once told me an experience he had with his branch president in the MTC:

> I remember thinking to myself, *Man, this branch president sees a new group of missionaries every couple weeks! How can he possibly know us by name? How can he possibly care about all of our individual needs?* Then I was called to be a district leader in the MTC. I was able to sit in meetings with the branch presidency. I marveled at how well they knew each individual missionary—more than just their names, they knew their needs. The Lord was guiding these men. I saw how much tender care was in their voices as they discussed struggling missionaries and how to help them. They really do know us because God knows us, and is guiding them to serve and minister to us.

Curriculum

On your first day as a missionary, you will receive a packet entitled *A Missionary's MTC Experience*. This handbook will work hand in hand with *Preach My Gospel* to teach you the skills you need to know as a missionary. In the introduction to *A Missionary's MTC Experience*, you will read,

> Each day you will plan, study, and teach. The daily pattern of planning, studying, and teaching activities fit together. Planning prepares you to study with a focus on your investigators. Studying prepares you to teach by the Spirit. Teaching helps you better understand

your investigators—and what to plan and study next. Each step is an opportunity to seek direction from the Lord and fulfill your purpose as a missionary.

Your teachers will help you become effective as you plan, study, and teach. Ultimately you will be able to conduct these activities on your own as you consistently focus on helping those you teach have faith in Jesus Christ and become converted.[1]

Take that pattern to heart! Planning, studying, and teaching will be the pattern of missionary life that will keep you centered on your purpose: to invite others to come unto Christ.

Planning: Missionaries can often feel that since the MTC is so structured, planning doesn't matter very much. "We already have our schedule" is often the response to planning sessions. However, planning goes beyond much more than just *what* you will be doing in the next day and week. It involves setting personal and companionship goals and deciding what to study and teach to investigators. It involves *seeking* and *receiving* inspiration! Planning sessions are so sacred, and as soon as you can embrace the sacredness of those minutes of your day, the Lord will bless and inspire you to know what He would have you do.

Studying: There is never a shortage of things to study as a missionary. Equally as important as *what* to study is *how* to study. Always remember to keep the missionary purpose at heart—in other words, study with your investigators in mind. Study *Preach My Gospel* and the doctrines that will assist you in teaching with the greatest effectiveness.

Teaching: The scriptures are the doctrine. They are the vast wealth of knowledge that we have been given by our Heavenly Father that we may know how to inherit eternal life. *Preach My Gospel* hones in on the specific principles and doctrines found in the scriptures that investigators need to learn in order to be baptized—the first step on the strait and narrow path to return to our Father in Heaven.

Preach My Gospel

Preach My Gospel is your magnificent missionary guide, with instructions on what you need to do and how to do it to be a successful and happy missionary. On page iii is the index, which will explain every topic contained in that wonderful book. I plead with you to study *Preach My Gospel* before you arrive at the MTC. Feast upon it—underline, highlight, and write in the margins. Digest this book and make it part of your life long before you enter the MTC. You will be grateful if you do.

Every topic is important, but some will be new to you.

Chapter 2: How Do I Study Effectively and Prepare To Teach (17–29)
Chapter 3: What Do I Study and Teach (29–89)
Chapter 8: How Do I Use Time Wisely (137–53)
    Key Indicators for Conversion (138)
    The Area Book and Planning and Reporting Tools (139–47)
    The Weekly Planning Session (147–53)
Chapter 9: How Do I Find People to Teach (155–74)
Chapter 10: How Can I Improve My Teaching Skills (175–95)
Chapter 11: How Do I Help People Make and Keep Commitments (195–203)
Chapter 12: How Do I Prepare People for Baptism and Confirmation (203–13)
Chapter 13: How Do I Work with Stake and Ward Leaders (213–25)[2]

Study. Ponder. Pray. Those three things will help you understand and appreciate this magnificent tool the Lord has given you to better fulfill your mission. Do these things with faith, diligence, and patience. Internalizing *Preach My Gospel* will help you become a pure disciple of Christ, with the ability to teach with the power and authority of God (see Alma 17:3).

Remember

Your experiences at the MTC, much like your mission and even your life on earth, will be what you make it. If you want it to change your life, put in the effort and be willing to sacrifice and to take a step out of your comfort zone—this is all new for you, but it is exciting, and inspired, and you will create friendships that will last an eternity!

CHAPTER 10

The Power of Knowledge

Come to a Knowledge of the Truth

Eternal truths come from God the Father through our Savior, Jesus Christ, by the power of the Holy Ghost. The Lord has taught, "He that keepeth his commandments receiveth truth and light, until he is glorified in truth and knoweth all things. Man was also in the beginning with God. Intelligence, or the light of truth, was not created or made, neither indeed can be. All truth is independent in that sphere in which God has placed it, to act for itself, as all intelligence also; otherwise there is no existence" (D&C 93:28–30).

As you strive to become a worthy disciple of Christ, you will develop a desire to know more about Him and His gospel; you will begin to "hunger and thirst" after this righteousness (3 Nephi 12:6). This in-depth study of the gospel is vital. *Preach My Gospel* encourages missionaries to teach from their hearts and by the Spirit, rather than from memorized dialogues. This is significant, because it requires your gospel knowledge to be written in your heart. We read in the Doctrine and Covenants, "Neither take ye thought beforehand what ye shall say; but treasure up in your minds continually the words of life, and it shall be given you in the very hour that portion that shall be meted unto every man" (D&C 84:85). If you obtain a deep base of gospel knowledge, the Lord can then give you inspiration at the moment you need it. You will obtain this knowledge by studying the scriptures, listening to the words of living prophets and leaders, and reading *Preach My Gospel* regularly during your teenage and mission years. These are the best missionary resources you will find—they have been written and spoken just for you. Study *Preach My Gospel* particularly as you prepare—this is your missionary manual. Underline it, mark it, write in the margins, and devour that precious book over and over again. As you do, you will be better prepared.

Also, remember the words of the Prophet Joseph: "In knowledge there is power. God has more power than all other beings, because he has greater knowledge; and hence he knows how to subject all other beings to Him. He has power over all."[1] In other words, the greater your knowledge, the greater your power to do good.

Gospel Knowledge

Think about the following notion: You want to go out on a mission, but is it really possible to prepare for this significant endeavor starting in the MTC? Elder Daryl Garn of the Seventy related the following:

> Three months into my mission, a new missionary from Idaho was assigned to be my companion. We had been together only a few days when I realized something very significant: my new companion knew the gospel, while I only knew the discussions. How I wished that I had prepared to be a missionary as hard as I had prepared to be a basketball player. My companion had prepared for his mission throughout his life and was immediately a valuable member of the team. How important it is for fathers and sons to work together on the basics in preparing for a mission.[2]

It's important for you to understand the many doctrines, principles, and teachings that allow you to be a better representative of Jesus Christ. As you study, understand, and come to appreciate the following doctrines, your own testimony will grow, and you will become a better instrument in the Lord's hands to help His children understand, appreciate, and accept the gospel in their lives. The following are some of the most important doctrines and principles you will need to understand and appreciate.

The Atonement

The doctrine of the Atonement of Jesus Christ is the center of the gospel. We read, "This is the gospel, the glad tidings, which the voice out of the heavens bore record unto us—That he came into the world, even Jesus, to be crucified for the world, and to bear the sins of the world, and to sanctify the world, and to cleanse it from all unrighteousness" (D&C 76:40–41). This is the heart the gospel. He suffered that you might not have to pay the price of justice. He sweat great drops of blood that you might be made pure. He died on the cross that you might live again. The principles of the Atonement that will allow you to live with God again are the first principles of the gospel: faith in the Lord Jesus Christ, repentance through the Lord Jesus Christ, baptism and taking upon yourself the name of Jesus Christ, receiving the Holy Ghost, and the ordinances and covenants of the temple.

I recommend a thorough, repeated study of 2 Nephi 9, Alma 34, and Doctrine and Covenants 19:15–19. By familiarizing yourself with these scriptures, you will come to understand the Atonement like you've never understood it before. Your gratitude for this sublime gift will deepen. You will recognize how tragic your destiny would have been had there been no Atonement.

In Alma, you will read of how the Atonement helps and lifts you:

> And he shall go forth, suffering pains and afflictions and temptations of every kind; and this that the word might be fulfilled which saith he will take upon him the pains and the sicknesses of his people.
>
> And he will take upon him death, that he may loose the bands of death which bind his people; and he will take upon him their infirmities, that his bowels may be filled with mercy, according to the flesh, that he may know according to the flesh how to succor his people according to their infirmities. (Alma 7:11–12)

Christ has been through it all: everyone's sins, pains, sufferings, and even temptations. He knows what you need and how to nurture you throughout your life. And most important, He wants you to enjoy happiness and succeed as a missionary.

The Atonement of Christ nurtures and blesses you through the grace of God. It helps you repent and overcome sin. Sin separates you from the Father; it causes you to lose the Spirit. The law of justice then demands that the sin be paid for. The law of mercy provides a way, through God's Only Begotten Son, to pay for these sins, as a price is required for each one. Earth life is not free; you understood this principle in the premortal life. Exaltation has a price—the grace of God, a gift given after all you can do (see 2 Nephi 25:23). Every needful thing has a price, and the Atonement of Jesus Christ, our Savior, is the price He paid to fulfill the demands of divine justice. We receive the fulness of the blessings of the infinite Atonement through repentance, keeping our covenants, and personal righteousness.

Doctrine and Covenants 19:15–21 teaches about the consequences if you don't repent. If you do not repent, the Lord has said that you must suffer even as He suffered. Justice requires payment, and if you are not willing to let the Savior's suffering pay the cost, then you must suffer yourself. The Atonement freely gives you immortality, but eternal life—or exaltation—comes only when you *apply* the Atonement in your life, through repentance and endurance to the end.

I encourage you to take time to write in your journal today about your feelings of gratitude for the Savior's atoning sacrifice. Commit to apply the Atonement in your life every day; you can make a covenant with the Lord regarding your behavior as you strive to apply His infinite, atoning sacrifice.

Faith

As discussed previously, the doctrine of faith has three elements: hope (or belief), action, and power. You are likely familiar with the definition of faith in Alma 32 and Hebrews 11: "Faith is the substance of things hoped for" (Hebrews 11:1). This is the first element of faith: belief. James added, "I will shew thee my faith by my works" (James 2:18). This is the second element of faith: action. In Ether, we read, "The brother of Jared said unto the mountain Zerin, Remove" (Ether 12:30). This is the final element of faith: power to do all things. The earth was created by faith. Faith is the vehicle of the priesthood. Faith is the foundation of all righteousness. If you want to read and understand more on faith as power, I would suggest the *Lectures on Faith* by the Prophet Joseph Smith.

Joseph Smith taught that before you can exercise faith, you must know the character of God—that He exists, that He is perfect, and that you are actually living according to His will. You cannot please God without faith (see Hebrews 11:6). You cannot exercise faith without love, and you can't have love without faith (see Galatians 5:6). Faith, love, and obedience are all intertwined. You cannot separate one from another. The greater your faith, the more you will love God, and if you love Him, you will obey Him. The Lord said, "If you love me, keep my commandments" (John 14:15). If you have faith, you will mentally and spiritually exert yourself and draw upon the powers of heaven.

The question is left for you to answer: What kind of life are you living? Does it make room for the Savior, Jesus Christ? When you look at your life, remember, it is only a reflection of your conversion to Jesus Christ and your faith in Him. When you exercise faith in Jesus Christ, you will repent and follow Him.

Prophets and Revelation

Another doctrine you must come to understand and appreciate to be an effective missionary concerns the prophets of God, the spokesmen for Jesus Christ. We read, "Surely the Lord God will do nothing, but he revealeth his secret unto his servants the prophets" (Amos 3:7). Prophets speak for our Savior, because they speak the words of Christ. The Lord said, in Doctrine and Covenants 1:38, "Whether by mine own voice or by the voice of my servants, it is the same." The prophet functions as the president of the Church, the presiding high priest, and the revelator for The Church of Jesus Christ of Latter-day Saints. The members of the Quorum of the

Twelve and the First Presidency are also prophets, seers, and revelators. They speak for the Lord.

It is also critical to understand that every person should be a prophet for himself or herself, regarding his or her own concerns. It was Moses who said, "Would God that all the Lord's people were prophets, and that the Lord would put his spirit upon them" (Numbers 11:29). Paul instructed us that we should "covet to prophesy" (1 Corinthians 14:39). In other words, you can be a prophet for your own soul, receiving revelation from God on things *you* should do. We must keep in mind, however, that the prophet of the Church is the only one who receives revelation for the Church and kingdom of God upon the earth.

The Lord has counseled us,

> Blessed are ye if ye shall give heed unto the words of these twelve whom I have chosen from among you to minister unto you, and to be your servants. . . .
>
> And again, more blessed are they who shall believe in your words because that ye shall testify that ye have seen me, and that ye know that I am. Yea, blessed are they who shall believe in your words, and come down into the depths of humility and be baptized, for they shall be visited with fire and with the Holy Ghost, and shall receive a remission of their sins. (3 Nephi 12:1–2)

The Lord later warned us to give heed to the prophets,

> And wo be unto him that will not hearken unto the words of Jesus, and also to them whom he hath chosen and sent among them; for whoso receiveth not the words of Jesus and the words of those whom he hath sent receiveth not him; and therefore he will not receive them at the last day;
>
> And it would be better for them if they had not been born. For do ye suppose that ye can get rid of the justice of an offended God, who hath been trampled under feet of men, that thereby salvation might come? (3 Nephi 28:34–35)

It is essential and imperative that we follow the prophets. It is your duty to sustain the prophet, which means supporting and following what he has asked you to do. In the battle against the offender Amalek, the Israelites, under Joshua, prevailed as long as Moses's hands were outstretched on the top of the hill, supported on either side by Aaron and Hur (see Exodus 17:9–13). This wonderful symbolic example helps us understand how important Church members are in regards to sustaining the prophet and assisting in building up the kingdom of God.

How grateful I am for a prophet—a living prophet of God. I bear testimony to you that as you follow the prophets, you will never be led astray.

The Divine Calling of Joseph Smith

How do you feel about the Prophet Joseph Smith? In the Doctrine and Covenants, we read, "Joseph Smith, the Prophet and Seer of the Lord, has done more, save Jesus only, for the salvation of men in this world, than any other man that ever lived in it" (D&C 135:3). Joseph Smith was the Prophet of the Restoration. He spoke for the Lord; he gave us the Book of Mormon, the Doctrine and Covenants, the Pearl of Great Price, and the inspired version of the Holy Bible. He established the Church and kingdom of God here upon the earth, as the Lord directed him.

You need to be able to bear testimony that Joseph Smith is the prophet of the Restoration. He holds the keys for the dispensation of the fulness of times. He is the Prophet who stands at the head of the Restoration. When you think of all that Joseph Smith has done—that he has done more, "save Jesus only," for your salvation and for the salvation of mankind, you will begin to feel gratitude for his divine calling and recognize that your life is what it is today because of the revelations he received from God by the power of the Holy Ghost.

Think of all the persecution that was heaped upon Joseph. He was tarred and feathered and left for dead in Hyrum, Ohio. He was beaten, thrown in jail, and finally martyred. How can anyone doubt the blessings of the gospel that have come to them because of what Joseph Smith did? Joseph Smith was full of the love of Christ. Even the day after he was tarred and feathered, he gave a talk on forgiveness and repentance, while some of the men who had done the deed were in attendance.

When you pray to Heavenly Father, you will know, as I know, that Joseph is the Prophet of the Restoration, and that the Church is likewise led by a prophet today.

The Truthfulness of the Book of Mormon

The Book of Mormon is the keystone of our religion; the fulness of the gospel is contained in its printed pages (see chapter 5 in *Preach My Gospel*). It is the word of God and the most correct book on earth. It will help you get closer to God than any other book (see the introduction to the Book of Mormon). The Book of Mormon is true—of this I testify. It is a record of God's dealings with man. And the purpose of the book is to show the goodness and mercies of God to His people and, above all, to teach that Jesus is the Christ, the Son of the living God. As President Heber J. Grant said, "I am convinced in my own mind, my dear brethren and sisters, that this book, the Book of Mormon, is the greatest converter of men and women as to the divinity of the gospel of Jesus Christ. It is in every way a true witness of God, and it sustains the Bible and is in harmony with the Bible."[3]

Oh, how I love the Book of Mormon. For twenty-seven glorious years, I have had the privilege of teaching this book at Brigham Young University and the Orem Institute of Religion. This book has made a wonderful difference in my family's life. When you read it on a daily basis, it will help you to live the word of God. There are legions of people who have read the book and then requested baptism because of the power of its words. The Spirit carried a confirmation of its truthfulness unto their hearts. The true seekers, the Lord's elect, believe.

When you study the Book of Mormon, remember to apply its teachings to your own life. Every teaching in the Book of Mormon is meant be applied to life. The prophet Nephi said, "I did liken all scriptures unto us . . . for our profit and learning" (1 Nephi 19:23).

When you study this way, the Book of Mormon will truly work miracles in your life. It will bring you unto Christ. As President Marion G. Romney said, "The Book of Mormon is the most effective piece of missionary literature we have."[4]

When you, or someone to whom you are teaching the gospel, accept the Book of Mormon as true, consider what happens:

1. If you accept the Book of Mormon, you know Jesus is the Christ and accept Joseph Smith as a prophet of God.
2. If you accept Joseph Smith as a prophet of God, you accept the First Vision as a reality.
3. If you accept the First Vision as a reality, you accept that God did establish this kingdom on earth and restored the priesthood to the earth.
4. If you accept that the priesthood of God was restored through angels under the direction of God, you accept that the Doctrine and Covenants, Pearl of Great Price, and other LDS scriptures and revelations are valid.
5. If you accept that the priesthood and the accompanying ordinances were restored, you accept that the organization we call The Church of Jesus Christ of Latter-day Saints is the institution of God restored on earth today—both in name and in fact.
6. If you accept that Christ's Church is restored, you accept that it is led by His prophets, to whom He continues to reveal His mind and will—His purposes for His children on earth.
7. If you accept and embrace the continuous revelation from God made possible through the prophets, you become aware of your eternal heritage and of eternal relationships and future possibilities.
8. If you accept and embrace all of these things, you will follow Jesus the Christ and seek to build up the kingdom of God on the earth.

The Holy Ghost

The following is just a short introduction to the Holy Ghost. Chapter 11 will discuss the glorious blessing and power of the Holy Ghost.

When the Savior was preaching to the Nephites, He instructed them to pray for that which they desired more than anything else. They prayed that they might have the gift of the Holy Ghost (see 3

Nephi 19:9). Why did they pray for the Holy Ghost? Why did they desire to have this gift so much? Because, as Elder Bruce R. McConkie taught, "He is the Comforter, Testator, Revelator, Sanctifier, Holy Spirit, Holy Spirit of Promise, Spirit of Truth, Spirit of the Lord, and Messenger of the Father and the Son, and His companionship is the greatest gift that mortal man can enjoy."[5]

Prayer

Sometimes missionaries say of their prayers, "Well, I just don't get an answer," or, "My investigators just don't get answers when they pray." When I hear these statements, I know that further knowledge and understanding of the pattern of prayer is needed. The pattern goes as follows: We must study things out to know of their truthfulness; then we make a decision based on what we have learned (see D&C 9:7–9). We then take that decision to the Lord and He will cause our bosom to burn—or sometimes we'll just feel peace, as the Lord pointed out to Oliver Cowdrey: "Did I not speak peace to your mind?" (D&C 6:23). A feeling of peace is also an answer to prayer

Do you remember the fruits of the Spirit we discussed earlier? When the Spirit confirms truth to your soul, you will feel good, you will be humble, and you will have a desire to deal justly with others. These are likewise the feelings that will tell you that the gospel is true. But, as with Oliver in Doctrine and Covenants section 9, asking the Lord a question is only part of the equation. The Lord said, "You took no thought save it was to ask me" (verse 7). You must ask with real intent, having faith and having done the things you need to do in preparation, and then your prayers will be answered. In other words, prayers are answered when you do your part. You just cannot say, "Give me, give me, give me." You must come before God in the name of Jesus Christ, with all your heart, might, mind, and strength, having faith with real intent—and then He will answer your prayers, either directly or through others.

Prayer is communicating with your Heavenly Father in and through the name of Jesus Christ. In 3 Nephi 18, note that the Savior consistently told the Nephites to pray in His name. We pray in the name of Jesus Christ because He is our Advocate and Mediator; He literally makes prayer possible and allows God your Father to help you. Know that God hears and answers prayers. Pray with real intent, without vain repetitions, with a sincere and faithful heart, and with every needful thing in place.

You can pray standing up, you can pray walking along on the street, and you can pray leaning against a building. The Lord said that when you cease your spoken prayers, you should keep a prayer in your heart (see 3 Nephi 20:1). Your prayers can and should be sent up to heaven continually. Prayer is the essence of knowing and worshipping your Heavenly Father. It is "the act by which the will of the Father and the will of the child are brought into correspondence with each other."[6] You must take the time to know the Father, and His will, through prayer. Always remember to use the pronouns *thee*, *thou*, and *thine* to show reverence. As you pray, ask for the courage to do the will of the Father.

Prayer is your way of communicating with Heavenly Father. It is an exchange of love with Heavenly Father. It is an earthly child checking in with his or her Heavenly Father. It is a servant seeking direction, comfort, and strength from the Father through the Master.

As you open your prayer and call upon Heavenly Father, I would counsel you to be still and wait for a feeling of love and closeness to come upon you. Listen to your heart and reach with your mind until you feel different from when you knelt down. That's when your spirit will connect with heaven.

Recall the moment in the Savior's life when He arrived in Jerusalem, and the crowds pressed about Him, trying to get close to Him. A woman, who had been diseased for twelve years, felt that if she could but touch Jesus's clothing, she would be made whole. So she found the hem of His garment and touched it. Jesus, even in the midst of the crowd, felt her touch His clothing. Her touch was different from the press of the crowds. She had connected with Him in faith, and He knew it. That's how sensitive He was, and that's how powerful the Spirit is. The woman was immediately healed; we read, "Jesus said, Somebody hath touched me: for I perceive that virtue [power] is gone out of me. And when the woman saw that she was not hid, she came trembling, and falling down before him, she declared unto him before all the people for what cause she had touched him, and how she was healed immediately. And he said unto her, Daughter, be of good comfort: thy faith hath made thee whole; go in peace" (Luke 8:46–48).

Please don't mumble a quick message or memorized prayer to Heavenly Father. Instead, take the time to consciously and intently have a conversation with your Heavenly Father. Please reflect upon and consider using some of the following:

- Communicate in humility with God the Father in the name of His Only Begotten Son, Jesus
- Have an exchange of love
- Share deep feelings of gratitude and ask for blessings you stand in need of
- Cleanse your soul through confession
- Plead for forgiveness
- Witness your resolve to do better
- Pray for those who despitefully use you
- Ask for guidance to find people waiting to be taught the gospel
- Seek understanding of gospel principles that are recorded in the scriptures
- Promise obedience
- Ask for strength to endure
- Seek help in learning a language and in learning teaching materials
- Search for ways to love others
- Cry out for confidence to do God's will
- Desire power to heal and bless
- Yearn for peace on earth and holiness among men

The scriptures are full of helpful counsel on prayer. A missionary must gain a testimony of the wisdom in daily personal prayer, the miracle of group prayer, the strength and learning in urgent prayer, and the growth and sense of well-being that comes from prayers of gratitude.

The scriptures give us the following counsel regarding prayer:

- "Pray always, lest ye enter into temptation and lose your reward" (D&C 31:12).
- "Pray always, and I will pour out my Spirit upon you" (D&C 19:38).
- "The prayers of the faithful shall be heard, and all those who have dwindled in unbelief shall not be forgotten" (2 Nephi 26:15).
- "Pray unto the Father with all the energy of heart" (Moroni 7:48).
- "Love endureth by diligence unto prayer" (Moroni 8:26).
- "Be thou humble; and the Lord thy God shall lead thee by the hand, and give thee answer to thy prayers" (D&C 112:10).
- "Draw near unto me and I will draw near unto you; seek me diligently and ye shall find me; ask, and ye shall receive; knock, and it shall be opened unto you" (D&C 88:63).

Many people think of Alma 34 as one of the most definitive statements concerning the plan of redemption—the crux of its message being that now is the time to prepare to meet God. The notes at the beginning of the chapter seem to concur. It is interesting to note that much of this chapter has to do with prayer and the way to communicate with God. I urge you to reread these exciting scriptures, particularly verses 17 through 27. Note how significant prayer is supposed to be in your life. The number of times we are commanded to "pray always" in the scriptures is telling. Here are just a few examples of this phrase. Ponder them carefully.

- Pray always to avoid temptation (3 Nephi 18:15–18).
- Pray always and not faint as you serve the Lord (2 Nephi 32:9).
- Pray always that mysteries will be revealed and that you may bring others to repentance (Alma 26:22).
- Pray in your heart continually for the welfare of yourself and others (Alma 34:27).
- Pray always lest the wicked one gain power (D&C 93:49).

- Pray always vocally and in your heart while proclaiming the gospel (D&C 81:3).
- Continue in prayer and fasting from this time forward (D&C 88:76).
- Pray always and be believing, and all things will work together for your good (D&C 90:24).
- Pray always lest you lose your reward (D&C 31:12).
- Pray always to understand the scriptures (D&C 32:4).
- Pray always to be ready for the Second Coming (D&C 33:17).
- Continue in prayer (Romans 12:12).
- Pray always for the welfare of the saints (part of the armor of God) (Ephesians 6:18).

Prayer is one of the most significant ways you worship your Heavenly Father (see Alma 33:3). Make it a special experience every time you pray.

Testimony

It will be hard—in fact, almost impossible—for you to be a minister of the Lord unless you have a testimony that Jesus is the Christ. Your testimony, when sincerely borne, is borne by the power of the Holy Ghost. This makes your testimony as strong as any person's testimony upon the earth, because true testimonies are borne by the power of the Holy Spirit.

Know that when you bear witness of the truthfulness of the gospel, the truthfulness of the Book of Mormon, the calling of the prophet, the truthfulness of the teachings of the gospel, and the reality of the kingdom of God on the earth, you do so by the power and authority of the Holy Ghost. The Holy Ghost is the testator of all truth, He is the revelator, and it is only by the Holy Ghost that you can testify to the truthfulness of the knowledge that Jesus is the Christ, the Son of God, and that The Church of Jesus Christ of Latter-day Saints is the true kingdom of God on the earth.

Can you see now that one of the most priceless possessions you have is your testimony? Bearing testimony means standing as a witness of revealed eternal truths and especially of the fact that Jesus is the Savior.

How do you get a testimony? Study, pray, live it, and bear it. It is interesting to note that this is the same thing you will ask investigators to do: study, pray, and live the commandments. This is because the gospel operates according to eternal truths. Nothing you ask investigators to do is arbitrary. Numberless prophets before you have preached these same patterns and doctrines. Again, to gain a testimony, you must study, pray, live it, and bear it, and then you will know the truth. President Hinckley reaffirmed this for you: "If there are any [of you] lacking that testimony, you can get it; and you must get it. . . . The Lord has said that he that doeth the will of the Father shall know of the doctrine, 'whether it be of God, or whether I speak of myself' (John 7:17)."[7]

When you bear your testimony, it becomes stronger because you are invoking the power of the Holy Ghost. The more experiences you have with the Holy Ghost, the stronger your testimony becomes. Sometimes your testimony will be strengthened simply by hearing the testimony of other people (see D&C 46:14). It is often the case that we must lean on others' testimonies until our own testimony is strong enough.

All good things are gifts from God, and the testimony that you possess, no matter how small or how great, is no exception. Think of the times when other people's testimonies have strengthened yours. Think of the times other people have been strengthened by your testimony. The greatest converting power of the gospel is the power of testimony, the word of God as given by the Spirit. Testimony is the purest form of the word of God, and we understand from scripture that the power of the word has greater power to change people's lives than anything else (see Alma 31:5).

Testify sincerely and often. This is what Alma did when his people were struggling: "And this he did that he himself might go forth among his people, or among the people of Nephi, that he might preach the word of God unto them, to stir them up in remembrance of their duty, and that he might pull down, by the word of God, all the pride and craftiness and all the contentions which were among his people, *seeing no way that he might reclaim them save it were in bearing down in pure testimony against them*" (Alma 4:19; emphasis added). Truth without testimony is hollow. The gospel is true, and you are the instrument through which the Lord works to share this truth with every nation, kindred, tongue, and people.

Your testimony will grow as you seek to understand the doctrines, principles, commandments, ordinances, and covenants of the gospel of Jesus Christ that lead to exaltation. As you seek to nurture your testimony and search for truth, keep the following principles in mind:

- The gospel truths are found in the word of God (see D&C 19:26).
- Truth will make you free (see John 8:32).
- In Christ is the fulness of truth and light (see John 14:6; D&C 84:45).
- You become sanctified through the truth (see John 17:17).
- The Spirit of truth is made manifest by those speaking by the Spirit of truth, which is indeed the Holy Spirit (see D&C 50:17–22).
- The Spirit testifies of the truth of all things (see Moroni 10:4–5).
- Truths must be confirmed by the power of the Holy Ghost (see Moroni 10:5).

It is critical for you to understand and appreciate the principles related to truth and testimony so that they become internalized in your life. It is also critical for you to embrace these truths by entering into and receiving all of the ordinances and covenants of the greater priesthood, which will lead you back to the presence of your Heavenly Father.

Your testimony begins with, and is strengthened by, coming to a knowledge of God the Father and His Beloved Son, Jesus Christ, by the power of the Holy Ghost. You do this as you learn of and live the doctrines of Christ, which the prophets and Apostles have taught both anciently and in modern times (see 2 Nephi 31). Likewise, the

Articles of Faith reiterate, "We believe that the first principles and ordinances of the Gospel are: first, Faith in the Lord Jesus Christ; second, Repentance; third, Baptism by immersion for the remission of sins; fourth, Laying on of hands for the gift of the Holy Ghost" (Articles of Faith 1:4).

It is interesting to note that the Lord commands parents to teach these doctrines: "And again, inasmuch as parents have children in Zion, or in any of her stakes which are organized, that teach them not to understand the doctrine of repentance, faith in Christ the Son of the living God, and of baptism and the gift of the Holy Ghost by the laying on of the hands, when eight years old, the sin be upon the heads of the parents" (D&C 68:25). Parents and teachers are responsible to teach the doctrines of the kingdom. In a way, the investigators you teach on your mission will be children to you in the sense that you will help guide them to a knowledge of the truth and help them grow and progress eternally.

The ways in which the Lord's children are brought to a knowledge of the truth are many and varied. You can come to a knowledge of the truth by doing the following:

1. You can study and learn by faith (see D&C 88:118; 109:7, 14).
2. You can live the doctrine and know that they are of God and true (see John 7:17).
3. You can know the doctrines are true by the power of the Holy Ghost (see D&C 9:7–9; 50:17–22; Moroni 10:5) and then proceed to live them.
4. You can feel that the gospel is true and then act upon those feelings and gain confirmation (see Alma 32:28; D&C 9:8).
5. You can grow in grace a little at a time and in the knowledge of truth (see D&C 50:40).
6. You can receive the truth by keeping the commandments (see D&C 93:28).

When you truly know, understand, and appreciate a truth, you will be filled with pure knowledge that enlarges your soul (see D&C 121:42). It is this knowledge from God the Father and your Savior Jesus Christ that will then bring salvation to your soul (see 3 Nephi

5:20). However, for you to receive truth by the power of the Holy Ghost, you must be *willing* to receive it. Then, as you come to understand and appreciate the knowledge that has been given you, you will act upon it because you will be filled with gratitude and the love of God. The desire to do good will move you to action.

Doctrines

Doctrines are truths taught by God and His messengers. They comprise your beliefs, your creeds, your knowledge of how to live, and your attitudes and attributes. Doctrines are literally the substance of the word of God, the gospel, the truths of salvation, and exaltation. Paul spoke of scripture being given from God as doctrine for reproof, correction, and instruction (see 2 Timothy 3:16). It is the knowledge of the doctrines of the gospel that teach you how to come to your Savior and be saved: "And at that day shall the remnant of our seed know that they are of the house of Israel, and that they are the covenant people of the Lord; and then shall they know and come to the knowledge of their forefathers, and also to the knowledge of the gospel of their Redeemer, which was ministered unto their fathers by him; wherefore, they shall come to the knowledge of their Redeemer and the very points of his doctrine, that they may know how to come unto him and be saved" (1 Nephi 15:14).

Your beloved Savior explained that the doctrine He taught was indeed the doctrine of the Father (see John 7:16). Nephi, likewise, explained that the doctrine he taught was the doctrine of Christ, which would yield wisdom (see 2 Nephi 31). "And now, my son, I have told you this that ye may learn wisdom, that ye may learn of me that there is no other way or means whereby man can be saved, only in and through Christ. Behold, he is the life and the light of the world. Behold, he is the word of truth and righteousness" (Alma 38:9).

Likewise, the doctrine you teach will be the doctrine of Christ (see 2 Nephi 31:12–21; 3 Nephi 11:21–41; 27:13–27; Alma 7:11–20; Ether 12). You teach faith in Jesus Christ (see 2 Nephi 31:19), repentance through Jesus Christ (see Mosiah 16:13), baptism for the remission of sins as you take the name of Christ upon you (see D&C 20:37), reception the Holy Ghost from the Father because you believe in Jesus Christ (see 3 Nephi 19:22), and endurance to the end with the pure love of Christ (see Moroni 7:45).

Principles

Principles of the gospel of Jesus Christ are the fundamental tenets, laws, or rules of action that support and underlie doctrines. They are the foundation of your beliefs. They will be the guidelines for your actions and behavior. Many of these principles are found in the fourth article of faith—faith in Christ, repentance, baptism, and receiving the Holy Ghost. Sometimes it is difficult to differentiate between principles and doctrines because they are so interconnected and entwined in every way. The most basic difference is that principles are the foundation for doctrines.

There are principles you must understand and appreciate that are specific to almost every calling and given situation. The Prophet Joseph taught, "I teach them correct principles, and they govern themselves."[8] These principles are based on eternal verities of light and truth, even the mysteries of the kingdom of God. As you seek to understand and appreciate these great life-changing and life-empowering principles, you will walk the path to eternal life.

Principles are not simply the why behind the doctrines; they also cover a gamut of truths: foundational truths, laws of action, fundamental tenets, and reasons behind actions. Many times, a doctrine will be simply described as a principle, a guideline for action as well as behavior; it may even include a list of things to do and implement into your life. Principles may also go beyond the "why" and include "whats" and "hows" that should be treasured up and then put into practice.

In this light, know that when I (or others) speak of principles, the term may include many of the eternal verities put into practice. For example, to increase our faith we can exert our mental capacities, and we can also hear the word of God, search the scriptures (see Romans 10:17), and fast and pray (see Helaman 3:35).

As we speak of principles, it is important to note that, as in all things, you must choose and govern yourself, for this is the doctrine of agency that you choose to act rather than be acted upon. This notion, in fact, is a principle itself—one you will observe as you teach your investigators as directed by the Holy Ghost. As you teach your investigators, you must plead for the Holy Spirit to be poured out upon them to touch their hearts so they will use their agency to come to know of the truthfulness of the principles being taught.

Commandments

Commandments are the laws, standards, statutes, and precepts by which the Lord has asked us to live. They are given of God for your welfare and growth. Regarding the commandments, the Lord promises, "He that hath my commandments, and keepeth them, he it is that loveth me: and he that loveth me shall be loved of my Father, and I will love him, and will manifest myself to him" (John 14:21). Every commandment has within it promised blessings. In the sacramental prayer, we covenant to take upon us the name of the Son and always remember Him and keep His commandments. The promised blessing is that we may always have His Spirit to be with us (see D&C 20:77).

The goodness of God your Father and your Savior Jesus Christ are manifest in all the doctrines, principles, commandments, ordinances, and covenants of the gospel of Jesus Christ. "Let us hear the conclusion of the whole matter: Fear God and keep his commandments: for this is the whole duty of man" (Ecclesiastes 12:13). The Lord reminds you, "Behold, this is your work, to keep my commandments, yea, with all your might, mind and strength" (D&C 11:20). It is in keeping these commandments that you are blessed with never-ending happiness (see Mosiah 2:41). Always remind and testify to your investigators of the promised blessings that come from living the gospel.

Ordinances

Ordinances are the sacred rites and ceremonies of the gospel of

Jesus Christ; they are usually connected to covenants. Some ordinances are in the form of blessing and healings, while others are in the form of rites and rituals that lead to salvation and exaltation. Elder John A. Widstoe said, "An ordinance is an earthly symbol of a spiritual reality. It is usually also an act of symbolizing a covenant or agreement with the Lord. Finally, it is nearly always an act in anticipation of a blessing from heaven. An ordinance, then, is distinctly an act that connects heaven and earth, the spiritual and the temporal."[9]

Each ordinance will likely require you to enter into a solemn covenant with the Lord. All ordinances are priesthood ordinances. Many ordinances are literally lifesaving—because they are necessary for you to receive in order to gain your exaltation. These include baptism by immersion (see Matthew 3:16; 3 Nephi 11:34–35; D&C 20:37; 72–74), confirmation to receive the gift of the Holy Ghost (see D&C 20:68; 33:15), reception of the priesthood (see D&C 84:6–16; 107:41–52), reception of temple ordinances (see D&C 84:19–22; 124:39), and marriage in the new and everlasting covenant (see D&C 131:2–4; 132:19–20). I encourage you to take a few minutes and immerse yourself in the noted scriptures that discuss these ordinances; they contain priceless words of eternal life.

Partaking of the ordinance of the sacrament (see D&C 20:77, 79) is integrally connected with all of the ordinances we will discuss. It may not be considered as a lifesaving ordinance, but it is essential for you to renew your covenants and promise to keep the commandments. As you do so, you will be given strength to endure to the end. The Lord introduced the sacrament to help you remember Him and keep the commandments so we can always have His Spirit to be with us. Remember that in partaking of the sacrament, you are renewing all of your covenants and commandments of God. Other ordinances of the priesthood include administration to the sick (see James 5:14–15) and the blessing of children (see D&C 20:70). Lastly the supernal and exalting ordinances of the holy temple!

Ordinances are essential to our obtaining eternal life. They exalt and prepare us. It is the greater priesthood that provides these blessings in our lives, particularly in the holy temples (see D&C 84:19–22). The temple is the only way to ultimately reach exaltation. The ordinances found within are truly lifesaving and life-exalting. Teach your investigators to look to the temple. This will strengthen them and help them through mortality.

Covenants

Covenants are sacred and solemn agreements or promises made between you and Heavenly Father. Indeed, you promise God that you will fulfill certain duties, and if you are faithful in your promise, He will shower you with blessings. It is through the great Abrahamic covenant that you, the seed of Abraham, will bless whole earth through spreading the gospel. The temple covenants and ordinances contain within them the power of exaltation if you keep them. You must remember that you are a child of the covenant. You are armed with righteousness, and with the power of God (see 1 Nephi 14:14). "And this shall be our covenant—that we will walk in all the ordinances of the Lord" (D&C 136:4 [2–4]).

Humility

You will recall that when Alma was teaching the Zoramites, many were humbled because they were cast out of the synagogues. These then listened to Alma and his message (see Alma 31–32). The wealthy and haughty Zoramites, those climbing up on the Rameumpton and praying, did not hear the word of God or feel the Spirit of the Lord. Humility is the beginning virtue in becoming a strong missionary.

As a missionary, your heart will resonate with President Lorenzo Snow's observation: "The Lord has not chosen the great and learned of the world to perform His work on the earth . . . but humble men [and women] devoted to His cause . . . who are willing to be led and guided by the Holy Spirit and who will of necessity give the glory unto Him, knowing that of themselves they can do nothing."[10]

Humility leads to righteousness and goodness. This is one of the many reasons I love to teach and generally just be around missionaries; missionaries are so willing to accept the teachings of the Lord. I feel great joy when I think what a great honor it is to work among missionaries; their righteousness, humility, and willingness to work is inspiring and touching.

I would like to tell you about two missionaries in particular, a companionship I worked with when I was a mission president. These two elders were my assistants. "President," they said to me one day, "we've only got a month left. We're training the new assistants, and they're doing really well. President, please let us go teach and baptize now." In other words, they didn't want the "honor" of being assistants to the president or any other honors of men. They said, "Let us just go find and teach. We feel that the power of God is upon us." And with that commitment and their strong desire, they went out and joyfully baptized twenty-three people in one month.

How was this possible? It happened because of the humility of two missionaries who gave their hearts to the Lord and humbly asked every day, "Father, what would thou have us do?" And then they went out and did it.

No matter how wonderful you are, there is always room for growth and change. None of us is perfect. However, we can all cultivate a willingness to serve and submit our hearts to the Lord—the greatest gift we can give him. Whenever the people in the Book of Mormon were prideful or disobedient, the Lord would work with them to bring about humility so that they could grow. Even when the people were doing well, the Lord would often send prophets, who would exhort them to become better. Sometimes the people were wicked, sinking into sinful behavior, and even then, the Lord still sought after them. Sometimes the people would change, and sometimes they wouldn't. Your challenge is to learn from these people's experiences and always be willing to change.

The task of becoming a true disciple and missionary of the Lord is up to you, and it depends on your willingness to be easily entreated (or humble) in receiving the word of God and acting upon it appropriately. As we learned previously, humility is the beginning of all spiritual growth. We must be willing to hearken to the Lord's anointed servants and prophets (see 3 Nephi 12:1–2; 28:34–35; D&C 1:38; 21:6).

The Lord has performed His infinite and eternal Atonement, and He stands at the door and knocks: "If any man hear my voice, and open the door, I will come in to him, and will sup with him, and he with me. To him that overcometh will I grant to sit with me in my throne, even as I also overcame, and am set down with my Father in his throne" (Revelation 3:20–21).

Will you humble yourself and let Him into your life? The Lord can surely make more out of your life if you turn it over to Him. You are here to become even as He is—and to help others come unto Christ the Lord. With humility and a knowledge of the truth, you will be armed to testify in the Lord's name by the power of the Holy Ghost.

Gaining knowledge and coming to a knowledge of the truth depends upon your humility. The Book of Mormon says that, as part of the perfection process, you must be humble or you will not learn (see 2 Nephi 9:42; Alma 7:23; 13:28). In Ether, you are told that becoming humble is part of the process of learning; recognizing your weaknesses is integral to becoming strong and great in the Lord's hands: "And if men come unto me I will show unto them their weakness. I give unto men weakness that they may be humble; and my grace is sufficient for all men that humble themselves before me; for if they humble themselves before me, and have faith in me, then will I make weak things become strong unto them" (Ether 12:27).

It is critical for you to be humble as you assist in this great work: "No one can assist in this work except he shall be humble and full of love, having faith, hope, and charity, being temperate in all things, whatsoever shall be entrusted to his care" (D&C 12:8). The Lord can assist *you* when you are humble: "Be thou humble; and the Lord thy God shall lead thee by the hand, and give thee answer to thy prayers" (D&C 112:10).

Certainly the people we read about in the Book of Mormon had a hard time with humility, and you might have a hard time too.

The scriptures also tell us that when God loves a people, He chastens them (see Hebrews 12:6). And He loves you. Chastening often results in humility, and you cannot grow without humility. So do not be surprised if at times you feel chastened.

Humility is the precursor of all spiritual growth. Until you are humble, you cannot grow. Elder Richard G. Scott described this virtue well:

> Humility is the precious, fertile soil of righteous character. It germinates the seeds of personal growth. When cultivated through the exercise of faith, pruned by repentance, and fortified by obedience and good works, such seeds produce the cherished fruit of spirituality (see Alma 26:22). Divine inspiration and power then result. Inspiration is to know the will of the Lord. Power is the capability to accomplish that inspired will. (See D&C 43:15–16.) Such power comes from God after we have done "all we can do" (2 Nephi 25:23).[11]

Remember, pride is of the devil and always leads to sin and sorrow. Humility will help you always hearken to the word of God and your leaders.

Remember

It will be critical for you to understand and appreciate the doctrines and principles of the gospel for you to put them into practice in your life. You must act upon them! Receive the commandments with gladness of heart, and then keep them. Receive, embrace, and honor the ordinances and covenants as you seek to keep them and gain the promised blessings. In the strongest way possible, I urge you to do these things for this is a matter of eternal life. Help your investigators know this too.

These are the things upon which you and your investigators must base your testimonies as you come to understand, appreciate, and do the will of the Lord by the power of the Holy Ghost. It will be necessary for you to hearken to the word of God, listen, and do His will. This is key to becoming the missionary the Lord knows you can become. Obedience rules.

Let us read the following once more: "There is a law, irrevocably decreed in heaven before the foundations of this world, upon which all blessings are predicated—And when we obtain any blessing from God, it is by obedience to that law upon which it is predicated" (D&C 130:20–21). You must obey, or act on, the knowledge and blessings you are given. You must ask, seek, and knock. You must choose to live your life in all holiness before the Lord: "And thus ye shall become instructed in the law of my church, and be sanctified by that which ye have received, and ye shall bind yourselves to act in all holiness before me" (D&C 43:9).

Always remember the following:

- Knowledge is power if you apply it in righteousness.
- Doctrines and principles are enlightening if you act upon them.
- Commandments yield a reward of the Spirit's companionship if you keep them.
- Ordinances and covenants are exalting if you are diligent and faithful.
- All spiritual growth begins with humility.

CHAPTER 11

The Holy Ghost Is the Key to Missionary Work

The Presence and Power of the Holy Ghost

You will need the Holy Spirit to be a missionary, because this work is totally dependent upon the presence and power of the Holy Ghost. Imagine your potential to be like the sons of Mosiah, who "waxed strong in the knowledge of the truth; for they were men of a sound understanding and they had searched the scriptures diligently, that they might know the word of God. But this is not all; they had given themselves to much prayer, and fasting; therefore they had the spirit of prophecy, and the spirit of revelation, and when they taught, they taught with power and authority of God" (Alma 17:2–3).

When the Holy Ghost is your companion, you will preach and teach with power, with the spirit of prophecy, and with the spirit of revelation. As you prepare yourself to be an instrument in the hand of the Lord, always remember that you must live and teach by the power of the Holy Ghost.

Peter, like the early disciples, became a magnificent missionary who was endowed with power and the Holy Ghost. We learn that he and the other disciples tarried in Jerusalem when instructed so that they could be endowed with this power: "I [Jesus] send the promise of my Father upon you: but tarry ye in the city of Jerusalem, until ye be endued with power from on high" (Luke 24:49). We then read that "when the day of Pentecost was fully come, they were all with one accord in one place. And suddenly there came a sound from heaven as of a rushing mighty wind, and it filled all the house where they were sitting. And there appeared unto them cloven tongues like as of fire, and it sat upon each of them. And they were all filled with the Holy Ghost, and began to speak with other tongues, as the Spirit gave them utterance" (Acts 2:1–4). The disciples had all power to teach and to bless because they had the power of the Holy Ghost. Peter became so righteous and powerful that the people "brought forth the sick into the streets, and laid them on beds and couches, that at the least the shadow of Peter passing by might overshadow some of them" (Acts 5:15).

This power of the Holy Ghost is key to all aspects of your missionary work. Even the Savior Himself was anointed with power and the Holy Ghost: "How God anointed Jesus of Nazareth with the Holy Ghost and with power: who went about doing good, and healing all that were oppressed of the devil; for God was with him" (Acts 10:38).

The Spirit will lead you to do good, to judge righteously, to be humble, to enlighten your mind, and to fill your soul with joy. The Spirit will fill your heart with love, joy, peace, longsuffering, gentleness, goodness, faith, meekness, and temperance (see D&C 11:12–13; Galatians 5:22–23). These are only a few of the blessings we are promised through the power of the Holy Ghost. The following are just some roles the Holy Ghost (also known as the Comforter) will play in your life:

- The Holy Ghost will testify of Christ (see John 15:26).
- The Holy Ghost will teach you all things and bring all things to your remembrance (see John 14:26).
- The Holy Ghost will bring the love of God into your heart (see Romans 5:5).
- The Holy Ghost will allow you to preach, teach, and speak truth effectively and with power (see 2 Peter 1:21; D&C 68:3–7).

- The Holy Ghost will show you all things you must do (see 2 Nephi 32:5).
- The Holy Ghost will make known to you the truth of all things (see Moroni 10:5).
- The Holy Ghost will sanctify you and make you pure (see 3 Nephi 27:20).

Can you see that it is the Holy Ghost who will empower you to be inspired, to understand, and to become the Lord's missionary?

When you understand the sublime blessings that are available through the companionship of the Holy Ghost, you will be inspired to seek the Spirit and pray for it continually to be with you as a constant companion (see 3 Nephi 19:9). You must also remember there is a price for this promised gift. To enjoy the companionship of the Spirit, you must increase your faith in Jesus Christ (see 1 Nephi 10:17) and remember that the Holy Spirit is bestowed only upon those who love God and purify themselves before Him (see D&C 76:116) and keep the commandments (see D&C 20:77, 79; chapter 4 of *Preach My Gospel*).

Regarding the Holy Ghost, the prophet Wilford Woodruff said, "You may have the administration of angels, you may see many miracles; you may see many wonders in the earth; but I claim that the gift of the Holy Ghost is the greatest gift that can be bestowed upon man."[1]

The prophet Brigham Young likewise emphasized the blessing of the companionship of the Holy Ghost when he said,

> If the Latter-day Saints will walk up to their privileges and exercise faith in the name of Jesus Christ and live in the enjoyment of the fulness of the Holy Ghost constantly day by day, there is nothing on the face of the earth that they could ask for that would not be given to them. The Lord is waiting to be very gracious unto this people and to pour out upon them riches, honor, glory, and power, even that they may possess all things according to the promises He has made through His apostles and prophets.[2]

Several years after Joseph Smith was martyred, he appeared to President Brigham Young. His message for the Saints at that time constitutes the theme of this chapter. Joseph said, "Tell the people to be humble and faithful, and be sure to keep the spirit of the Lord and it will lead them right. Be careful and not turn away the still small voice; it will teach you what to do and where to go; it will yield the fruits of the kingdom. Tell the brethren to keep their hearts open to conviction, so that when the Holy Ghost comes to them, their hearts will be ready to receive it."[3]

Oh, how I yearn for the companionship of the Holy Ghost in my life. When I feel it and recognize it, I am literally transformed. It leads me to do good and to focus on those around me. And in turn, when I focus on those around me, I seem to have a greater abundance of the Spirit. When I think only of myself, I don't feel so much of that sweet Spirit. It is marvelous to think that God our Father loves us so much that He commissioned a member of the Godhead to function as our prompter for life. The Holy Ghost will be your Comforter and guide in all things. Oh, how Father loves you!

The Holy Ghost Helps You Serve in Righteousness

Remember the following principles as you strive to keep the Spirit with you at all times:

- You cannot teach by the Spirit without the prayer of faith (see D&C 42:14).
- You cannot come to the knowledge of the truth without the power of the Holy Ghost (see Moroni 10:5, 7; 3 Nephi 16:4; 1 Nephi 10:17; D&C 46:13, 15–16; 124:5).
- You cannot receive confirmation or answers to prayers in both your heart and mind without the power of the Holy Ghost (see Galatians 5:22–23; Moroni 8:26; 1 Nephi 17:45; D&C 6:23; 8:2; 9:7–9).
- You cannot be directed in all things without the power of the Holy Ghost (see D&C 11:12–13; 1 Nephi 4:6; 2 Nephi 32:2–3, 5; Helaman 5:45; Mark 13:11; D&C 68:3–4).
- You cannot become clean and pure, sanctified and holy, without the power of the Holy Ghost (see 3 Nephi 27:20; Mosiah 3:19; Alma 5:54; 13:12; Moroni 6:4).

What can you do on a daily basis to receive the great blessings of the Holy Ghost in your life?

- Increase your faith through fasting and prayer (see Helaman 3:35).
- Feast upon the word of God (see Romans 10:17).
- Love God and your Savior with all your heart, mind, and soul (see Matthew 22:36–40).
- Purify your soul through the Atonement of Christ (see Mosiah 3:19; Jacob 4:11; D&C 76:116).
- Be obedient. By keeping the commandments, you will always have the Holy Spirit to be with you (see D&C 20:77).

Recognizing the Holy Spirit

Of all the questions I have been asked as a priesthood leader and a teacher, the most common (and of the seemingly greatest concern to the Saints) has been, "How will I recognize the Holy Spirit?" Hopefully I can explain myself sufficiently so that all may come to an understanding of this most important question.

Initially, most people are looking for too much when it comes to the Spirit, even a type of sign, if you will—something visible or a definite physical sensation. This is not usually the case. In this section, we will discuss how the Holy Spirit is perceived and how the Spirit works so that you will know what to look for. The presence and manifestation of the Holy Ghost can be categorized in several ways that you have almost certainly felt at some time in your life. Recognizing them as the Holy Spirit is the key.

Please remember that I, like you, am just trying to do the best I can. I do not set myself up as the ultimate example but rather as a regular member of the Lord's Church—which all of us are. Each of us has the same right and privilege to receive the blessings of the Holy Ghost in our lives, for God is no respecter of persons and is the same yesterday, today, and forever (see D&C 1:35; 38:16; Acts 10:34; 2 Nephi 27:23; Mormon 9:9; Moroni 10:19).

I will describe the expressions of the Holy Ghost in four ways: physical awareness and sensations, spiritual and emotional feelings, distinct impressions to act upon, and thoughts and ideas given after prayerful pleadings to the Lord.

Physical awareness and sensations. Your bodies can be filled with the Holy Spirit, light, and truth as if by fire (see Alma 36:20). Words may come to you as fast as you can speak (see D&C 100:6). You may feel power within your soul, stemming from somewhere outside yourself (see Alma 26:16). Sometimes you may feel a tingling sensation and, yes, a burning in the bosom can be felt (see D&C 9:7–9). Nephi expressed the following sentiment: "Behold, I am full of the Spirit of God, insomuch that my frame has no strength." His brothers were so angry that they wanted to throw him into the sea, but Nephi warned them, "I command you that ye touch me not, for I am filled with the power of God, even unto the consuming of my flesh; and whoso shall lay his hands upon me shall wither even as a dried reed" (1 Nephi 17:47–48).

Following a physical manifestation with the Holy Spirit, your body may be left in a weakened state (see 1 Nephi 19:20). These experiences are rare and personal, and for those who experience them, there is no question where the experience has come from.

Spiritual and emotional feelings. Just as many prophets have said regarding the feelings that accompany the Spirit, you will know them when they happen. I too testify that this is true. The emotions that come as a manifestation of the Spirit are hard to describe, yet clearly recognizable. The Prophet Joseph felt these feelings when reading James 1:5–6. He stated, "Never did any passage of scripture come with more power to the heart of man than this did at this time to mine. It seemed to enter with great force into *every feeling of my heart*" (Joseph Smith—History 1:12; emphasis added).

The emotions that are fruits of the Spirit are simple and amazing, and when you feel them you should thank the Lord and *recognize that they have come from the Holy Spirit.* Among them are "love, joy, peace, longsuffering, gentleness, goodness, faith, meekness, temperance" (Galatians 5:22–23).

Feeling the love of God and a sensation of being in the arms of His love are distinct expressions of the Holy Spirit. Nephi, when conversing with the Holy Spirit and an angel of God (see 1 Nephi 11), spoke of the love of God and the way he felt. Paul likewise taught, "Hope maketh not ashamed; because the love of God is shed abroad in our hearts by the Holy Ghost which is given unto us" (Romans 5:5). The love you feel for anyone is an expression of the Holy Spirit. We read, "Seeing ye have purified your souls in obeying the truth through the Spirit unto unfeigned love of the brethren, see that ye love one another with a pure heart fervently" (1 Peter 1:22).

As you become a saint and allow these feelings of the Holy Spirit to become part of you, you will become "as a child, submissive, *meek, humble, patient, full of love*" (Mosiah 3:19; emphasis added). Alma described what happens as you allow the Holy Ghost to be your companion. You will "be led by the Holy Spirit, becoming humble, meek, submissive, patient, full of love and all long-suffering" (Alma 13:28).

Feelings of joy are mentioned as a "fruit" of the Spirit, and one of the purposes of the Holy Spirit (see Galatians 5:22; D&C 11:13). The scriptures are replete with examples of the Spirit filling individuals' hearts with joy and rejoicing (see Mosiah 4:3, 20; Alma 7:17, 26; 19:13–14; 22:15).

Peace is another feeling associated with the Spirit. Peace was given to Oliver Cowdery when he was struggling: "If you desire a further witness, cast your mind upon the night that you cried unto me in your heart, that you might know concerning the truth of these things. *Did I not speak peace to your mind concerning the matter?* What greater witness can you have than from God? And now, behold, you have received a witness; for if I have told you things which no man knoweth have you not received a witness?" (D&C 6:22–24; emphasis added).

This peace is so precious. As you get older, you will come to treasure such peace more and more. This special manifestation of the Holy Spirit is especially dear to me. I plead for peace often. The Lord has said, "Learn of me, and listen to my words; walk in the meekness of my Spirit, and you shall have peace in me" (D&C 19:23). I have learned that peace comes by the Spirit from following the word of God in meekness.

Alma experienced the blessing of peace as he learned of his people's promised deliverance: "Yea, and it came to pass that the Lord our God did visit us with assurances that he would deliver us; yea, insomuch that *he did speak peace to our souls*, and did grant unto us great faith, and did cause us that we should hope for our deliverance in him" (Alma 58:10–11; emphasis added).

The Holy Spirit will be a great blessing in your life, as a missionary and forever. Without it, your life would be lonely, without direction and without power. The goodness of God is remarkable. He sent us the Holy Ghost because of our faith in His Beloved Son: "Father, thou hast given them the Holy Ghost because they believe in me; and thou seest that they believe in me because thou hearest them, and they pray unto me; and they pray unto me because I am with them" (3 Nephi 19:22).

Distinct impressions to act. Nephi is an excellent example of someone who was led by the Spirit not knowing beforehand the things he would be asked to do (see 1 Nephi 4:6). Many times people have told me, "I had a distinct impression that I should. . . ." Heavenly Father has given you the precious gift of direction by the Spirit to use throughout your life. Just as the Lord used the spindles on the Liahona to point the way Nephi's family should travel and gave instructions written on the ball, He will likewise instruct and direct you in your life. As with both the Liahona and the gift of direction by the Spirit, you will be guided according to your faith and diligence (see 1 Nephi 16:10, 16, 26–30). And the Liahona is like unto the word of God, which will tell you all things to do (see 2 Nephi 32:3; Alma 37:44).

These promptings to act will have a dramatic effect on your behavior. They will inspire you to do good and to become more like your Savior: "And they all cried with one voice, saying: Yea, we believe all the words which thou hast spoken unto us; and also, we know of their surety and truth, because of the Spirit of the Lord Omnipotent, which has wrought a mighty change in us, or in our hearts, *that we have no more disposition to do evil, but to do good continually*" (Mosiah 5:2; emphasis added). Surely, these were the feelings of President Joseph F. Smith when he said,

I speak of the influence and power of the Holy Spirit

The feeling that came upon me was that of pure peace, of love and of light. I felt in my soul that if I had sinned—and surely I was not without sin—that it had been forgiven me; that I was indeed cleansed from sin; my heart was touched, and I felt that I would not injure the smallest insect beneath my feet. I felt as if I wanted to do good everywhere to everybody and to everything. I felt a newness of life, a newness of desire to do that which was right. There was not one particle of desire for evil left in my soul.[4]

The Holy Spirit will always lead you to do good (see D&C 11:12). It is interesting to note that this is exactly what happened to your Savior, following His anointing by God, "*who went about doing good . . . for God was with him*" (Acts 10:38; emphasis added).

Thoughts and Ideas. The Prophet Joseph taught,

The Spirit of Revelation is in connection with these blessings. A person may profit by noticing the first intimation of the spirit of revelation; for instance when you feel *pure intelligence* flowing into you, it may give you *sudden strokes of ideas,* so that by noticing it, you may find it fulfilled the same day or soon; (i.e.) those things that were presented unto your minds by the Spirit of God, will come to pass; and thus by learning the Spirit of God and understanding it, you may grow into the principle of revelation.[5]

The Holy Spirit will enlighten your mind with ideas and inspiration (see D&C 11:13) and give to you the words which you should say: "Angels speak by the power of the Holy Ghost; wherefore, they speak the words of Christ. Wherefore, I said unto you, feast upon the words of Christ; for behold, the words of Christ will tell you all things what ye should do" (2 Nephi 32:3). For example, we read that it was an angel who delivered the message to King Benjamin that he delivered to his people (see Mosiah 3:2).

One important key in understanding this principle is found

in the doctrine that the spirit of prophecy and revelation comes by the power of the Holy Ghost: "For the prophecy came not in old time by the will of man: but holy men of God spake as they were moved by the Holy Ghost" (2 Peter 1:21). We, likewise, read in the Doctrine and Covenants that "to some it is given by the Holy Ghost . . . to prophesy" (D&C 46:13, 22). Whenever you read the words *prophecy* or *revelation* in the scriptures, you will know that the power of the Holy Ghost is functioning. Other examples from scripture include the sons of Mosiah (see Alma 17:2–3) and Samuel when he was told to prophesy the things that came into his heart (see Helaman 13:3, 5). The spirit of prophecy is demonstrated countless times in the Book of Mormon as well (see Alma 4:20; 5:47; 6:48; 8:24; 9:21; 10:12; 13:26; 16:5; 37:5; 43:2; Helaman 4:12, 23; 3 Nephi 3:19).

Each of the expressions of the Holy Spirit are perceived and felt in a variety of ways, whether that be a sense of urgency to act (see 1 Nephi 4:6), a still small voice, a clear sense of instruction, or even a demonstrative power that is felt by others.

It is interesting to note the words that are used in the scriptures regarding how the Holy Spirit is made manifest. It is often described as being *poured out* (see Jacob 7:7–8; Mosiah 25:24; D&C 19:38). It sounds as if you are a container or conduit for the Holy Spirit, and indeed you are. The Holy Spirit works through you so that you might feel the power and blessing of His presence. In other scriptures, the words *filled with the Holy Ghost* are used (see Alma 8:30; 1:36; 36:24; Helaman 5:45; 3 Nephi 12:6; 19:13; 26:17; 30:2). These scriptures teach, and you must realize that, the Spirit dwells within you, for you are a temple of God (see 1 Corinthians 3:16), and the Holy Spirit will not always strive with you unless you are clean, pure and free from iniquity (see Mormon 1:14; 1 Corinthians 3:17; 1 Timothy 4:1; 2 Nephi 33:2; Mosiah 2:36; Helaman 4:24; D&C 64:16).

Being worthy is the most important key to recognizing the Holy Ghost in any form. I urge you to be worthy and thus receive the direction of the Holy Ghost.

As a young bishop I learned this lesson. It was about 1969, when a young girl named Susan Gerszewski came to see me. She began, "Bishop, you've got to take my name off the records of the Church."

I said, "Oh, Susan, what's wrong?"

"My brothers think I'm a dork for being here at BYU, and I can't stand the pressure when I go home, and my parents are wondering what's going on with me."

And then, all of a sudden, the Lord stepped in, and words came out of my mouth by the power of the Holy Ghost like this: "Susan, I promise you that if you stay faithful, your brothers will join the Church, and your parents' hearts will soften." How could I say that? I couldn't. Only the Holy Spirit could.

She said, "Oh, I just don't know, Bishop, I just don't know."

I said, "Well, Susan, is the Book of Mormon true?"

"Well, of course it is, Bishop."

"Do you love the Savior and do you believe in Heavenly Father?"

"Yes, I do."

"Is the prophet the head of the Church today?"

"Of course."

"Is this the true Church?"

"Of course it is. But I just can't stand the pressure."

I said, "Susan, will you be willing exercise your faith? Because the Lord just gave you a promise."

She said, "Well, I guess I can try."

She exercised her faith. That year, she moved out of the ward and I lost track of her.

At Brigham Young University (BYU) in 1972, I volunteered to teach another religion class, besides the Book of Mormon, before going to my dental office. It was the Gospel Principles and Practices class. There were about sixty students in the class, and life was going just merrily along, and on the last day to drop the class, this student came up to me, and he said, "I've got to drop your class."

I asked, "How come?"

He said, "Well, I'm on scholarship, and if I don't get a B or a B+, I could lose my scholarship; and I got a C+ on the test, and besides, I'm not a Mormon."

I looked at his little information sheet I had him fill out before class. He'd checked the "nonmember" box so close to the "member" box that I'd missed it.

I said, "Well, Jim, you mean you're just afraid you won't get a B?"

He said, "Well, how can I? I'm not a member, and I just can't risk it."

I said, "Jim, I've got an idea. Do you normally study once a week for this class?"

He answered, "Yes."

I said, "Jim, I've got it. Would you mind studying with me Tuesday nights before Wednesday class for an hour?"

He said, "Yes, but what will that do?"

I continued, "Well, Jim, you want a B, right? Do you know who makes out the grade?"

He answered, "Well, you do."

I smiled. "That's right, Jim, I'm guaranteeing you a B or a B+."

"You mean you'll guaran—"

"I guarantee it. Look, I'm going to teach you every Tuesday night. If you're in my house for an hour, well, I'll make up the test too. I'll even help you prepare for the test. Jim, I'm guaranteeing you this."

Jim said, "Well, that's a deal, I'm going to study with you."

So Jim came up to my house, and this went on for a couple of weeks, and then one day he asked, "Hey, Brother Ed, could I bring my brother and my roommate too? I mean, you and I have banana splits and root beer floats and doughnuts every study night; we might as well have parties when you teach."

And so I said, "You bet. You bring them up." So we went along for several weeks, and then one night they came up and they were kind of kidding around a lot, so I said, "You guys are sure having a hoot tonight. What's up around here?" They looked at each other as if to say, "Okay, who's going to tell him?" Jim finally said, "Brother Ed, we've been thinking, and we talked to our bishop, and we all want to be baptized, and will you baptize us and confirm us members of the Church next week?" As I floated down from the ceiling, I said, "Yes Jim. I will, I will, I will."

Well, his name was Jim Gerszewski, but I had mispronounced his name. Jim was Susan's brother; Susan was at the baptism, and it was a joyful occasion. I baptized Jim and Don, and their roommate baptized Larry Kacher.

Now, you tell me that God our Father and Jesus Christ are not in charge of everything on this earth. How could those words come out of my mouth: "Your brothers will join the Church"? How, three years later, could one of those brothers be in my class? There were twenty thousand plus students at BYU at the time. Why did I add that class to teach that semester? Why didn't he drop the class from the religion office? Why did he get a low score and come and talk to me about dropping the class? Don't tell me that the Lord's hand isn't in all things that are good. All three boys served missions. All three were married in the temple and have served well. Yes, Jim and Don Gerszewski and Larry Kacher are stalwarts in the Church. Elder Larry Kacher was just called to the Quorum of the Seventy. The Spirit is the key! The Lord is the master of "coincidences."

How and Why the Holy Ghost Withdraws

Understanding the ways in which the companionship of the Holy Ghost may be lost is of critical importance. Without the Spirit's guidance, we are left alone with no sure direction in life and with no power to learn, teach, preach, testify, or do good. It is primarily through disobedience and sin that you separate yourself from the Holy Ghost:

> And now, I say unto you, my brethren, that after ye have known and have been taught all these things, if ye should transgress and go contrary to that which has been spoken, that ye do withdraw yourselves from the Spirit of the Lord, that it may have no place in you to guide you in wisdom's paths that ye may be blessed, prospered, and preserved—
>
> I say unto you, that the man that doeth this, the same cometh out in open rebellion against God; therefore he listeth to obey the evil spirit, and becometh an enemy to all righteousness; therefore, the Lord has no place in him, for he dwelleth not in unholy temples. (Mosiah 2:36–37; see also Helaman 4:24)

You must realize that anytime you do not keep the commandments, the Holy Ghost will withdraw from you (see Mormon 1:13–14). You must remember that you are at war with the devil. You are constantly being harassed by the evil one to yield to his temptations of the flesh and the desires of the carnal mind. Paul counseled,

> Walk in the Spirit, and ye shall not fulfil the lust of the flesh.
>
> For the flesh lusteth against the Spirit, and the Spirit against the flesh: and these are contrary the one to the other: so that ye cannot do the things that ye would.
>
> But if ye be led of the Spirit, ye are not under the law.
>
> Now the works of the flesh are manifest, which are these; Adultery, fornication, uncleanness, lasciviousness,
>
> Idolatry, witchcraft, hatred, variance, emulations, wrath, strife, seditions, heresies,
>
> Envyings, murders, drunkenness, revellings, and such like: of the which I tell you before, as I have also told you in time past, that they which do such things shall not inherit the kingdom of God. (Galatians 5:16–21)

When you don't walk in the Spirit—when you do things that are contrary to God's plan—you literally don't have the Spirit to be with you. You literally become subject to the devil, for without the Holy Spirit, sin quickly enters in the door. Simply put, if you don't keep the commandments, the devil will have power over your heart. "But behold, the Spirit of the Lord had ceased striving with them, and Satan had full power over the hearts of the people; for they were given up unto the hardness of their hearts, and the blindness of their minds that they might be destroyed; wherefore they went again to battle" (Ether 15:19).

It is critical for you to understand that failing to hearken to the words of the prophets will cause you to lose the Spirit: "For behold, the Spirit of the Lord ceaseth soon to strive with them; for behold, they have rejected the prophets" (1 Nephi 7:14).

The messengers, representatives, and special witnesses of our Savior represent Him and therefore merit your greatest respect and obedience. Criticizing the Lord's anointed is a step toward apostasy and a sure way to lose the companionship of the Holy Ghost.

The Holy Spirit is so sensitive that it will not strive with us in the presence of pride (see Moroni 8:27–28). At the first sign of wickedness and unbelief, the Holy Spirit will depart (see Mormon 1:14). A hardened heart likewise dispels the Spirit (see 2 Nephi 33:2). Failure to repent and acknowledge the light you have received will cause the precious Holy Spirit to depart (see D&C 1:33). Even thoughts and attitudes such as lust or jealousy can make the Spirit flee (see D&C 42:23).

The Holy Ghost may also be lost if we willingly and knowingly break covenants, particularly the most sacred covenants of the temple, which we have received by the power of the fulness of the Holy Ghost: We read,

> All people who shall enter upon the threshold of the Lord's house may feel thy power, and feel constrained to acknowledge that thou hast sanctified it, and that it is thy house, a place of thy holiness.
>
> And do thou grant, Holy Father, that all those who shall worship in this house may be taught words of wisdom out of the best books, and that they may seek learning even by study, and also by faith, as thou hast said;
>
> And that they may grow up in thee, and receive a fulness of the Holy Ghost, and be organized according to thy laws, and be prepared to obtain every needful thing. (D&C 109:13–15)

This means in part that as you "grow up unto the Lord" and enter the temple, you receive a fulness of the Holy Ghost and thereby become accountable for that knowledge—and thus, you have a greater condemnation and loss of the Spirit if you turn away from this knowledge. You will receive in the temple the ordinances of the greater priesthood; symbolically, the Lord's prophets in His holy house teach you the law of the Lord. Of all ways in which the Holy Ghost may be lost, this is the most serious and significant. Why? We read, "For do ye suppose that ye can get rid of the justice of an offended God, who hath been trampled under feet of men, that thereby salvation might come?" (3 Nephi 28:35). These words are both literal and symbolic. Living by the word of God is a matter of eternal lives and exaltations. When we trample them, the Spirit flees.

Remember

As you exercise obedience and humility, the Spirit will infuse all aspects of your life. Seek to be worthy of the Spirit as you prepare for your mission; it will be one of the most important things you do. As you are worthy, you will be led by the Spirit, not knowing beforehand the things you should do (see 1 Nephi 4:6). You can have the Spirit's companionship all day long, every day. The question is, will you allow it?

When the Spirit is with you, you will desire to do good. You will want to search the scriptures, say your prayers, and be kind to your companion. The Spirit will show you and help you do all things you should do. Sometimes, when you receive a prompting, you might think, *I'm not ready. I don't know how to do this. How could I ever do it?* The Lord and the Spirit will assist you in these situations. The Lord has said, "I will go before your face. I will be on your right hand and on your left, and my Spirit shall be in your hearts, and mine angels round about you, to bear you up" (D&C 84:88). The Lord will help His missionaries and every person who strives to live by the power of the Spirit. Become an instrument for the Lord and a conduit for the Spirit and give credit to the Lord for all good things.

One of the most important things you can do to prepare for your mission is to understand and appreciate the power of the Holy Ghost in your life, including how to recognize this supernal gift. There are many promised blessings for keeping the commandments—and the blessings of the Holy Ghost in your life is empowering (see D&C 20:77, 79; Acts 10:38; 2 Nephi 32:5; Alma 17:3; and many more).

CHAPTER 12

Advice from Missionaries

I have observed and spoken with many missionaries and future missionaries over the years. They have taught me a great deal, and the advice and lessons they have shared with me will be helpful to you as well as you prepare to go into the mission field.

Empowerment and Inspiration in Letters

Heavenly Father and our Savior communicate the word of God to us through Their words. The scriptures are literally letters from heaven. Angels, messengers, and prophets speak the word of God. Revelatory talks are given and recorded at general conference. Leaders and teachers teach the word of God: "whatsoever they shall speak when moved upon by the Holy Ghost shall be scripture, shall be the will of the Lord, shall be the mind of the Lord, shall be the word of the Lord, shall be the voice of the Lord, and the power of God unto salvation" (D&C 68:4). We receive answers to our prayers, which we call inspiration and revelation. We have received a special guide, which we call the Holy Ghost and which will "show unto you all things what ye should do" (2 Nephi 32:5). Communication through revelation is vital. We need to live by the word of God (see D&C 84:44).

Letters and emails can be the lifeblood of your mission and your inspiration to others. You and your family need to commit to weekly writing. It will bring a closeness that will last forever. These epistles to and from your family and friends will be a sustaining influence in your missionary effor,t and your letters to family and friends at home will inspire them to greater spirituality. Like Nephi wrote, "For we labor diligently to write, to persuade our children [our missionaries and each other], and also our brethren, to believe in Christ, and to be reconciled to God" (2 Nephi 25:23). Earlier, Nephi had said, "And upon these I write the things of my soul, and many of the scriptures which are engraven upon the plates of brass. For my soul delighteth in the scriptures, and my heart pondereth them, and writeth them for the learning and the profit of my children. Behold, my soul delighteth in the things of the Lord; and my heart pondereth continually upon the things which I have seen and heard" (2 Nephi 4:15–16).

This principle taught by Nephi is the essence of the letters to and from your missionary that all might learn and profit by the things that you write to one another. Letters aren't simply "I took a test at school," or, "Dad received a new calling," or, "Mom just got a new hairdo." You need to write "the things of your soul" for "learning and profit" that you might be an instrument in the hands of the Lord "to persuade your children and your brethren, to believe in Christ, and be reconciled to God." You are writing the things of your soul like Nephi.

Everyone will be on a new level of communication. Everyone will grow and change. Your letters will inspire. The pure love of Christ will grow within everyone's soul as they take upon themselves the divine nature of Christ. You will become instruments in the hand of the Lord as you receive with humility and write in meekness and love that all will be blessed.

As a missionary, your weekly letters to your mission president will have a different feel as your epistles become full of gospel truths and how they have helped you as the Lord's disciple.

My daughter, Traci, reminded her missionary son, Grayson, to write an inspirational paragraph at the end of each letter. These paragraphs are becoming the highlight of his letters and have become cherished advice, inspiration, and revelation to everyone. Epistles of love are empowering!

Meeting Your President and His Wife

Your mission president and his wife have been called of God to preside over your mission. They are full of charity and will love you instantly and seek your eternal welfare. Learn to hearken to their words, and they will lead you in righteousness. As you learn to obey, you will learn to love the work more deeply.

When you meet them the first time, you will be able to feel their love for you. They will radiate the pure love of Christ. Pray for them like you pray for the prophet. They, like you, have given up much to serve the Lord.

Your mission president will interview you periodically to determine your well-being in every aspect of your life because he cares about you. He will ask you how your companion is doing. Remember, you are your brother's or sister's keeper. He will inquire of the work and how he can help in your efforts to bring souls unto Christ. He will listen to you and your needs. Don't be afraid to ask for help or a blessing, according to your needs.

Your First Missionary Companion

You will have a special twelve-week training period to help you adjust to missionary life and be better prepared to serve the Lord, assisting you in hastening the work as you invite souls to come unto Christ.

Your mission president has prayed concerning you and providing you with the best "trainer" for you. Your trainer should be an obedient and righteous example. If you have concerns, have the courage to give your mission president the information he needs so he can strengthen your trainer. Never ever hide facts from your president. He seeks your eternal welfare. Be strong and of good courage so your mission president can help you be the kind of missionary you want to be. The habits established in your first twelve weeks will have a dynamic effect upon your entire mission, as well as your life.

Your trainer can teach and train you in regard to the principles of having a good day every day as a missionary. It is all about doing your very best. Trust in the Lord knowing that "whoso receiveth you, there I will be also, for I will go before your face. I will be on your right hand and on your left, and my Spirit shall be in your hearts, and mine angels round about you, to bear you up" (D&C 84:88).

Learn to Study and Practice

One of the biggest failings before a missionary leaves on his or her mission (and in the mission field as well) is a failure to study and practice. In the mission field, you will usually have two hours every morning to study. Sometimes you will mistakenly think you know enough and don't need to do your studying. You will then lose the knowledge you might have gained, which might have given you power. You lose the preparation that precedes this power. It is situations like this that allows fear and hesitation to creep in because you are not well prepared. We read, "If ye are prepared ye shall not fear" (see D&C 38:30), and the opposite is also true. Studying and preparing to serve will allow you to have a great day on your mission each and every day, no matter what happens.

Elder Kramer, a wonderful missionary, wrote me, saying, "Dear President, I had a wonderful experience this last week. It shows you that if you study hard it really pays off." He had read Doctrine and Covenants 22:2, where it says if a man is baptized one hundred times, it "availeth him nothing" if the baptism wasn't performed with proper authority. He continued,

> One of my investigators was all ready to be baptized when he said, "Elder Kramer, I've decided I'm not going to be baptized because I've been baptized before." But President, then I remembered what I had studied. I asked him if he had read the Doctrine and Covenants. "Oh yes, I love the Doctrine and Covenants," he said. So I turned to section twenty-two and read verse two, where it asks what good it does to be baptized one hundred times without the proper authority. And then the man said, "Elder Kramer you're right, I must be baptized the right way. I'll be baptized Sunday as planned."

Because Elder Kramer had the power and the knowledge, he had the answer when his investigator had a question. And he had studied to find that answer.

On one occasion, when I was out teaching with the elders, one of their investigators said, "President Pinegar, I want to talk to you; come with me." The elders stood there visiting in the living room, and the investigator and I walked outside. He said, "I want to tell you something about your missionaries." (They weren't actually mine—they were the Lord's—but they were like my sons because I loved them so much.) He said, "I'm joining the Church next month, and you know one of the reasons I am?"

I said, "Well, it's because you know the Church is true and you feel the Spirit."

He said, "Yes, but it's also something about your missionaries."

I said, "What is it?"

He said, "You know, President Pinegar, they always have the answers I need, and the way they give them to me, well, I just want to believe them." These elders had the power of the Holy Spirit with them to answer this man's questions because they had studied and worked hard.

Sometimes, despite your preparation, an investigator may say, "I don't want to hear from you anymore." This might happen for a few reasons. It might happen because they are not yet prepared to hear the gospel message. Maybe they see no apparent need for it. Remember, you must always honor others' agency. Sometimes, regardless who is teaching, the person listening is not fully prepared or ready to hear the word of God. Do not let your lack of study and practice be the reason for someone's rejection of the true Gospel. You must study the scriptures, *Preach My Gospel,* the discussions presentations, and your investigator records; you must study and organize every needful thing so that you can preach the gospel with the power and authority of God.

Learn Missionary Skills

As you prepare to be a missionary, be aware that there are particular skills that will be of great use to you—skills like being able to talk to people, being socially graceful, and being able to carry on a conversation and turn it into a missionary opportunity. Learn to talk to people. Learn to learn to open your mouth, and remember that the Spirit will give you the words you need to say at the very moment you need to say them (see D&C 100:5–6). Learning these skills takes time. There is no speed course known to mankind. Countless hours of practice—and learning to step out of your comfort zone—will be the best form of preparation.

Gain a testimony of the fact that teaching is the greatest calling on this earth and then learn how to teach effectively by reading and practicing the principles in *Preach My Gospel* and *Teaching, No Greater Calling*. Alma was the chief judge, but he conferred the chief judgeship seat upon Nephihah so he could teach. He said he wanted to go out and teach all the people by bearing pure testimony (see Alma 4:18–19). Mothers and fathers, likewise, teach as one of the most important parts of their stewardship. Teaching is the highest and noblest calling, and there are few things more satisfying than teaching the word of God, because you help people come unto Christ and experience true happiness.

Missionaries often talk about the many things they learned in a missionary preparation course in their ward or stakes. When possible, you should attend a missionary preparation course. You can also take missionary preparation classes and religion classes at all of the Church universities and institutes of religion.

It will be valuable for you to learn some domestic skills: learn how to cook, wash, iron, and clean. Check out the videos *Called to Serve* and *Labor of Love* from your ward library. There are other great videos as well, like *Heavenly Father's Plan, What Is Real,* and *Together Forever,* to name a few. There is also a plethora of material on the Church's website, lds.org. All these materials will help you prepare to become a good missionary and help you as you present the actual lessons in the mission field.

There are usually missionaries called to the area in which you live. The missionaries I have spoken with have found it helpful for youth to go out and teach with them. They will let you read a scripture, bear your testimony, or just smile a lot—however you contribute, it's okay. Helping the missionaries teach is a great feeling, and you will love it. Every day can be a missionary day in your life, whether you are serving a full time mission yet, or not. Listen to the CD *60 Minutes to a Great Mission*. It can inspire you.

Learn How to Build Relationships of Trust

One lesson that all missionaries learn is that it will be critical for you to build relationships of trust so people will trust, love, and respect you. This is the first thing you do as a missionary, even before you teach: you build relationships of trust. The most successful missionaries I have worked with know this principle well. They have learned how to talk to people and build up a relationship to a point that those people will allow them to teach the gospel. You must be an example of all that you believe, including the principles you preach, such as love and patience, because what you are speaks so loudly, people sometimes don't hear a word you say. You teach what you are. If you are full of love, then they'll want to listen to you. Relationships are the key. You must learn to be a true and honest friend. Then people will trust you to the point where you can teach them. It has been said that it is better to be trusted than loved—be both ,and you will teach "with power and authority of God" (Alma 17:3).

Learn to Open Your Mouth

In his epistle to the Romans, Paul proclaimed, "For I am not ashamed of the gospel of Christ: for it is the power of God unto salvation to every one that believeth" (Romans 1:16). It is critical for you to understand that you have nothing to be ashamed of in communicating the love of God to the world. You have no reason to fear; you must simply learn to open your mouth and share it.

I will never forget a moment in the MTC, at the last meeting before the missionaries would go out into the field. I spoke about opening your mouth. I spoke about being bold, obedient, full of love, and courageous in opening one's mouth. I would say, "Do not be afraid. The worth of souls is great. You have a mighty role in the kingdom." Well, some of my missionaries were still afraid. I would ask them to have an experience in which they could practice opening their mouths. One sweet young sister wrote me a letter after she'd been out in the mission field two weeks:

Dear President,

After your talk Sunday night I was so nervous, I didn't know what to do. I knew I'd be leaving Wednesday, and I was going to have to open my mouth. And I thought, *I can't do it, I can't do it.* So I fasted and I prayed and I left Wednesday on the plane, and to my joy I had a window seat and my companion sat next to me. So I said, "Oh dear, I won't be able to talk to anybody on the plane," and I was so relieved. But then, I got into the airport and I sat down, and there was a man sitting across from me. He was old and different looking, and I didn't know what to do. And all I could remember was your voice telling us, "Open your mouths, and they will be filled, I promise you." Well, I girded up my loins and I opened my mouth and said, "Hi, where you headed?" From that little beginning, we began an hour-long conversation. Pretty soon we became friends. And after a bit I said, "If you knew there was another book written about Jesus Christ, would you be interested in reading that? The Book of Mormon?"

He said, "Oh, I have a Book of Mormon." I committed him right there to read the book, and then he told me, "My daughter is taking the discussions too."

And then I said, "Is it okay if the missionaries come by and see you?" He said, "That would just be fine." Oh, President, it's so easy to open your mouth. The Lord will fill it. There's nothing to it.

I always read that letter to departing missionaries because it helps them realize that we can all have the courage to open our mouths. All of us, member missionaries and full-time proselyting missionaries, can open our mouths, and they will be filled.

Sometimes as a missionary, you might feel afraid to do your duty. Sometimes the tasks will seem impossibly hard. However, in my experience, missionaries who had the hardest time in the mission field were the ones who were afraid, filled with doubt, and thought they couldn't do it. I would encourage you to learn how to overcome fear, to cast it away from you.

The following are six ways, tested and true by countless missionaries, to help you overcome fear: faith, love, knowledge, preparation, experience, and prayer.

Faith in the Lord Jesus Christ. If you exercise faith and mentally exert this power, fear and doubt will flee. The Apostles of old asked the Savior to increase their faith (see Luke 17:5). Faith comes by hearing the word of the Lord. Every time you read the scriptures, hear your mission president speak, counsel together with your companion, or listen to good advice from your parents, the word of the Lord will come into your heart, and your faith will increase. You will become like Nephi and Lehi and the sons of Helaman, whose faith was so strong that they converted thousands of people (see Ether 12:14). Faith destroys doubt and fear, as we learn from the scriptures: "They did fast and pray oft, and did wax stronger and stronger in their humility, and firmer and firmer in [their] faith" (Helaman 3:35). Faith is the first step toward overcoming your fear.

Love. Perfect love casteth out all fear (see 1 John 4:18). Think about it—if you're full of love, then there's no room for fear. When love is in your heart, you will feel an overwhelming appreciation for the worth of souls. You will have such concern that you will do anything to help them come unto Christ. You won't fear doing a single thing. Such was the example of the sons of Mosiah, who were so concerned for others that the thought of any of them living without the knowledge of God was physically painful (see Mosiah 28:3).

Knowledge. Knowledge is power. When you see things as they are, you will have no reason to fear. I remember once when I was little, I saw a scary movie. It was something like *Frankenstein Meets the Werewolf with the Mummy.* I know that sounds silly—today, it would be a G-rated movie, and we'd say, "Oh, look how funny it is." But in those days, I was just a little nine-year-old boy, and I hid behind the seats.

At that time, we lived on a farm. To irrigate our orchards, we would receive water from Strawberry Reservoir. Well, it so happened on the day of the movie, it was our turn to use the irrigation water at midnight. Now, my duty as the youngest boy, the baby of the family, was to do whatever my big brothers said. So my job was to go down to the end of the furrow, and when the water got there, say, "The water's here." That was it.

But, you must understand, it was midnight, and there was a full moon. I knew the werewolf was going to come and get me—there was no way out of it. I was frightened, but I couldn't chicken out in front of my brothers. So I started walking down the row, and the pheasants were flying by, and I thought, *Heavenly Father, I'm going to be a good boy. Don't let me die.* I was afraid. Why was I so afraid? Because I couldn't see. There was no light. I was afraid because of the past experience of that movie. Likewise, when you don't have enough knowledge and understanding, it is as if you are walking in darkness. You are full of fear, and you fear what others will think or what may happen to you. When you gain enough knowledge, you see things clearly; it's as if a light has been turned on to make the darkness flee. You have power, and then fear will leave. That's how knowledge overpowers fear.

Preparation. When you're prepared, you will overcome fear. We read this in the scriptures: "If ye are prepared ye shall not fear" (D&C 38:30). Preparation, like knowledge, is power. Your self-confidence will increase with your level of preparation.

When you have a clear vision of the importance of the work and a desire to do it, preparation becomes the master. It takes time, effort, dedication, and often sacrifice to prepare well. Make yourself fully capable of doing all that is required. Be sure you are spiritually, emotionally, and mentally prepared with every needful thing. The greatest act of preparation is allowing the Holy Ghost to help you form an uncompromising vision of success in the objectives you have committed yourself to achieve.

Make a detailed checklist of things you need to do in your preparation. What are your target goals, objectives, deadlines, and milestones? Select target dates along the way to be sure your preparation is on schedule. How will you know you have succeeded? By measuring and evaluating as you go along. Make midcourse corrections as you go—preparation is an ongoing process that must become a permanent part of your life. You must organize your time well so that preparation and planning have adequate time to help you achieve your goals. When preparation is a part of your mission, you will feel more in control, fear will depart, and you will have success. Make a goal to prepare well, and then enjoy the blessings of success in your life.

Experience. The more you do something, or the more experience you gain from it, the more fear decreases. On their first full day in our mission, my assistants would teach the new missionaries the skills and dialogues to open their mouths. Then we would send them out on the streets with their new companions just to practice opening their mouths.

The experience went something like this: "Would you be so kind and friendly as to answer a few questions that could bless your life? It'll only take a minute." That was the big number-one question, after which the missionaries would ask questions about life, the Savior, families, the Book of Mormon, and so on. But it all started with one simple question. Then they would practice that approach over and over until they were confident in that approach. And after a few hours, the experience helped them conquer the fear of opening their mouths.

Prayer. When you recognize that you are an instrument in God's hands—a disciple of Jesus Christ, and filled with love—you will find it natural to pray unceasingly for the strength of the Lord. The scriptures state, "Open your mouths and they shall be filled, and you shall become even as Nephi of old, who journeyed from Jerusalem in the wilderness. Yea, open your mouths and spare not, and you shall be laden with sheaves upon your backs, for lo, I am with you. Yea, open your mouths and they shall be filled, saying: Repent, repent, and prepare ye the way of the Lord, and make his paths straight; for the kingdom of heaven is at hand" (D&C 33:8–10). And yet again, the Lord promises,

> Lift up your voices unto this people; speak the thoughts that I shall put into your hearts, and you shall not be confounded before men;

For it shall be given you in the very hour, yea, in the very moment, what ye shall say.

But a commandment I give unto you, that ye shall declare whatsoever thing ye declare in my name, in solemnity of heart, in the spirit of meekness, in all things.

And I give unto you this promise, that inasmuch as ye do this the Holy Ghost shall be shed forth in bearing record unto all things whatsoever ye shall say. (D&C 100:5–8)

The Lord will give you specific instructions as you seek them in prayer. We read of Samuel the Lamanite, when "the voice of the Lord came unto him, that he should return again, and prophesy unto the people whatsoever things should come into his heart" (Helaman 13:3).

You are not alone in this work. Remember that it is the Lord's work, and you are the instrument though which He works to bless His children. He will help you and guide you as you ask Him through prayer.

A Typical Day on Your Mission

Every day can be a great day on your mission, knowing you have done your best and that is all the Lord requires of you. There will be days of disappointment when someone tells you not to come back, or that they choose not to be baptized or go to church, and your heart will ache. Sometimes you will have tears well up in your eyes, and you will have pain in your being, and then you will ask as the Lord asked in the allegory of the olive tree: "The Lord of the vineyard wept, and said unto the servant: What could I have done more for my vineyard?" (Jacob 5:41). The Lord repeated this again in verse 49. He is in charge of the work here upon the earth and that is why you have been called at an earlier age to labor in His vineyard. "Behold, I will hasten my work in its time" (D&C 88:73). You are the ones chosen to hasten His work throughout the earth.

This is a typical daily schedule.[1] This may change according to individual missions.

Missionary Daily Schedule

6:30 a.m. Arise, pray, exercise (thirty minutes), and prepare for the day.

7:30 a.m. Breakfast.

8:00 a.m. Personal study: the Book of Mormon, other scriptures, doctrines of the missionary lessons, other chapters from *Preach My Gospel*, the *Missionary Handbook*, and the *Missionary Health Guide*.

9:00 a.m. Companion study: share what you have learned during personal study, prepare to teach, practice teaching, study chapters from *Preach My Gospel*, and confirm plans for the day.

10:00 a.m. Begin proselyting. Missionaries learning a language study that language for an additional thirty to sixty minutes, including planning language learning activities to use during the day. Missionaries may take an hour for lunch and additional study, and an hour for dinner at times during the day that fit best with their proselyting. Normally, dinner should be finished no later than 6:00 p.m.

9:00 p.m. Return to living quarters (unless teaching a lesson, then return by 9:30) and plan the next day's activities (thirty minutes). Write in journal, prepare for bed, and pray.

10:30 p.m. Retire to bed.

There is additional training for twelve weeks for new missionaries in the mission field. It includes everything you need to study and know in regard to missionary work. There is a suggested companion study schedule that focuses on *Preach My Gospel* and the *Missionary's MTC Experience* and specific lessons.

These lessons include

- "The Doctrine of Christ—The Missionary Purpose"
- "The Role of the Holy Ghost in Conversion"
- "Revelation through Prayer"
- "Revelation through The Book of Mormon"
- "Revelation through Church Attendance"
- "Teach People, Not Lessons"
- "We Invite, They commit, We Follow Up"
- "How to Begin Teaching"[2]

If you become familiar with *Preach My Gospel* and the *Missionary Handbook* (online at lds.org) and the lesson topics prior to your mission, you will learn at a greater rate, and your stress will be lessened markedly because you are well prepared. In your first twelve weeks, you are given an additional hour of companionship study, which will really enhance your knowledge and skills as a missionary. From your study, you will seek to make applications in your proselyting effort.

Each week, you have an assigned area to study, and many of those will include video segments to enhance your learning. Then you evaluate your progress periodically in regard to the eight lessons you study. As you progress in your mission, your companion study time will usually focus on the needs of your investigators.

The Lord's Promise to Assist You in His Work

I will never forget a story that two sister missionaries told me. It was a dark, dark night in the heart of London—so dark that they were nervous. A large man came up to them in the shadows of the bus stop, and they were nervous. Then they said they remembered what I had told them: "Don't fear, the Lord is before your face. He's on your right hand, he's on your left hand, His Spirit is in your heart, His angels round about you" (see D&C 84:88). So these two sister missionaries spoke to this man. They said, "Excuse me, sir, would you be so kind and friendly as to answer a few questions that might bring you happiness?"

And he said, "Well, I'd be glad to, young ladies." And he did. His name was Peter Salaka, and he was from the Solomon Islands. He would be staying in England for four weeks. He heard the message and wanted to hear more. Because the sisters cannot teach a man alone, the elders were contacted to teach him the rest of the discussions.

After he had been taught several discussions, Peter said, "I want to meet your mission president." So I went with the missionaries to a discussion. I recognized that Peter Salaka is an elect man of God, like those we read about in the Doctrine and Covenants; he is elect because he heard the Lord's voice and knew the words were true (see D&C 29:7). These two sisters and the elders had taught him. We arranged for a baptism. Peter Salaka spoke at his own baptism. It was the greatest talk I have ever heard at a baptism. He spoke with the wisdom of a bishop, as if he'd been in the Church all of his life. I thought, *Who is this man?*

When he came to church on Sunday, he was interviewed and ordained to the office of a priest. He then left for the Solomon Islands, which was in one of the Australian missions at the time. I called the Australian mission president and informed him of Peter's baptism. He said, "I think we have one member on that island. We'll see what we can do."

Time went by, and Elder Sonnenberg of the Quorum of the Seventy (who was the president of the Australian area) and Elder James E. Faust (then a member of the Twelve) went on a visit to the Solomon Islands to see what they could do to form branches there. Peter Salaka greeted them at the airport. He said, "I am Peter Salaka, and this is my son. I am a priest in The Church of Jesus Christ of Latter-day Saints. How can I help you build up the Church here?" Elder Sonnenberg sent me a picture of Elder Faust, himself, and Brother Salaka.

What would have happened if those two magnificent sisters had not opened their mouths? So many blessings and so much growth might have been missed. Do your best to give everybody an opportunity to hear the gospel and find great joy in this life. This isn't a matter of business; this is a matter of spiritual life and death. I am grateful that those faithful sisters opened their mouths and acted as instruments in the hands of the Lord to bless this great brother.

Always open your mouth. Do not be afraid. You never know who will be a golden contact unless you do. You must remember that we mortals cannot be the judge of who will or will not be receptive to the gospel message. But if you are dedicated to the work, the Lord will help you find them; if you're obedient, the Lord will remove your fears and gladden your heart and fill your mouth. "Therefore, dearly beloved brethren, Let us cheerfully do all things that lie in our power and then may we stand still, with the utmost assurance, to see the salvation of God, and for his arm to be revealed" (D&C 123:17).

Do you believe those words? I testify that whenever you open your mouth, it will be filled. The concept is simple. Plead with the Lord to soften the hearts of the people you meet so that they will receive you. Exercise your faith. The Lord promised that He would go before you to prepare the hearts and minds of the people to accept the gospel. He will lead you to those who are prepared.

Things You Have to Learn by Your Own Experience

There are many new and different things you will have to do and learn on your mission. Sometimes the learning curve is steep. Sometimes sacrifice is required. Here are some things to remember that will be required of you as you serve with all your hearts.

1. You will learn to be separated from love ones and friends.
2. You will need to learn to live with someone 24/7. This requires patience and understanding. You are never alone.
3. There are many new skills you will have to learn, as well as procedures, policies, and subject matter, which will assist you in this life-saving work.
4. You will have to learn and appreciate a new culture or language and what matters to the people you serve.
5. Never judge!
6. There are no vacations.
7. Sometimes there will be new foods to get used to.
8. You will need to learn to be flexible and hold your opinions to yourself.
9. You will need to learn that your smart phone is not available every moment to play and communicate with friends.
10. You will learn to be exactly, immediately and courageously obedient every day.
11. Always do your best. Work hard. Be diligent.
12. You are an example to someone every moment of every day.
13. Learn to face disappointment, especially when an investigator chooses not to continue the discussions or be baptized.

14. Never let contention, in any degree, enter into your relationships, else you will lose the Holy Spirit.
15. Never "Bible bash" or contend with anyone.
16. Opposition does not go away. Temptation is still operating. Agency is supreme. You have the power to choose.
17. There will be spiritual experiences that are priceless and there will be moments of frustration and pain.
18. You may not know the answer to every question. Have the courage to say you don't know, but still tell your questioner that you will seek out an answer.
19. The best two years of your life will require *sacrifice.*
20. Love the apparently unlovable. Everyone needs love.

Missionary work is hard work, but the price is worth it, and the promised blessings are amazing and everlasting.

Leadership Skills

As a missionary, you will need to learn many aspects of leadership. Great leaders must have many skills and qualities, but above all they must have character, as selfless servants of the Lord. Great leaders do not force; they motivate with love unfeigned, gentleness and meekness, persuasion, long-suffering, and a shared vision (see D&C 121:41). They lead by example and truly love the people they serve and the causes they support. Below is a list of helpful hints on how to prepare to become a good leader.

- Become a person of high character, built on Christlike virtues.
- Share the vision and purpose of your work with those you lead.
- Build relationships of trust with all those in your stewardship. This will help build unity.
- Where possible, get feedback and reports from people in regard to their personal areas of responsibility.
- Delegate, but make sure that assignments are understood and that there is appropriate accountability and follow-up.
- Give PIE: Praise often. Instruct and Inspire. Encourage always.
- Be sure everyone knows his or her duties and responsibilities.
- Communicate with everyone so they understand and appreciate not only the cause but also their role within the work.

- Never gossip, complain, or lay blame on others. When there are concerns, go to the individual in a private setting.
- Be a good listener. Obtain feedback regularly.
- Be cheerful and have a good sense of humor.
- Never neglect the weightier matters.
- You must always exhibit honesty and integrity in everything you do.
- Remember—leaders are servants and teachers.

You will lead your investigators carefully and with love to our Savior. You may have the opportunity to lead a new missionary as you serve as a trainer. You may have other opportunities in leadership roles within your mission. When you return from your mission, you will become the ultimate leaders of society and the kingdom of God as you serve as mothers and fathers, as well as serving in opportunities within the Church.

Media in the Mission Field

In the mission field today, you will have many tools at your disposal that are new and different from those that were available in the past, such as cell phones, email, blogs, chat features, and media referrals. Not all missions have integrated these approaches, but it is important for you to be familiar with them in case you are asked to use some of them.

In all of your media use, it is critical that you have integrity—to use it only for the purpose for which it is intended: building up the kingdom of God and bringing souls to Christ. Much of the media you use will be to assist in keeping in touch with contacts, making appointments, and staying in touch with your leaders. However, you will also be allowed to use some media for personal enrichment. You will be able to communicate with your family and use lds.org to help you and to teach your investigators. The guidelines on music will vary from mission to mission, but in all cases the music should direct your thoughts to the Savior.

Cell phones are becoming fairly common in the mission field. You will likely share one cell phone with your companion; the phone should only be used as a teaching tool and to make appointments and contacts. The use of iPads is increasing to help in your presentations, planning, and access to lds.org.

You will also likely see media referrals used in your mission. A media referral results when someone requests a copy of the Book of Mormon or other Church materials online. The request is then sent (within twenty-four hours by either text or email) to the missionaries in the area corresponding the person's address. You may be asked to deliver a DVD or Book of Mormon or Bible, which allows you to then share a brief message about the media or watch the media with the person who requested it.

Many new programs are also at work in the mission field, integrating many forms of media to more effectively keep track of contacts and share the message of the gospel. It's possible that you will participate in one of these new programs. The Church is always searching for ways to help facilitate the spreading of the gospel and to more effectively reach people. In this era, that often means using technology. Do not be surprised to see adaptations and new forms of media being used in moving the work forward.

Pleasing God

Jesus Christ is your example in seeking to please God: "I can of mine own self do nothing: as I hear, I judge: and my judgment is just; because I seek not mine own will, but the will of the Father which hath sent me" (John 5:30). He went on to say, "I do nothing of myself; but as my Father hath taught me, I speak these things. And he that sent me is with me: the Father hath not left me alone; for I do always those things that please him" (John 8:28–29). This oft-repeated scripture will be shared again and again, for it must be embedded into your mind, heart, and soul. You must always ask yourself, "Will what I am doing really please my Heavenly Father and my Savior?"

To please your Father in Heaven, you must yield your thoughts, actions, and behavior to God. You must keep His commandments. You must, in essence, submit your will to His will. As you do so,

you make clear to Him that you have received His love with gratitude and thanksgiving, for you have partaken of the fruit of the
tree of life. You signify that you have received the Atonement of
His Beloved Son. God rejoices in your righteousness as you do
these things. In the end, it is you, His child, who brings glory and
gratification to God for this is His work. You can be as Alma, who
said,

> I know that which the Lord hath commanded me, and I glory in
> it. I do not glory of myself, but I glory in that which the Lord hath
> commanded me; yea, and this is my glory, that perhaps I may be an
> instrument in the hands of God to bring some soul to repentance;
> and this is my joy.
>
> And behold, when I see many of my brethren truly penitent, and
> coming to the Lord their God, then is my soul filled with joy; then
> do I remember what the Lord has done for me, yea, even that he hath
> heard my prayer; yea, then do I remember his merciful arm which he
> extended towards me. (Alma 29:9–10)

As you come to the end of your full-time mission, go out with
a blaze of glory, working faithfully and diligently. Carry on doing
good.

Consider the following as you seek to please Heavenly Father,
even as the Savior did (see John 8:28–29):

- Love God and your Savior, Jesus Christ—seek to follow Christ
  and do the will of God the Father.
- Be obedient—keep the commandments (see D&C 20:77; John
  14:15, 21).
- Exercise faith (see Hebrews 11:6).
- Repent often (see Alma 34:15–17; D&C 18:13).
- Sacrifice (see 3 Nephi 9:20).
- Feed our Savior's sheep (see John 21:15–17).
- Express thanksgiving and gratitude (see D&C 46:7; 58:17, 21;
  62:7; 78:19; Alma 34:38).
- Have a pure heart and ponder all the Beatitudes (see Psalm
  24:4; 1 Timothy 1:5; 3 Nephi 12:3–11).
- Live by the word of God—nurture the word with faith,
  diligence, and patience (see D&C 84:43–46; Alma 32:40–43).

- Become clean, pure, holy, and sanctified (see D&C 133:5; Alma 5:19; 3 Nephi 27:20).
- Consecrate your lives to do the will of the Father with desire, dedication, and diligence.
- Seek charity (see Moroni 7:44–48).
- Receive the temple ordinances and covenants (see D&C 84:19–22; 38:32, 38; 43:16; 95:8; 105:11; 109:35).
- Proclaim the gospel (see Mormon 9:22; D&C 15:6).
- Redeem the dead (see D&C 128:15, 22–25).
- Perfect the Saints through Christ the Lord (see Moroni 10:32–33).
- Assist the poor and needy (see Alma 34:28–29).
- Worship God your Father and Jesus Christ (see Moses 1:15; 2 Nephi 25:16, 29).
- Live under the guidance of the Holy Ghost (see D&C 11:12–13).

The happiness and joy of your Heavenly Father and your Savior is in your receiving the blessings of eternal life.

In contrast, beware of these things that displease Them:

- Failing to express gratitude and to acknowledge His hand in all things (see D&C 59:21; Alma 34:38).
- Failing to open your mouth to share the gospel (see D&C 60:2–3).
- Seeking signs (see D&C 63:12; Mark 8:12; Luke 11:29).
- Exalting yourselves (see D&C 53:55–56; 09:19–20).
- Idleness, greediness, and materialism (see D&C 68:31; James 4:17; Matthew 6:19–21, 24; Luke 12:15–34; 16:9, 11,13; 1 Timothy 6:9–10).
- Not having your heart right before the God (see D&C 112:2–3).
- Lust (see 1 Corinthians 10:5–6).
- Idolatry (see Exodus 20:2; Moses 5:13; 1 Corinthians 10:5–7).
- Murmuring (see 1 Corinthians 10:5,10; 1 Nephi 2:11–12; 16:20).

When we seek to please God, He blesses us greatly in return:

- We are endowed with power from on high (see D&C 84:19–22; 38:32, 38; 43:16; 95:8; 105 11; 109:35).

- We are given a feeling of peace (see Alma 38:8; 40:12; D&C 6:23; 19:23; 111:8; 138:22; Romans 5:1; Galatians 5:22–23).
- We are given freedom from guilt and pain (see Enos 1:5–8; Alma 36:16–20; D&C 18:13).
- We are blessed in a state of never-ending happiness (see Mosiah 2:41; Alma 42:8; 4 Nephi 1:15–16).

And if you are faithful, the Lord will bless you: "If you keep my commandments and endure to the end you shall have eternal life, which gift is the greatest of all the gifts of God" (D&C 14:7).

Remember

When you learn to love and care so much for your brothers and sisters, you will find that you would do anything to bring them to a knowledge of the gospel so that they might find joy. You will gladly pay the price to learn to communicate—with love, knowledge, and faith. Understand that it won't always be easy—in fact, it can be tough. There will be times when you want to walk away, when you want to say, "I don't care." It is at times like this, more than ever, that you must cling to your faith and your hope in the Atonement. As you grow in the gospel, as you gain a greater desire to show and give love, you will become a mighty missionary in the hands of the Lord. When the Spirit is with you, you will fulfill your mission honorably.

Pay the price to learn how to communicate in love. This skill, above all others, will help you become a great disciple of the Lord, because it puts your faith into action.

The work you are doing is the Lord's will. It is important. Some of the most transcendent events of your life will occur when you communicate with people to bless them. Never forget that communication with your Heavenly Father is important. Fall upon your knees and ask Him to help you in all things as you seek to help your brothers and sisters to come unto Christ.

CHAPTER 13

Nurturing New Converts and Rescuing the Struggling Saints

The worth of souls is great in the sight of God. You learn in John 15:16 that the Savior was praying that the Apostles' fruit might remain—that is, that the Saints, after baptism, would be retained in the kingdom of God. The balanced effort in missionary work is this: you should simultaneously emphasize conversion, retention, and activation. In other words, just because people are baptized, it doesn't mean the work is over. The work with them is forever. As missionaries and as members, we are working together to help bring souls truly to Christ.

After their baptism, you should always help converts prepare for the temple, to be sealed for time and all eternity, and in some cases to prepare for their missions. You always let people know there's more to the kingdom than just being baptized. You want enduring conversions. They have to acquire a deep and abiding testimony of the gospel of Jesus Christ and the Church. Most importantly, they must make a social transition in the Church. They must make friends—find a support group—so that they want to change their lifestyles, to abandon habits and activities that are inappropriate.

You see, people need to know that they're loved. People need to find joy within the Church and kingdom of God. Why is this important? Because, as President Hinckley taught, every one of

Heavenly Father's children needs a friend and a responsibility and to be nurtured by the good word of God.[1]

The worth of souls is great in the eyes of the Lord. The Lord said that His work and His glory is to bring to pass our immortality and eternal life (see Moses 1:39). Souls are precious, but to gain eternal life, they must come into the Church and receive all the ordinances and covenants of the gospel, including the life-exalting ordinances and covenants of the temple. This is not all, they must also endure to the end.

Utilizing the New and Returning Member Progress Form with New Converts

Can you retain these new precious souls? The answer is yes. You must be as anxious to retain your converts as you are to baptize. The *New and Returning Member Progress Form* should be used with utmost accuracy, in every phase of the work. If you follow it—making sure your converts have met the bishop and ward leaders, have had all their interviews and discussions, have set up goals for the temple, and so on—the chances of retention are much higher.

As a missionary, you should follow up to make sure that everything on the progress form has been taken care of and that the new convert has had an opportunity to receive a calling—and if he is a man, an opportunity to receive the priesthood. You should do everything in your power when a person comes into the Church, to help them remain active.

Continually Visit and Make Contact with Your New Converts

What's the second thing in helping converts remain active? Always make continual visits and keep contact in any way possible. People often say, "I don't care how much you know, until I know how much you care." Do you really care about your new converts? Do you really want to help them to stay active? We baptize people so they can come unto Christ. Our duty as missionaries is to help them press forward with steadfastness; this is why you make contact with them.

Remember, when we're making visits to people, it is important that we live Doctrine and Covenants, where the Lord says, "Therefore, strengthen your brethren in all your conversation, in all your prayers, in all your exhortations, and in all your doings" (D&C 108:7). In other words, in all that you and your companion do with the new converts—at every moment as you open your mouth, in your conversation, as you pray, as you exhort them to stay strong in the Lord, in all of your doings—do everything you can to help them walk in the ways of the Lord. Make sure you enter their names in the record for your area so the missionaries that follow you will continue to make contact with them. Carefully follow the baptismal checklist. Visits with members are important too. Whenever possible, take a member with you to your appointments.

The Five Lessons following Baptism

Ensure that the new converts review the five lessons (the five lessons from *Preach My Gospel*'s chapter 3, entitled "Study and Teach"), because you want them to be nurtured by the word of God and the Spirit. Following their baptisms, and over next few months, you need to teach and review the five lessons taught prior to baptism. Sometimes you must initiate those. Sometimes you go with the ward missionaries, or sometimes you go with the home teachers. Moroni 6:1–4 says that once they've been baptized and entered into the Church and kingdom, their names are kept that they might be continually nourished with the good word of God. Those five lessons are essential.

Home teaching and visiting teaching visits are a must. It is crucial that new converts attend Gospel Essentials classes. Every chance you have, you want to assure that these people are nurtured. People are nurtured by the Spirit of the Lord, by the power of the word, by faithful and obedient missionaries, and members praying with all their hearts, mights, minds, and souls. Many of your new converts will be struggling and lonely. You must do everything to make them feel comfortable and at ease in the Church and kingdom of God.

As you seek to serve, you need to remember the lost and weary. One of the great lessons President Monson has taught us by precept and example is that we are to rescue those lost and struggling Saints. You are to seek the lost, the lonely, and the weary. This was always the Savior's admonition, as described in the three great parables of the lost coin, the lost sheep, and the prodigal son. The Lord was always seeking to bless the less fortunate and those with heavy burdens to bear. You are to lift up the hand that hangs down. You are to "strengthen your brethren in all your conversation, in all your prayers, in all your exhortations, and in all your doings" (D&C 108:7). This is what you are about. This is your work. Every soul is precious.

The rescue effort is of prime importance. There are those who have struggled and find themselves estranged from the Church. Every ward should have a plan to visit and bring back to activity all who have strayed. This is missionary work too. The home teaching and visiting teaching efforts are always seeking to help the weary and downtrodden. Visit with the bishop or Relief Society president, and they will help you find people who need your love. You may be just the one to bring a soul back into full fellowship, and this is joy. Remember, these efforts are always correlated with the ward missionaries.

Utilizing the New and Returning Member Progress Form *with Those Who Are Less Active*

You work with new converts and those less active—those who have strayed, people who have not made the best choices. I have found in the Church that many stray through misunderstanding, loneliness, and lack of knowledge.

Another reason people become less active is that they feel a lack of love. The psalmist wrote in Psalm 142:4, "I looked on [my] right hand, and beheld, but [there was] no man that would know me: refuge failed me; no man cared for my soul." Feeling unloved is a major cause of inactivity in the Church. By using the *New and Returning Member Progress Form,* you will be able to follow through with every needful thing to help the struggling Saints return to full activity.

Personal Paths of Righteousness

When working with those less active, it's important that you get them on the path of righteousness—the path to eternal life, the strait and narrow path. Privately, people must begin to do two things: pray and search the scriptures.

In your introduction to the missionary lessons, you will find one of the first things discussed is teaching your investigators how to pray and committing them to pray.

The Lord said, "Verily, verily I say unto you, ye must watch and pray always, lest ye be tempted." And later on, He said, "Verily, verily I say unto you [pray lest ye be tempted] for Satan desireth to . . . sift you as wheat" (3 Nephi 18:15, 18). Even in your own individual lives, if you don't pray or search the scriptures, you will lose the constant companionship of the Holy Ghost and be tempted.

In another lesson, you are taught how to invite people to read and study and ponder the Book of Mormon. A person who is less active must be diligent in searching the scriptures so temptation will not lead them astray.

Laman and Lemuel asked Nephi, "What meaneth the rod of iron?" Nephi responded, "The [rod of iron is the] word of God" (see 1 Nephi 15:24). The only way you can get to the tree of life is by holding to the rod, the word of the Lord. There is no other way. And when temptations come over us—the mists of darkness—there's only one way through, and that is by holding to the rod. You live by every word that proceedeth forth from the mouth of the Lord (see D&C 84:43–46), for the words of Christ will tell you all things that you should do (see 2 Nephi 32:3). You learn that the word is indeed a key to avoiding temptation.

Whether you are a missionary, mother, father, or teenager, you need to search the scriptures and fast and pray so that you not be tempted beyond that which you can endure. That is the way you get other people on the strait and narrow path too.

Fellowship in the Community of Saints

Now that they are on the path that is part and parcel of righteous behavior, the second part is equally important. When people know you care, they are willing to change. I wrote the new English converts and asked them to tell me about their conversion. They often replied, "The reason I was converted, President Pinegar, was this: I felt the love of the missionaries so much, I had to listen to what they said. While listening, I felt the Spirit and came to the knowledge of the truth and I knew I just had to be baptized." You see, knowledge and love are important and must be felt.

Another factor in activation is the sociality, the fellowship, the coming to church, and the going to meetings so people will tell them how nice it is to see them. And when they start doing that, their lives will change because they feel part of the great entity of the Church. You might call it a community of the Saints. When you feel that community, you want to be involved with it.

Recently, I was ready to teach my institute class, and I looked at one girl whose close friend hadn't arrived yet. And I said, "Hi! How you doing today?"

"Oh, good, Brother Ed. I'm great." Her name was Alicia. She was sitting there, and pretty soon her friend Angela walked in the door. Angela caught Alicia's eye, came in, and sat down. "Hi!" They smiled as they greeted one another, and they were just so happy together. And I thought, *They come to this class to learn, but they also come because of the sociality and love they feel.*

Never, ever let a person feel unnoticed or unloved. When you go to your ward and see a little boy or girl going to Primary, walk up and say, "Hi there, young man (young woman), you're going to be a great missionary." That's going to make him or her feel good. In other words, let everybody know that you care about them and give them hope and confidence. That's the sociality of the Saints—fellowshipping and loving because you truly, truly care.

Goals in Visiting Those Less Active

When you start working with those who are less active, you need to visit them. There are four basic groups: lifetime inactive members who often raise their families in inactivity; new converts who have fallen away, usually in their first year as members; active members who slip into transgression, or for some other reason fall away; and youth who fall away because of the philosophies of the world and the influence of their peers.

Whatever the excuses for inactivity, there are some things to remember as you prepare to visit less-active people. Gather as much information as you can about them before the visit. Visit with the bishop or their former home teachers. Seek only the information that's proper and reasonably possible. Let their home teachers know about your plan to visit. Remember that in the Church, the missionaries are to visit those less active as part of their member work in missionary service. This is part of being a full-time minister for the Lord.

Some valuable information to gather might be: Is this a part-member family? What is their marital status? When were they baptized? When was the last time they came to Church? When was the last time they had home teachers? What are their hobbies and birthdates? Are there children or youth in the family, and what are their ages? Would it be helpful to invite a member to accompany you, such as the primary president or the Mia Maid leader? You need to care about what they care about so it is easier to make a connection and begin to build a relationship of trust.

These kinds of things are valuable to know. Then, before your first visit, pray for the Spirit of the Lord to tell you all things you need to do before you go. Remember, the Lord will prepare a way.

Your first visit should always be short. Be sincere and show love and concern for the people. Introduce yourself and tell them you'd like to visit with them. Ask if this is a convenient time—if not, set up a time to return. Tell them a little about yourself. Ask them about the missionaries who taught them. There is something that happens when that occurs. When converts recall the missionaries who taught them, they become tender and sensitive to the Spirit.

For example, I remember once that I sent an elder to High Wycombe for his first area. He arrived in England on the day when the missionaries were making less-active visits (they usually did one every day). He was taught these things—to ask about the missionary who taught them. Well, Elder Kennard asked, and the man answered, "Oh, she was a wonderful lady. Her name was Sister Loretta Johnson."

Elder Kennard paled, and then he blurted out, "That's my mother. My mother taught you." They were so excited they could hardly stand it, to think that here he was, called on a mission. His first area was High Wycombe, and during the first week, when he goes to make visits, who does he visit? His mother's less-active convert. Needless to say, the fire was rekindled. Brother Eastley, the inactive member, came back to the Church. Not only that, but his wife, who was not a member, joined the Church as well. Those feelings that converts have about their missionaries are always special in their hearts. The Lord knows that, and He certainly works in marvelous ways.

Be sure you express sincere interest in their feelings and concerns and discuss any anxieties. You should be sweetly bold in order to get their concerns out in the open, but most of all, use love and tenderness so as to better understand their true concerns.

In every visit, be sure you encourage them to make and keep at least one commitment. Whether it's just the commitment for a return visit, a commitment to read the Book of Mormon, or a commitment to pray, it is important that a return appointment be set up. As you continue to make these visits, always remember that everyone is different and special. What might be best for one may not be best for another.

As you are planning your visits to those who are less active, be sure you correlate this with the ward council and especially the ward mission leader. If there are Primary-age children in the family who haven't yet been baptized, be sure you talk to the Primary president.

Or if there is a young woman who's about fourteen years old, make sure the Young Women's presidency and the Mia Maid class can visit her. It is important to correlate your work so everyone in the ward is involved, and they too can reap the blessings of missionary work. This is absolutely essential. This is why it is important to correlate with the ward mission leader and attend the ward council whenever possible. Regular visits to less-active families are important in helping them feel the Spirit and return to activity and fellowship in the Church.

Remember

Here are some things to ask and think about when working with any who are hesitant and less active:

Remember that their souls are precious; they must know that you really care. Do you really know how they feel and what they are thinking? Have you asked enough find-out questions? For example: "How did you feel when you attended church? How did you feel when you read the Book of Mormon? Will you come with us to visit Sister So-and-So?" Suddenly, some unrealized concerns may surface. But you must understand, you'll never know their real condition until you've asked enough questions to know how they really feel and what they are really thinking. Have you used the Book of Mormon as a tool? Is there something in the Book of Mormon that can strengthen them? Have they felt the Spirit and are they aware of it? You must help them identify it and recognize it in their lives. Invite them to make a commitment. All this is done in a conversational approach and with love.

We must be like Alma. Alma said, as they were going to visit the Zoramites who had gone astray, "Oh Lord, will thou grant unto us that we may have success in bringing them again unto thee in Christ. Behold, O Lord, their souls are precious, and many of them are our brethren; therefore, give unto us O Lord, power and wisdom that we may bring these, our brethren, again unto thee" (Alma 31:34–35).

Once your less-active brothers and sisters have felt that Spirit and been made aware of it, help them resolve their concerns and make and keep their commitments. Make sure that you invite them properly, so that they'll have the staying power to keep the commitments that the Lord would have them keep. Arrange for a follow-up to help them.

May you remember your duty, not just to baptize, but to retain and keep active all those children of your Heavenly Father by helping them feel the Spirit and make and keep commitments.

CHAPTER 14

Forever Called: Starting Another Phase of Your Life

Saying Good-bye and Keeping in Touch

Saying good-bye can be a tender time when you finish your mission. You have loved the people and served them with all your heart, might, mind, and strength. You truly care for them and their happiness. They will be friends forever—the people you have served, the converts that you have assisted in coming unto Christ, ward members, missionary companions, and friends. Keep a good address book with emails, phones, and addresses. You will be glad you did. When you return home, you will have a desire to stay in touch. Remember to contact your converts often. They still need your love.

You can return home from your mission with joy and satisfaction. You have changed. You have become a selfless servant of others. You blessed and served others. You are more Christlike. During returned missionaries' welcome-home talks, they often say, "It was the best two years," or, "It was the greatest two years," or, "It was the happiest time of my life." Why do missionaries say such words?

Why the Best Two Years?

You will refer to your mission as "the best two years" because you were devoted to the Lord; you spent all your time and all your effort in His behalf, blessing His children. You were happy because you spent your time building up the kingdom of God and helping people come unto Christ. On your mission, you worked hard. You were busy. You had a regular schedule. You were always thinking of others and praying for others, pleading with the Lord that they'll come unto Christ.

Sometimes there were days that were frustrating because your investigators didn't keep their commitments. Sometimes you felt rejected, as people had no desire to hear the word. Oftentimes you did not have enough money and you were off your budget. There were challenges and trials, but all that did not matter because you had one goal: Who can I bless today? Who can I invite to come unto Christ? This is why you will have experienced happiness on your mission, despite all the trials and adversity and hard times, and you can keep this mind-set the rest of your life as you go to school, get married, and have a family. You don't compartmentalize the gospel. You live the gospel every day and in every phase of your life.

Every morning on your mission, you arose early. You searched the scriptures alone, and then studied with your companion. Then you prayed morning, noon, and night. You prayed for your investigators, your companions, the whole world—that they might come unto Christ (see Alma 6:6). You prayed to do the Father's will and build up the kingdom of God. Your life was focused. You set goals and you made plans: How many people can we find today? How many are we going to invite to church? How many copies of the Book of Mormon can we place? Thus you were able to prepare people to come unto Christ, and your life was focused on one thing: Jesus Christ and His kingdom. When you return from your mission, you can do this in an abbreviated time frame and still do all that is expected of you.

As you strive to do this, the Spirit will nurture and lead you. You will teach and testify by the Spirit. You will enjoy all the blessings of the Spirit that come from choosing to do good, to do justly, to walk humbly, to judge righteously; your mind will be enlightened, your soul filled with joy, and you will have love, peace, gentleness, goodness, faith, meekness, and temperance. As a missionary, you enjoyed these feelings of the Spirit's companionship. That's why you now can feel so good building up His kingdom—serving your fellowmen and the Lord every moment of your life.

Why do we do this? Because of the Atonement of Jesus Christ. Christ died so that everyone might live. For the whole world, He suffered and died that all might return to the presence of our Heavenly Father. And that is why you served. So you must continue to hold up the "light." The Lord said you are the "light unto the world, and to be the saviors of men" (D&C 103:9). You recognize the worth of souls. The Lord said, "How great [shall be your] joy [over] the soul that repenteth" (D&C 18:13 [13–15]). As a missionary, you were thinking only of blessing other people. When you achieved your goals, you tasted the fruit of your labors; you brought souls unto Christ and were consumed with the Spirit. You had an overwhelming desire to do good.

On your mission, you continually received support and praise for all that you were doing: letters from parents and friends, the support of the bishopric, and praise and thanks from your mission president for building up the kingdom. You enjoyed the confirmation from the Spirit that you were doing good things. You received letters of praise and support and gratitude from converts. Above all, you felt the love of God, knowing that you were on the errand of the Lord Jesus Christ. These wholesome relationships and feelings you had were not built upon lust, greed, power, or vanity; they were built on your desire to help someone. Yes, as a missionary, you have had the vision of the work of the Lord: to bring to pass the immortality and eternal life of men. You were always applying correct principles to your life. That is what happens on a mission.

Maintaining the Vision

But when you return home from your mission, things are different—*really* different. There are young men and young women, and you don't have to be one full arm's length away—you can actually hold their hands. You can even ask them out on dates! Yes, when you return home, things really are different. Many people will have changed; your little brother may be driving your car. He may have even used your bedroom, and it's still his. You're not quite as organized when you get back. There is a lot less praise and appreciation. It is easy to become self-focused—"I want to do this. I need to do that." There are many pivotal decisions to be made, and suddenly life can become "all about me." Some days you may feel unfulfilled. Your life may become a little undisciplined. You may not recognize the Spirit as much as you did before. You may find yourself not seeking to bless others, but rather just to get things done. You may feel lost because you are not receiving the blessings that you did in the mission field. There are no regular interviews with a mission president who asks, "How are you doing? I love you." Your social life may become stressful because you don't remember how to ask, "Hi! Would you like to go to Church with me?" or, "Would you like to go on a date?" or, "Will you please hold my hand?"

You feel like you're home, you've done your work, you did your mission. It's over—your mission is over. And that is a *big* mistake. Missions are for life!

Now, you're anxious to get back in the flow of life, but temptations are prevalent and sometimes because you may say to yourself, "I've worked so hard for two years (or eighteen months), I need to rest. Hallelujah, I don't have to do scripture study. I don't have to get up at 6:30 a.m. anymore." So you sleep in, and when you sleep in, you don't have time to search the scriptures, and you could become self-indulgent and idle. Whenever you are idle, you will not be happy, for you are not achieving anything worthwhile. You become pleasure seeking, the "me" syndrome happens: my job, my class, my things. Gradually, instead of reaching out to other people to bless them and serve them, you could turn inward and get out of the habits that you need to be happy.

Returned missionaries want to do what's right, but sometimes they don't remember the things they did that brought them happiness. When I was a bishop a few years ago, an elder had just returned from his mission about five or six months before, and he came in and said, "Bishop Ed, I've got to talk to you right now." He was a big, strong football player. He said, "I'm not happy anymore," and he began to cry. "My mission was great, and now I don't know what's going wrong. Life is not good. It's the pits. I just wish I was back there, and yet I want to be here. I'm just, I'm just. . . ." He was frustrated, overwhelmed, and downright discouraged. And then he blurted out, "And I know why. I'm not doing what the Lord wants me to do. Bishop Ed, every day on my mission I searched the scriptures, I studied with my companion, and I prayed with real intent to bless people's lives. Now I don't do anything like that at all."

Too many missionaries come home saying, "I've got to adjust to a new way of living because I'm going to live differently now," and that is a mistake. Life is your mission, and you were called to serve on the earth. We came on this earth to perform a mission, to live here and help people be happy. Sometimes, when you are out of the mode of full-time proselyting missionary, you forget that you are always a missionary. The young women of the Church stand up each Sunday and say, "We are daughters of our Heavenly Father, and He loves us and we love Him, and we will stand as witnesses for God at all times in all things and all places as we strive to live the Young Women's values."[1] You think about that. Young women, between ages twelve and eighteen, have the values and standards to stand as witnesses for God at all times, in all things, and all places. That teaches a principle. Don't seek to adjust to a new way of life; rather, make your life as a missionary part and parcel of your future life. In other words, the only way to be happy and adjust well is to continue to live by the Spirit. Your life must be a Spirit-directed life. It's a different time in life, but the same principles are involved.

In the mission field, you wanted to find people to whom you could teach the gospel. Well guess what? Now you get to find an eternal companion. Doesn't that sound kind of exciting? You want to find that one who you can be sealed to in the temple of your God. And this should be a desire—a goal. This isn't something that will just happen. This is something toward which you must work.

You need to get an education. The Spirit can help you choose, and it can guide and direct you toward that which you are best qualified to do. Time moves on, and you get married, and guess what?

You will need the Spirit to raise a family. And then you will realize, "I am a son (or daughter) of God, the Eternal Father. I am a disciple of Jesus Christ. My duty and obligation here on the earth is always the same: to help people." Whether as a home teacher, a visiting teacher, a Sunday School teacher, or a Primary teacher—your job is to help people.

Well, the same commitment pattern you learned in the mission field applies in the family, at work, at play, and at school. You find out how people are feeling. You present messages. You help them recognize the Spirit because you have taken the time to build a relationship of trust, so your credibility is strong. You'll follow up and see how they're feeling. You'll resolve any concerns. The commitment pattern is a methodology of the way the Spirit works.

One time, when I was a bishop, a young returned missionary, who had been home for about four or five months, came up and said, "Bishop Ed, I've got this new home teaching assignment. I'm going to be seeing Bill, and I don't know what to do to help him." Now mind you, he had just returned from a mission. He knew how to commit people to live the gospel. But you see what happens—as missionaries, we often compartmentalize the things we learned in the mission field and come home and try to be a new person, and that is the mistake in the adjustment.

I said to him, "Do you know him very well?"

"No, not really."

"Well, maybe the first thing you ought to do is get acquainted so you can build a relationship of trust and love. You mentioned he doesn't come to church. Well, after you get to know him and find out what he likes to do, you could take him fishing, skiing, or whatever he likes to do. Build on common interests and become better acquainted. Your credibility will be there, and you could present him a little message about coming to church, or going on a double date, or doing something fun. Then pretty soon, you could find out how he feels, and when he feels good, and then invite him to come to priesthood with you on Sunday morning. 'I'll pick you up about eight.'"

All of a sudden, the elder said, "Wait a minute, Bishop Ed, that's the way we helped people commit to living the gospel."

I said, "That's right, my son. That's the commitment pattern. You use it in everything you do."

Don't set aside the things that you learned in the mission field, but rather implement and integrate them into your life. You must be a disciple to lift up the hands that hang down and strengthen the feeble knees (see D&C 81:5).

And when you're converted, you strengthen your brethren. How? In all your conversations, prayers, doings, exhortations (see D&C 108:7). Your mind is still the same. You don't change your lifetime focus of serving others just because you are home from your mission; you merely focus on different people. Because once you change focus from the gospel of Jesus Christ in your life, your focus will become blurred and the world will ensnare you. Why? Because you will love the things of the world more than the things of God.

This happened even in Adam's time. When Adam and Eve were cast out of the garden, Jehovah taught them the plan of redemption (see Moses 5:11–13). After they had been taught, they thought it was important to make these things known unto their children, and so they did. Then, in verse 13 (a sad scripture), Satan came among them, saying, "I am also a son of God," and then he said to "believe it [the gospel] not." And "they loved Satan more than God," and from that time forth they became "carnal, sensual and devilish."

Whenever you set your mind on things of the world—clothes, labels, titles, championships, or any other thing of the world—you will find the world is merely a representation of the adversary. If you love the things of the world, then you don't love God as you should. And as the scripture says, "They loved Satan [and the world] more than God."

Keep the Commandments

So how do you maintain your focus on Christ and building up the kingdom? The Lord said, "If ye love me, keep my commandments"

(John 14:15). This becomes an important solution to being happy in the adjustment from your mission.

As the emphasis changes from a full-time proselyting mission to that of a lifelong mission, one thing should be constant—that you do Heavenly Father's will. If you don't, and it's not in your plans, then righteousness is not yours, and you lose. And what do you lose? You lose happiness. King Benjamin said if you keep the commandments, you will be happy and enter into a state of never-ending happiness (see Mosiah 2:41).

Goals and Self-Discipline

The phase of life following your full-time mission should merely be an extension of your growth, not a separate, compartmentalized time of life. Never compartmentalize the gospel of Jesus Christ. How do you avoid doing this? The solution is clear. You have the Spirit, but you must organize every needful thing. You must have the vision of what you want to accomplish. In the mission field, you planned every day: who to visit, who to see, who to bless, and how to help. At home, you also need to plan out your day to do your school work or your job to the best of your ability, to visit your home teaching family and the women you visit teach, to read your scriptures, to pray. . . . You make a list, a little list of planning to organize every needful time and thing. Your use of time will be better, your educational experience will be better, and your life will be better.

I'll never forget one elder. He had returned home from his mission and was going to school, and he wrote me a letter.

Dear President Pinegar,

School's going great, everything's good, life is good, life after the mission is terrific. You know what President? You know when you taught us to set goals and make plans? I thought, well that works in the mission field; it ought to work in school. So I took our planner and where it had everything to do with teaching people, I would substitute classes and work and educational experiences and things, and I made my plan to achieve in all those areas. President I just thought you'd want to know that I got a 4.0 this semester, and boy, do I feel good."

In other words, he was happy because he had achieved, because he had set his goals and made his plans.

Beginning August 2015, the Church created a new online course for full-time missionaries, entitled *My Plan*. A booklet will be available where the Internet is not readily accessible. *My Plan* will be used throughout your mission to set goals and make plans for a spiritual foundation for your life.

My Plan includes eight lessons. The first is completed prior to entering the MTC. The second is completed at the halfway point of your mission. The last six learning experiences are to be completed during your last six weeks of your mission. Each experience can be completed in one hour of your personal study time on the computer. Your post-mission plan will automatically be shared with your mission president, and he will be able to give you counsel during your last interview. This will be a wonderful time to visit your mission president and set your goals as you leave the mission field.

Upon returning home, it is important to share your goals with your parents and priesthood leaders so they can support you in your efforts. You will find that having sustaining influence of others will help you along your way. Once you have realized the benefit of putting into practice *My Plan*, you will be able to help other returned missionaries when they come home. *My Plan* can make the difference in your life.

What kind of goals should you set? The whole point of setting goals, of course, is to keep you on track. The most easily achieved goals are *smart* goals. *Smart* stands for the five traits of well-designed goals.

Specific: Goals must be clear and definite. When goals are specific, you are more able to achieve them. Only with specific goals are you able to make progress.

Measurable: You need to measure your progress to make sure you are on track. If goals are not measurable, you will have a difficult time accomplishing anything. It is hard to stay motivated to complete the goals if there are no measuring points along the way.

Attainable: Goals must be realistic and attainable. If goals are set too high or low, they become meaningless. They need to be real and practical.

Relevant: Goals must be an important to your overall plan and vision for life. Relevant goals will keep you connected to your values and things that matter most.

Time-Bound: Effective goals have target dates for competition and check points along the way. Goals without schedules, checkpoints, and time limits tend to get lost in your everyday activities. Writing them down and reviewing your progress is vital to keeping you on schedule.

Goals are important, and so is the self-discipline you need to accomplish them. In the mission field, you had mission rules, and they blessed you and kept you safe. Sometimes when you return home, you are so anxious to rid yourselves of the rules that you become totally undisciplined, and you do not have the standards that you once had. Some of the saddest moments I've ever had as a bishop are when missionaries return and in a few months decide they want to do what they want to do. They become complacent in their scripture study, prayers, and church attendence. They also become a little mischievous, to say the least.

Never let your standards down because if you do, you will feel guilt. And when that guilt comes upon you, you will be unhappy. So if you let down your standards, you get guilt, you don't feel good, and then you lose the Spirit. You feel upset, and you think that adjustment to your new life is the pits. And why is it the pits? Because you chose to not be obedient and disciplined.

Most important, you must remember that as you make your goals and plans, you must balance your life. Intellectual, social, emotional, physical, and (above all) spiritual areas are all important. You can balance them so everything has adequate time in relationship to your life.

Remember to fast and pray for all things and express gratitude to Heavenly Father and the Savior. Feast upon the scriptures daily, for they will tell you all things to do (see 2 Nephi 32:3). Continue to be a missionary, even a member missionary the way you wished the members had been when you were on your mission.

Making the Transition

How do you adjust to a whole new way of life? Life hasn't changed; you are just on the mission of education, getting a job, and (most important) finding your eternal companion. As you adjusted in the mission field, you'll now need to make that small adjustment as you return. You'll need to build some more relationships of trust.

Remember this—time is your ally. Do not be overwhelmed because of the situation and pressures of the day. Don't be impatient. Remember how the Liahona worked? Remember how you plant the seed and nurture it with faith, diligence, and patience? So likewise, your patience will be tested as you return home. Allow yourself time to recognize that you will be serving a different kind of mission: the mission of life. Building up the kingdom of God is still a priority, but with family and friends, and at school and work. Now, we simply broaden our focus a little. Our lives are still dedicated to building up the kingdom of God—to perfect the Saints, redeem the dead, proclaim the gospel, and assist the poor and needy.

I want you to remember with care the things you learned on your mission and apply them to your mission in life. As you start to date, remember the decency, patience, kindness, and respect that you learned as a missionary. Respect your date like an investigator. Remember how you were so tender, loving, and thoughtful with your investigators because you cared, and you wanted them to hear the gospel? Well, don't become commanding and demanding just because you're home. You should treat everyone like an investigator. Why did you treat your investigators so nicely? Because you wanted them to come unto Christ. You know what? When you are married and have children, they become your investigators. If you treat everybody that way, life will be sweeter in all that you do, and you will help each other come into the kingdom.

Remember to stay focused on living the gospel every day. Rely on the Lord, just like you relied on Him before. Be patient in all things and be sure that your expectation of others is not so high that you cannot make life fun and happy.

Above all, stay busy. Never, ever lower your standards. Guilt and sin will bring great sorrow.

You might say to yourself, "Well, I know those things." That's right, you do know everything you have read, but here's the question: Will you remember and apply these things to your life? Life will be sweet if you continue on your course of coming unto Christ, accepting and applying His atoning sacrifice, and being perfected by Him in all that you do.

Remember: The Joy and Glory of the Work

Each of us grows step by step in the gospel plan, and you will find that the same is true as you prepare for your mission. During each step of the way, you will find joy in being strengthened by the Holy Spirit. You will find joy in knowing that you are doing the will of the Father. When opposition arises, you will even experience joy in knowing that you have power to respond by evaluating the situation, setting goals, and planning. As President Kimball's desk plaque said, simply "just do it." Repeat this process as often as necessary to achieve success in your labors.

We become the fulfillment of God's purpose for mankind here on earth. We help build up the kingdom of God and assist in the Lord's work—"the immortality and eternal life of man" (Moses 1:39). We bring joy to others and ourselves and cause our Heavenly Father's and our Savior's joy to be full because of our faith.

Through humility and faith, you can tap the strength of the Lord. You can become independent of the world as you gain strength in the Lord so that you will be able to do all things whatsoever you are commanded. You will truly become "even as He is" at those precious moments when you act and teach by the Spirit. You are His disciple. You have the ability to become one with the Lord, therefore you are His.

As a missionary and a member of the Church, you are on His errand. You shall not fail. You came to succeed. You are of God, and you are to be His anointed servant. You are a true disciple of Jesus Christ. You will be an example to others. The principles and values you live are what you will become. And this will bring you great joy.

You will be led by the Spirit in the "how" of being obedient to the commandments. I testify that you will find security in knowing that you are led and motivated by Jesus Christ, and you will find joy and glory in being an instrument in the hands of God. You will find that the Spirit will both guide you and empower you, for you have been literally called of God through His holy prophet. All of these things will turn your heart to others and show how you can help them come to Christ. In turn, they will help others, and the process will continue.

Your perception and vision of the work will lead you to action and a sense of how your goals should be accomplished. All things will be possible for you to accomplish in the strength of the Lord. You will continually improve as you adapt to new approaches to missionary work with a positive attitude and a willing spirit. Your perception of yourself and the work will grow and improve as you seek to build up the kingdom of God.

Let the purpose of your mission be ingrained within your heart. It is to bring souls to Christ through the waters of baptism. Your end goal should be conversion to Christ, that all may partake of His goodness. Let your mind be consumed with this thought. Strive each day to do the right things and be obedient and motivated by your faith and your love of God. And with time, effort, study, training—and by preparing every needful thing—you will truly become a pure disciple of Jesus Christ. Let your motive be pure—a love of Christ and your fellowmen. This will unlock your divine potential as you truly seek to enlighten and liberate the children of God with the gospel of Jesus Christ.

Let us conclude with the words of a modern-day prophet: "I

feel sorry for the man or the woman who has never experienced the sweet joy which comes to the missionary who proclaims the gospel of Jesus Christ, and brings honest souls to a knowledge of the truth, and who hears the expressions of gratitude and thanksgiving that come from the hearts of those who have been brought by his labor to a comprehension of life eternal."[2] It is up to you to become not just a missionary but a devoted servant of the Lord who will live up to this message of the restoration of the gospel of Jesus Christ. In this, you will find joy.

On your mission, you will find the joy of loving all mankind. You will learn to love everyone, including the seemingly unlovable, the difficult companion, the downtrodden, the haughty, the prideful, the unconcerned, and even the hateful. You will learn to love them all with a perfect love, to the point that your concern for their welfare is your ultimate concern.

You will also discover the joy of forgiving, including those who speak evil of you, judge you unrighteously, reject you, disregard you, and do not understand. You will forgive and love all of them, even as your Savior does.

You will learn the joy of serving steadfastly, knowing you are doing the will of God, and enduring to the end in blessing your brothers and sisters and nurturing those who stand in need.

Most of all, you will become a true disciple of the Lord. You will truly come to know the feeling of joy in the gospel, joy in preaching and teaching, joy in the soul that repents, and joy in bringing others to Christ.

ENDNOTES

Chapter 1

1. "I Hope They Call Me on a Mission," *Children's Songbook*, 169.
2. Ezra Taft Benson, *Ezra Taft Benson Remembers the Joys of Christmas* (Salt Lake City: Deseret Book, 1988), 11.
3. Joseph Smith, *History of The Church of Jesus Christ of Latter-day Saints*, 2nd ed. (Salt Lake City: Desert Book, 1980), 2:478.
4. *True to the Faith* (Salt Lake City: The Church of Jesus Christ of Latter-day Saints, 2004), 78–79.
5. *For the Strength of Youth* (Salt Lake City: Intellectual Reserve, 2011), 18.
6. Ezra Taft Benson, *Teachings of Ezra Taft Benson* (Salt Lake City: Deseret Book, 1974), 363.

Chapter 2

1. M. Russell Ballard, "The Greatest Generation of Young Adults," *Ensign*, May 2015.
2. *Meridian Magazine* July 13, 2014.
3. Bruce R. McConkie, "How Great Is My Calling," (address delivered while serving as president of the Australian Mission, 1961–64).

Endnotes

Chapter 3

1. "President Monson: Missionary Work," lds.org, accessed February 29, 2016, https://www.lds.org/prophets-and-apostles/unto-all-the-world/prepare-to-be-a-missionary?lang=eng.
2. Ibid.
3. Gordon B. Hinckley, *Teachings of Gordon B. Hinckley* (Salt Lake City: Deseret Book, 1997), 374.
4. Joseph Smith, *History of The Church of Jesus Christ of Latter-day Saints*, 2nd ed. (Salt Lake City: Desert Book, 1980), 2:478.
5. Smith, *History of the Church*, 4:540.

Chapter 4

1. Howard W. Hunter, "Your Temple Recommend," *New Era*, April 1995.
2. Gordon B. Hinckley, *Teachings of Gordon B. Hinckley* (Salt Lake City: Deseret Book, 1997), 608–9.
3. Howard W. Hunter, *Teachings of Howard W. Hunter* (Salt Lake City: Deseret Book, 1997), 36.
4. Howard W Hunter, *The Teachings of Howard W. Hunter*, edited by Clyde J. Williams (Salt Lake City: Bookcraft, 1997), 36–37.
5. Monte S. Nyman and Charles D. Tate Jr., eds., *Mosiah: Salvation Only through Christ* (Provo: BYU Religious Studies Center, 1991), 240.
6. Ezra Taft Benson, in a mission presidents' seminar, August 1982.
7. M. Russell Ballard, "The Greatest Generation of Young Adults," *Ensign*, April 2015, 67–70.

Chapter 5

1. Hans B. Ringger, "Choose You This Day," *Ensign*, May 1990, 25.
2. *I Know That My Redeemer Lives: Latter Day Prophets Testify of the Savior* (Salt Lake City: Deseret Book, 1990), 203.

3. Joseph Fielding Smith, *Church History and Modern Revelation*, vol. 2 (Packard Technologies, 2008), 108.

4. Joseph Smith, *Lectures on Faith* (Salt Lake City: Deseret Book, 1985), 1:12.

5. Smith, *Lectures on Faith*, 1:24.

6. Ezra Taft Benson, *A Witness for Christ* (Salt Lake City: Deseret Book, 1983), 132.

7. Gordon B. Hinckley, *Teachings of Gordon B. Hinckley* (Salt Lake City: Deseret Book, 1997), 186.

8. Ibid., 373.

9. Ezra Taft Benson, *The Teachings of Ezra Taft Benson* (Salt Lake City: Bookcraft, 1988), 275.

10. Adapted from Patricia P. Pinegar, "Peace, Hope, and Direction." *Ensign*, November 1999.

Chapter 6

1. Dallin H. Oaks, "The Keys and Authority of the Priesthood," *Ensign*, May 2014, 49, 51.

2. "Excerpts from Recent Addresses of Gordon B. Hinckley," lds.org, accessed February 29, 2016, https://www.lds.org/ensign/1997/07/excerpts-from-recent-addresses-of-president-gordon-b-hinckley?lang=eng.

3. Howard W. Hunter, "The Great Symbol of Our Membership," *Ensign*, October 1994.

4. Howard W. Hunter, "Your Temple Recommend," *New Era*, April 1995, 6.

5. Ibid.

6. Adapted from Donald M. Parry, " 'Who Shall Ascend into the Mountain of the Lord?': Three Biblical Temple Entrance Hymns," *Reason, Revelation, and Faith: Essays in Honor of Truman G. Madsen*, edited with Daniel C. Peterson and Stephen D. Ricks (Provo: FARMS, 2002), 729–42.

7. Truman G. Madsen, *The Radiant Life* (Salt Lake City: Bookcraft, 1994), 125.

8. Ibid., 125–26.

Chapter 7

1. Adapted from Alma Burton, "Endowment," *Encyclopedia of Mormonism*, ed. Daniel H. Ludlow, 5 vols., (New York: Macmillan, 1992), 454–55.

2. John A. Widtsoe, comp., *Discourses of Brigham Young* (Salt Lake City: Deseret Book, 1926), 637, quoted in *Encyclopedia of Mormonism*, ed. Daniel H. Ludlow, 5 vols., (New York: Macmillan, 1992).

3. Spencer W. Kimball, 534–35, quoted in Daniel H. Ludlow, ed., "Endowment," *Encyclopedia of Mormonism*, 5 vols. (New York: Macmillan, 1992).

4. Adapted from Alma Burton, "Endowment," *Encyclopedia of Mormonism*, ed. Daniel H. Ludlow, 5 vols., (New York: Macmillan, 1992), 454–55.

5. John A. Widtsoe, comp., *Discourses of Brigham Young* (Salt Lake City: Deseret Book, 1926), 416.

6. Daniel H. Ludlow, ed., *Encyclopedia of Mormonism*, 5 vols. (New York: Macmillan, 1992), 1444.

7. Ibid., 1551.

8. Guide to the Scriptures, "Wash, Washed, Washings," scriptures.lds.org, accessed February 29, 2016, https://www.lds.org/scriptures/gs/wash-washed-washings?lang=eng.

9. J. Richard Clarke, "The Temple—What It Means to You," *New Era*, April 1993, 4.

10. Joseph Fielding Smith, *Church History and Modern Revelation*, vol. 1 (Packard Technologies, 2008), 162–63.

11. Wilford Woodruff, "No Man Can Build Up the Church of Christ Without the Priesthood. . . ." *Journal of Discourses*, vol. 21 (London: Latter-day Saints' Book Depot 1881), 122.

12. *I Know That My Redeemer Lives: Latter day Prophets Testify of the Savior* (Salt Lake City: Deseret Book, 1990), 203.

13. Joseph Smith, *History of The Church of Jesus Christ of Latter-day Saints*, vol. 5 (Salt Lake City: Deseret Book, 1909), 424.

Chapter 8

1. Joseph Smith, *Teachings of the Prophet Joseph Smith,* selected by Joseph Fielding Smith (Salt Lake City: Deseret Book, 1977), 121.

2. Wilford Woodruff, Address, March 5, 1889, *Deseret News Weekly,* Vol. 38: 451, quoted in G. Homer Durham, ed., *The Discourses of Wilford Woodruff* (Salt Lake City: Bookcraft, 1946), 5.

3. Brigham Young, "Summary of Instructions," *Journal of Discourses,* vol. 11 (London: Latter-day Saints' Book Depot, 1865), 114.

4. John A. Widtsoe, "Temple Worship," *The Utah Genealogical and Historical Magazine,* vol. 12 (Salt Lake City: The Deseret News Press, 1921), 58.

5. John A. Widtsoe, comp., *Discourses of Brigham Young* (Salt Lake City: Deseret Book, 1926), 416. Italics added for emphasis.

6. G. Homer Durham, ed., *The Gospel Kingdom: Selections from the Writings and Discourses of John Taylor* (Salt Lake City: Deseret Book, 1943), 278.

7. *Preparing to Enter the Holy Temple* (Salt Lake City: Intellectual Reserve, 2002), 20.

8. Evelyn T. Marshall, "Garments," in *Encyclopedia of Mormonism,* ed. Daniel H. Ludlow 5 vols., (New York: Macmillan, 1992), 2:534.

9. Carlos E. Asay, "The Temple Garment: 'An Outward Expression of an Inward Commitment,'" *Ensign,* August 1997.

10. Quoted in Carlos E. Asay, "The Temple Garment: 'An Outward Expression of an Inward Commitment,'" *Ensign,* August 1997.

11. Joseph Fielding Smith, *Doctrines of Salvation* vol. 2 (Salt Lake City: Bookcraft, 1992), 143.

12. Orson F. Whitney, *Conference Reports,* vol. 99 (Salt Lake

City: The Church of Jesus Christ of Latter-day Saints, 1929), 110.

13. Richard H. Winkel, "The Temple Is about Families," *Ensign*, November 2006, 9.

14. Ibid., 11.

15. Joseph Smith, *History of The Church of Jesus Christ of Latter-day Saints*, 2nd ed. (Salt Lake City: Desert Book, 1980), 6:184.

16. *Teachings of the Presidents of the Church—Joseph Smith* (Salt Lake City: The Church of Jesus Christ of Latter-day Saints, 2007), 472–73.

Chapter 9

1. *A Missionary's MTC Experience*, 4.

2. *Preach My Gospel* ((Salt Lake City: The Church of Jesus Christ of Latter-day Saints, 2004).

Chapter 10

1. Joseph Smith, *Teachings of the Prophet Joseph Smith,* selected by Joseph Fielding Smith (Salt Lake City: Deseret Book, 1977), 287.

2. Daryl H. Garn, "Preparing for Missionary Service," *Ensign*, May 2003, 46.

3. Quoted in Joseph L. Wirthlin, *Conference Reports* vol. 23 (Salt Lake City: The Church of Jesus Christ of Latter-day Saints, 1947), 84.

4. Marion G. Romney, "Drink Deeply from the Divine Fountain," *Improvement Era*, vol. 63, no. 06 (Salt Lake City: The Church of Jesus Christ of Latter-day Saints, 1960), 435.

5. Bruce R. McConkie, *Mormon Doctrine*, 2d ed. (Salt Lake City: Bookcraft, 1966), 359.

6. Bible Dictionary, "Prayer."

7. Gordon B. Hinckley, *Teachings of Gordon B. Hinckley* (Salt Lake City: Deseret Book, 1997), 648.

8. Quoted in John Taylor, "The Organization of the Church,"

Millennial Star, vol. 13, no. 22 (Liverpool: 1851), 339.

9. John A. Widtsoe, *Priesthood and Church Government in the Church of Jesus Christ of Latter-day Saints* (Salt Lake City: Deseret Book, 1950), 366.

10. Lorenzo Snow, *Teachings of Lorenzo Snow* (Salt Lake City: Bookcraft, 1984), 77.

11. Richard G. Scott, "The Plan for Happiness and Exaltation," *Ensign,* November 1981, 11.

Chapter 11

1. Address, March 5, 1889, *Deseret News Weekly,* vol. 38: 451, quoted in G. Homer Durham, comp., *The Discourses of Wilford Woodruff,* (Salt Lake City: Bookcraft, 1946), 5.

2. Brigham Young, "Summary of Instructions," *Journal of Discourses,* vol. 11 (London: Latter-day Saints' Book Depot, 1865), 114.

3. Brigham Young and Elden Jay Watson, *Manuscript History of Brigham Young* (J. Watson, 1971), 529.

4. Joseph F. Smith, *Gospel Doctrine,* (Salt Lake City: Deseret Book, 1963), 96.

5. Joseph Smith, *Teachings of the Prophet Joseph Smith,* selected by Joseph Fielding Smith (Salt Lake City: Deseret Book, 1977), 151. Emphasis added.

Chapter 12

1. *Preach My Gospel* (Salt Lake City: The Church of Jesus Christ of Latter-day Saints, 2004), viii.

2. *A Missionary's MTC Experience,* 10.

Chapter 13

1. John L. Hart "Strengthening New Members," *LDS Church News,* published November 29, 1997, accessed April 1, 2016, http://www.ldschurchnewsarchive.com/articles/29287/Strengthening-new-members.html

Endnotes

Chapter 14

1. "Young Women Theme," *Young Women Personal Progress* (Salt Lake City: Intellectual Reserve, 2009), 3.
2. Heber J. Grant, *Conference Reports*, vol. 23 (Salt Lake City: The Church of Jesus Christ of Latter-day Saints, 1907), 23.

ABOUT THE AUTHOR

E d J. Pinegar is the author of over sixty nonfiction books and
audio tapes—most recently *The Temple: Gaining Knowledge and
Power in the House of the Lord* and the bestselling Christmas story
The Christmas Code. He has taught part time at the BYU College
of Religion for nineteen years and full time at the Orem institute
for ten years. He has also taught early morning seminary for five
years and as a volunteer teacher at the Provo MTC for ten years. He
has served in many positions of leadership in The Church of Jesus
Christ of Latter-day Saints, including bishop, stake president, mission president, and president of the Provo MTC and Manti Temple.
He and his wife, Pat, are parents of eight, grandparents of thirty-
eight, and great-grandparents of twenty-two. Ed and his wife live in
Orem, Utah.